Judy Ferris

For my Writing Partner.
-Jim

Satir Transformational Systemic Therapy

Satir Transformational Systemic Therapy

Edited by

John Banmen

Printed in the United States of America

Library of Congress Card Number 00-133439

ISBN 978-0-8314-0092-7

Cover design by: Jim Marin
Typesetting by: Jocelyn Paul

Contents

FOREWARD

by William C. Nichols, Ed.D., ABPP (Clinical)

This book had it origins in my invitation several years ago to John Banmen to serve as guest editor for a special issue of *Contemporary Family Therapy* on "Satir Today." As a long time clinician and family therapist and editor of family and family therapy journals, as well as an unreconstructed historian, I thought it would be interesting and appropriate to see what kind of legacy remained from this towering pioneer's career, what kind of impact she had left. I knew that like several other early family therapists—Nathan Ackerman, who is memorialized in the Ackerman Family Therapy Institute, Don Jackson through the Mental Research Institute, and Murray Bowen in the American Family Therapy Academy, for example--Virginia Satir had a legacy: the Avanta Network. What better place to turn than to her colleagues in the Avanta Network to answer the question: How is this charismatic clinician being remembered and represented today, nearly two decades since her death?

My impressions of Virginia Satir—one of the few persons who generally would be recognized in the field simply by utterance of her first name—swing between 1965, when I first saw her work with a family in a live demonstration during a meeting of what was then the American Association of Marriage Counselors, and 1988, when the opening session of the annual conference of the grownup American Association for Marriage and Family Therapy was devoted to her memory. In the first instance, she was regarded by the group of professionals largely with a mixture of awe, questions, and intrigued interest, and rejected by a few whose conservative theoretical orientations did not jibe with the young and growing family therapy revolution she represented. At the latter conference, the expressions were uniformly those of bereavement, loss, affection, and respect, as Satir had become simply "Virginia."

Would she be remembered as a cult figure, her teachings frozen into dogma to be followed unquestioningly by her devotees, her writings to be revered as holy scripture? The psychotherapy field certainly has not been immune to having some of its major characters treated as gods, or demigods, by their disciples. All too vividly, I remember quietly leaving a monthly gathering of a psychotherapy society several decades ago when it suddenly struck me that the meeting was a deification of a deceased founder conducted by adoring subjects listening reverently as a veteran clinician described wonderful days of the past at the feet of the master founder. Orthodoxy and unwavering adherence to old ideas obviously were the norm among the society members, making my resolve to depart and not return quite easy to maintain. Despite the high esteem and affection accorded Satir by her followers, there appears little indication that she will similarly be thrust into the role of a cult figure whose ideas are to be permanently repeated verbatim and whose practices are to be imitated without question or change.

Consistent with her strong emphasis on growth, Virginia Satir founded the Avanta Network in 1977 "as a forum for the continued evolution of Satir theory and practice" (Avanta Network, 2005). The organization has members in more than twenty countries and institutes on five continents, and maintains a free listing of professionals from several different backgrounds who have in common their self-identification as following the Satir model and process in their work. It appears that Satir's work embodies an invitation to her disciples to "go forth and grow" rather than doing things exactly as she did them. In other words, a broad framework of ideas and values, rather than a narrow and explicit list of prescriptions to be followed without deviation, seems to be the path and pattern expected of Satir-model practitioners.

As charismatic as the person sometimes referred to as "the mother of family therapy" was, it is doubtful that memories of charisma would be sufficient to maintain her legacy. Perhaps it would, but as the years have accumulated since she was active around the globe, it appears that other factors may play a more significant role in keeping her approach and practice alive and evolving. Not the least of these may be the impact of the experiences of the therapeutic and relational actions on persons encountering Satir-model therapy, consultation, workshops, and mentoring. Other factors, in my judgment, that encourage people to follow the model's outlines broadly and as creatively as they can include the emphasis on selfhood, the individual's capability of growth, the straightforward nature of interventions, and a legacy of techniques that are relatively easy to grasp, all combined with the absence of esoteric, obscure meanings.

How, then, is Virginia Satir's work remembered and represented today? John Banmen has produced an edited work that does two things: First, it represents an excellent guide to Satir theory and practice and, second, it not only shows us where Satir's legacy is on he current scene but also illustrates to an interesting degree some of the ways in which her approach continues to evolve.

John Banmen and most of the colleagues whose chapters appear in this volume are practicing their versions of Satir Transformation Systemic Therapy and most also are leading training programs based on that approach. They emphasize that this form of therapy is systemic and offers deep transformational changes—in clients' relationships with themselves, in their lives, and in relationships with others—that can be brought forth in a comparatively short time. My intention in this foreword is to sketch some of the important elements in the picture of Satir today set forth by these authors. To attempt to be comprehensive would require much more space than is typically allotted for a foreword.

Banmen, a long-time colleague of Satir, attempts to update some of the more salient portions of the Satir model, indicating that it focuses on the intrapsychic, the interactive, and the family –of origin as major areas for therapeutic intervention. He describes the Personal Iceberg metaphor as representing the intrapsychic emphasis. Human experience, according to Satir, occurs at six levels: behavior, coping, perceptions, feelings, unmet expectations, and longings. These levels form the basis of the Personal Iceberg metaphor, described by Banmen and others (e.g., Innes and Lee) in this volume. This metaphor has been used clinically to engage clients to do internal process work.

The idea of family parts inside people has been developed into an Internal Family Systems therapy model by Richard C. Schwartz (1995). This model is based on the premise that these subpersonalities interact and change much as other human groups such as families interact and change. Referring to her as a trailblazer, he gives Satir credit for doing much the preliminary work leading to the combining study of systems theory with intrapsychic subpersonalities.

Although the content of the metaphor is quite different from the ideas in Freud's personality theory, the personal iceberg metaphor may be somewhat reminiscent of some of the emphasis in psychoanalysis on conscious, pre-conscious, and unconscious layers of awareness. One large difference between the two approaches is that in the Satir model, people are much more readily capable of change than in classic psychoanalytic theory. Banmen offers, among other things, an outline reflecting the general features of the Satir model and a description of important therapeutic beliefs that many find intriguing. Pointing out that Satir made little effort to record or explain the theoretical basis of her work, Banmen says that examination of her practice, training programs, and recorded demonstrations have "indicated a deep, consistent psychological base," adding that "few family therapy authors have captured the depth and significance of her contributions."

While Satir identified six stages of change from observing what occurred among the people she worked with, Banmen added transformation as a seventh stage. This results in the following seven changes: (1) Status Quo, (2) Foreign Element, (3) Chaos, (4) Transformation, (5) Integration, (6) Practice, and (7) New Status Quo (Banmen, 1998). Carl Sayles describes these change stages in detail in his chapter, including some case illustration material. Max Innes, who is not a Satir-model therapist, makes a decided effort to understand and represent Satir and her work. Besides outlining the model's conceptual foundations, organizing it clearly in terms of presuppositions, basic constructs, methods, and therapeutic process, he observes that the Satir model has not been accepted in the mainstream of the family therapy movement and offers a brief but perceptive analysis of why this is the case. It is well worth reading and pondering. One point he sets forth is that without the charisma that Satir possessed and minus the principles of practice to formulate their own approach, her followers' outcomes have been less convincing to other therapists. Bonnie K. Lee also notes the "under-valuation" and "marginal status" of Satir in the family therapy field and attributes the absence of critical analysis and appraisal of her ideas and theory to the fact that she used experiential workshops to teach her model.

Satir, in the later years of her life, incorporated a spiritual element into her work. Similar to developments that have occurred in recent years in the wider field of family therapy and psychotherapy in general, spiritually has continued and expanded as a matter of interest in the work of Satir-model therapists. This theme is picked up by Bonnie Lee, who defines spirituality as a subset of religion. She examines the spiritual and religious significance of congruence in the Satir model and attempts to demonstrate correlations between certain aspects of Satir's approach and theologian Paul Tillich's religious quest and philosophical understanding of "salvation." Satir's emphasis regarding acceptance of one's self and relationships is akin to some religious conceptions regarding "grace" and the specific idea that humans are accepted by deity and that we have to "accept our acceptance," while we also must act to free our life force to fulfill their positive possibilities (Satir, 1988).

Several other aspects of Satir's thought and work are set forth in this book. Reconstruction is described in several different settings. Gilles Beaudry characterizes the family reconstruction process and its continuing evolution (Satir's transformational process) as focusing on wellness and as a new way to regain, and own, our wholeness. Beaudry is highly optimistic that Satir's model of human communication and growth "continues to be a major alternative for the present stage of history." It should be noted that some critics have indicated that Satir's approach is more in tune with earlier periods of time in which individualism characterized U.S. culture. It remains to be seen, as Satir-model therapy evolves, whether this criticism is valid and up-to-date. Certainly, the clinicians writing in this book seem to be quite convinced that what they are doing is effective in working toward transformation with people.

Continued refinement of approaches is reflected in the work of Gloria Taylor, who also writes on family reconstruction, describing it essentially as an unparalleled vehicle for transformation at all levels of congruence. People at the first level accept their feelings as they are. At the second level, they are in harmony with the Self. At level three, congruence consists of being in harmony with the Self and life energy, spirituality, or God (Satir et al., 1991). Taylor uses a case example to demonstrate how a reconstruction can be conducted in a much abbreviated fashion. By using specified steps and principles, she cuts the time for such work down to three hours.

Satir-model therapists (e.g., Stephen Smith in this book) emphasize that not only is therapy transformational for clients but also that training is transformational for therapists. John Banmen and Kathlyne Maki-Banmen (2000) continue to provide training in their modified Satir model that they call Transformational Systemic Therapy, which they do in Canada, Hong Kong, Korea, Singapore, Taiwan, the United States, and Europe. Wendy Lum emphasizes that the Banmen updating of the personal iceberg metaphor has provided a valid method by which to train therapists to develop the use of Self.

Some limited research has been conducted on the results of that training, specifically about the integration of the Personal Iceberg metaphor into the personal and professional life of the therapist (Lum, 2000). Among the results from the data of the nine-participant study were a reported increase in awareness, a feeling of respect and reverence for the client and for themselves, and a shift from observing events and behavior to looking at the impact of the experience. Smith notes that whereas participants in the training may have gone into the program seeking a new way to do therapy, they found a new way of being, a new way of experiencing themselves. Another step forward in the research area has been taken by Bonnie Lee, who has developed a congruence scale based on the Satir model, which she reports on in this book.

One of the questions sometimes raised regarding therapeutic approaches is: Is it used only with "problems in living" or does it help with "serious" problems? There are few social issues more significant and troublesome than suicidal behaviors among the youth. Wendy Lum, Jim Smith, and Judy Ferris survey therapies commonly used for suicidal adolescents and focus on Satir-model therapy as it is used with this population. Informed by their therapeutic work, their involvement with the Suicide Intervention and Treatment Task Force at the Institute of the Pacific, and their work in behavioral investigation of child, youth, and adult suicides, the authors comment on a case study of record from the coroner's office of an adolescent who successfully took his own life. They describe how a therapist using the Satir model might have worked therapeutically with the youngster while he was still alive, using the Satir model as a framework encompassing an holistic and integrative approach to inner experiences that can be effectively applied to prevention, intervention, and treatment with suicidal youth.

Another serious problem area to which the Satir model is applied is to working with adult female survivors of childhood sexual abuse. Anne Morrison and Judy Ferris provide a case study with detailed notes on interventions, goals, and results of treating such persons with a Satir model.

Two authors from Hong Kong, Grace Cheung and Cecilia Chan, emphasize the cultural sensitivity of Virginia Satir and propose adopting an approach in Hong Kong that draws from traditional culture and maintains continuity with hierarchical collectivism while protecting individual desires for freedom, equality, and independence. Having benefited from Satir's 1983 training visit to Hong Kong and years of follow-up by therapists from the West, they now feel that it is their task to adapt the Satir model and/or develop a practice based in their own culture.

Many other developments seem to indicate that Satir's work and legacy are alive and well. One can go to North America, Hong Kong, and elsewhere to find them. For example, at the Satir Centre of Australia for the Family, the family chess board, a way of adapting the familiar notion of sculpting families when moving family members around and placing them physically is not desirable or practical, has been developed (Neil, 2004; Neil & Silverberg, 1995).

Whether in the mainstream or not, whether driven by the personal charisma of Virginia or not, the Satir legacy is a different and growing phenomenon throughout much of the world.

John Banmen and his colleagues have produced a fine product in committing to paper interesting descriptions of a vivid, experiential model of therapy and training that virtually defy being captured in ink.

References

Avanta Network. What is Avanta? Internet, downloaded 9/28/05.

Banmen, J. (1998). Stages of change. Presentation at the Intensive Residential Training Program. Federal Way, WA.

Banmen, J., & Maki-Banmen, K. (2000). *Satir's systemic brief therapy training program, level II.* Richmond, BC: Satir Institute of the Pacific.

Lum, W. (2000). *The lived experience of using the personal iceberg metaphor from Satir's systemic brief therapy training.* Unpublished master's thesis. University of British Columbia, Vancouver, Canada.

Neil, S. E. S. (2004). The family chessboard and projective genogramming: Two tools for exploring family systems. In W. C. Nichols (Ed.), *Family therapy around theworld: A festschrift for Florence W. Kaslow* (pp. 173–86). New York: Haworth Press.

Neil, S. E. S., & Silverberg, R. L. N. (1995). *The family chessboard: Sound moves for a sounder family.* Melbourne: Satir Centre of Australia.

Satir, V. (1988). *The new peoplemaking.* Palo Alto, CA: Science and Behavior Books.

Satir, V., Banmen, J., Gerber, J., & Gomori, M. (1991). *The Satir model.* Palo Alto, CA: Science and Behavior Books.

Schwartz, R. C. (1995). *Internal family systems therapy.* New York: Guilford Press.

PREFACE

Virginia Satir (1916–1988) was one of the original founders of the family therapy movement. She was born in Neillsville, Wisconsin, USA, to a farming family, the eldest of five children. Eighteen months after her birth, her twin brothers arrived, then a sister and, finally, another boy. She often talked about taking care of her siblings during their time growing up together on the farm. Her formal schooling began in a one-room rural school. She attended high school in Milwaukee, graduating just before she turned sixteen. By the time she was twenty, in 1936, she had completed her bachelor's degree in education from the University of Wisconsin. She started teaching the same year in a small rural community and quickly learned that her relationship with her students' families played a large role in her success as a teacher. In 1948, she earned a master's degree in social work from the University of Chicago.

The therapeutic community in Chicago at the time was very psychoanalytic and male dominated. Satir said that she tried to follow the practice of the day, seeing only individuals and avoiding seeing more than one member of the same family even separately, but this was not comfortable for her. By 1951, she had seen her first family (Satir, Banmen, Gerber & Gomori, 1991). In 1959, she joined Don Jackson and Jules Riskin as co-founders of the Mental Research Institute (MRI) at Menlo Park, California. That same year she taught her first family therapy course at MRI . Her interest was more toward clinical work and teaching than research, and she soon became the Director of Training at MRI . In 1962, MRI received a National Institute for Mental Health grant to offer its first formal family therapy training program.

In 1964, Virginia Satir published her first book, *Conjoint Family Therapy*, in which she presented her views on the importance of working with families and the tremendous impact that family systems have on individuals. The book caught on, and she then devoted much of her time to traveling around the world offering workshops and training programs in family therapy. Her aims included helping people become "more fully human."

She started annual month-long training programs in 1969 and continued them until her death in 1988. I first met Virginia in 1970 in Manitoba, Canada, at a five-day residential training program. As so many other people have before and since that time, I experienced her work with people as magical and very powerful. Just the month before I met her, I had received my doctorate in psychology; but my experience with Virginia Satir made it seem that my therapy training had begun all over again.

In 1972, Virginia spent three months in Manitoba, Canada, working with several groups: the provincial government, including the premier and his cabinet members; helping professionals from various fields; and the public. It was a rich time in which I experienced the best learning in my life. By 1981, I joined her month-long training programs as part of her faculty. Much of what she did and taught was the subject of *The Satir Model: Family Therapy and Beyond* (1991), which I co-authored with her, Jane Gerber, and Maria Gomori. It was published three years after Virginia's death.

During the 1980s, Virginia focused most of her time and efforts on working with large groups. During that time, she developed and extensively used the two therapeutic vehicles with which she is most commonly associated: Family Reconstruction and the Parts Party. Both are well described in *The Satir Model.* In this book, the chapter by *Gilles Beaudry* describes new developments in the Family Reconstruction process.

In these large-group workshops, Virginia focused on promoting and facilitating personal and professional growth. Many participants reported experiencing major improvements in their lives as a result of the changes they made during and after attending such workshops. However, what seemed to be missing for many therapeutic practitioners were he skills to translate what they experienced in the large-group workshops to their own places of work. They wanted to become more competent in doing therapy with individuals and families using the Satir model.

This has become my goal during the years since Virginia's death in 1988. Since then, colleagues and I have taught the Satir model in a form that is useful for practicing therapists in office settings working with individuals and families. We call this Satir's Systemic Brief Therapy, which suggests her legacy is a form of therapy that is systemic and offers deep transformational change in a relatively short period. In this book, all but one of the contributing authors practice Satir's systemic brief therapy with clients. Most are training other therapists to do so, as well.)

In our therapeutic practices, we have learned to assist clients in setting positive directional goals that meet the requirements of the whole person, inside and out. A key aspect of the Satir model is that of working on major changes, or transformations. The focus integrates both intrapsychic and interactive approaches, as Virginia demonstrated throughout her clinical work.

We build on the resources of each individual client and of the family system. Into each therapy session, we bring our hope and belief that change is possible. We work on bringing about transformation at the levels of feelings, perceptions, and expectations and help our clients find ways to meet their deepest yearnings.

The therapeutic focus is on facilitating change so that people become different at a deep level, not just on doing things differently or on feeling differently. Similarly, in our Satir's Systemic Brief Therapy trainings, we stress that each therapist must become as congruent, as wholesome, and as internally harmonious as possible and live life that way, especially during therapy sessions.

The ensuing chapters describe aspects of our way of working therapeutically. The results are significant. Our clients need much less time in therapy, and they make much greater changes in their lives, including their relationships with themselves and others.

I hope this book gives a clear sense of how the Satir model has evolved and is applied in various situations. Also, I hope it informs readers of useful and practical therapeutic approaches.

John Banmen

Contributing Authors

- John Banmen, R.Psych, AAMFT, director of training, Satir Institute of the Pacific.
- Gilles Beaudry, Ph.D., clinical supervisor and therapist, Service de Conseiller; and professor, College Universitaire de Saint-Boniface, Winnipeg, Manitoba, Canada.
- Cecilia L.W. Chan, Director, Centre on Behavioral Health; and professor, Department of Social Work and Social Administration, University of Hong Kong.
- Grace Y. K. Cheung, honorary assistant professor, Department of Social Work and Social Administration, University of Hong Kong; and director, Resculpt —Center for Personal and Relational Reconstruction.
- Judy Ferris, M.A., M.Ed., Child, Youth, and Family therapist in Langley, B.C., Canada.
- Max Innes, Ph.D., AAMFT-approved supervisor; and individual, couples and family therapist in Vancouver, B.C., Canada.
- Bonnie Lee, Ph.D., assistant professor in addictions counseling, School of Health Sciences, University of Lethbridge, Alberta, Canada; and AAMFT-approved supervisor and marriage and family therapist.
- Lenley Lewis, M.A., psychotherapist and freelance writer/editor, Waynesburg, PA, USA.
- Wendy Lum, M.A., RCC, Counselor at the University of Victoria, B.C., Canada.
- Anne K. Morrison, MSW, RSW, RMFT, therapist, consultant, and trainer, Abbotsford, B.C., Canada.
- William C. Nichols, Ed.D., ABPP (Clinical), Athens, Georgia, USA, Former president of the American Association of Marriage and Family Therapy; former president of the International Family Therapy Association; and editor of *Contemporary Family Therapy Journal.*
- Carl Sayles, Psy.D., licensed marriage and family therapist, trainer, and supervisor in Roseville, CA, USA.
- Jim Smith, BPE, RCC, RSW, director of Langley Youth & Family Services, Langley, B.C., Canada.
- Stephen Smith, MSW, addictions therapist with the Surrey Alcohol and Drug Outpatient Clinic, Surrey, B.C., Canada.
- Gloria Taylor, M.A., AAMFT-approved supervisor and individual, couples and family therapist in Kitchener-Waterloo, ON, Canada.

1

THE SATIR MODEL: YESTERDAY AND TODAY

John Banmen

Virginia Satir is considered to be one of the pioneers of family therapy. One of her earliest contributions was the idea and practice of seeing more than one member of the same family at the same time (Satir, Banmen, Gerber & Gomori, 1991). What a daring challenge that she and others—such as John Elderkin Bell, Nathan Ackerman, and Murray Bowen—made to the existing practice of the day. And that was only the beginning of her contributions to family therapy and personal growth. Now, most therapists, and especially family therapists, consider such a practice not only normal, but essential in their work.

Satir was an innovator at the practical level. She put little effort on recording or even explaining her theoretical base. Nevertheless, over the years, her practice, her training programs, and her recorded demonstrations have indicated a deep, consistent psychological and therapeutic theoretical base. Few family therapy authors have captured the depth and significance of her contributions.

This chapter will be an attempt to share a small part of the Satir model and how it is presently practiced.

The Theory of the Satir Model

The Satir model, as Satir's contributions have become known, can best be placed in the humanistic/transpersonal psychological schools. From a therapeutic perspective, the Satir model falls within the experiential family therapy frame.

Therapy models are based on a foundation of beliefs, assumptions, and hypotheses. Without going into the philosophical antecedents of the Satir model, let us look at a few therapeutic beliefs that set the context for this chapter.

1. Change is always possible, even if change can only take place inside of the person. These changes might include feelings, perceptions, and expectations.
2. Therapy sessions need to be experiential to bring about second-level change. This involves a change in being, not only in doing or feeling.
3. The problem is not the problem; coping is the problem. Therefore, therapy focuses on improving one's coping instead of just solving one's problems.
4. Feelings belong to us and, therefore, we can learn to change them, manage them, and enjoy them.
5. Therapy sets positively directional goals and resolves the impact of negative experiences.
6. Therapy is systemic, both intrapsychically and interactively.
7. People have the resources they need to cope and grow. Therapy is one vehicle to harness these resources to help people change.
8. Most people choose familiarity over the discomfort or fear of change, especially during times of stress.

These, and similar therapeutic beliefs (Satir et al., 1991) help guide the therapist with a base from which to view human beings, relationships, and change.

The Three Areas of Therapeutic Intervention

The Satir model focuses on three major areas for therapeutic intervention: the intrapsychic, the interactive, and the family of origin.

The Intrapsychic System

The intrapsychic focus has been identified in terms of an Iceberg

Metaphor. Many of the articles in this issue will include some reference to the Iceberg Metaphor. Basically, it is a way of conceptualizing human experience and recognizing that most human experience is actually internal. The components of the internal experience are very interactive and systemic. Changes in one area often result in some changes in other areas. In a linear, two dimensional framework, the areas, or components, that are included in the Iceberg Metaphor are: a) behavior, b) perceptions, c) expectations, d) yearnings, and e) the Self. A detailed diagram of the Satir model Iceberg Metaphor is shown below.

Assume that a client comes to see you for help. Let us say that he is unhappy because his wife left him for another man. After the therapist makes some contact with him by asking the client some personal questions with genuine interest, the therapist might say something like this: "Well, tell me, what brings you here today?"

This kind of question usually brings about some description of some events. It is the story of his unhappiness and what brings him for therapy. The Satir model advocates keeping the story to a minimum and only using the story to provide part of the context in which the therapeutic work will take place.

It is now up to the therapist to explore the internal experience of the client. This will involve asking various questions related to the person's feelings, perceptions, expectations, and yearnings. Sample questions might include the following:

- "How do you feel right now?"
- "How did you feel when your wife left?"
- "How did you express or handle your feelings?"
- "How do you see yourself now that your wife left?"
- "How do you see your wife now that she left you?"
- "What other feelings are you aware of?"
- "What hopes and expectations did you have of your marriage?"
- "What did you possibly contribute to make the break up take place?"
- "What deeper longings are you aware of?"

These questions give an example of how to explore the internal, or intrapsychic, experience of the client. As these types of questions are being considered, the therapist now wants to start setting some goals. It is hoped that these goals relate to the internal experiences of the client. The client wants to feel better and more positive. The client wants to resolve his unmet expectations that have given him a lot of reactive, negative feelings lately. He needs to find ways of meeting his yearnings, possibly forgiving himself, loving and accepting himself, and appreciating what he has done and who he is. While setting such goals, the client needs to be helped to make some commitments to work on these goals.

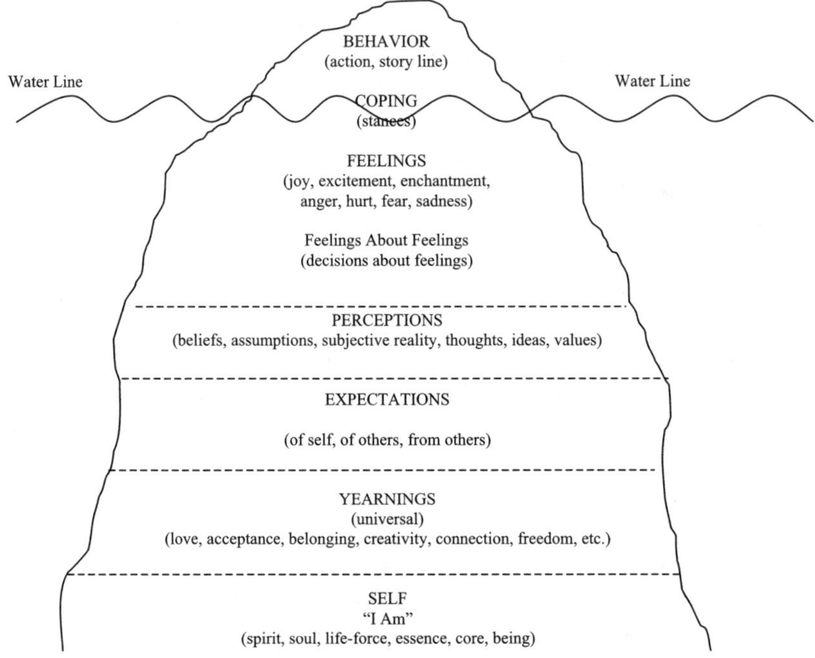

Figure 1.1

The Personal Iceburg Metaphor

Now, the therapist helps the client to change whatever is in the way of experiencing some harmony, some self-worth, and some sense of accepting and empowering himself. He needs to resolve his disappointment, his possible guilt, his anger, hurt and sadness.

The focus, initially, is to work on the intrapsychic area before focusing on the interactive area of his life. Goals are positively directionally framed to provide the client with a focus for change.

The Satir model has set four meta-goals as its positively directional focus for change. These are:

1. Raising the self-esteem of the clients. Self-esteem is considered as one's own judgment, or experience, of one's own value.

2. Helping clients to be their own choice makers. Satir encouraged people to consider at least three choices in any situation. She wanted to empower people to become their own choice makers. At the mechanistic, reductionist level of viewing humanity, we often find ourselves at one or the other end of a polarity: right or wrong, good or bad, for example. The Satir model, in simple terms, tries to avoid dilemmas such as "either/or" choices and advocates looking at one's situation in terms of three or more possibilities. The model also advocates a more integrative view instead of "either/or" thinking. Choices are not only decisions about one's actions; they include different responses to unmet expectations instead of a person's usual reactions.
3. Helping clients to be more responsible. Responsibility includes being in charge of one's internal experiences, not only one's behavior. The main focus here often is being responsible fore one's own feelings. This includes being in charge of them, managing them and enjoying them. Written works of such authors as Damasio (1999), Le Doux (1996), and Pert (1997), detail how the responsibility of individuals could move deeper inside towards the molecular level of responsibility and change. The Satir model is open to such possibilities in its therapeutic work.
4. Helping clients become congruent. Congruence is a state of internal and external harmony. It is a sense of calmness, wholeness, peace, and tranquility. Congruence is a state therapists are encouraged to be in during their therapy sessions. It is a sense of empowerment, which means that the individual is not controlled or triggered negatively by the outside world, but responds to the world from a state of internal harmony with one's deepest Self, as well as with others and within the context of the situation.

With these meta-goals as background and a framework, the therapist helps each client and each family formulate their own specific positively directional goals. These goals need to include the whole person, not only one aspect of life such as behavior or feelings. In Satir model terms, goals need to include changes in behavior, feelings, feelings about feelings, perceptions, expectations, and yearnings. That is, goals need to include every part of the Iceberg Metaphor. The Satir model in the 21st century is best described as positively directional goal focused and transformational change based.

The Interactive System

In relationships, whether it is couples or families, people often report their problems as conflicts. The Satir model looks at people's relationships in terms of sameness and differences. Satir used to say that sameness attracts and differences help us grow. She missed telling us the other l ess effective ways to deal with differences. In the therapeutic field, we often hear about conflict resolution. The Satir model advocates resolving differences from a congruent place of interacting. Differences are handled in various ways. There are five ways that people might use to handle differences:

1. *Conflict as a solution.* This method of handling differences includes physical or verbal fights and disagreements. It is an either/or position with only one right possibility. It often builds on the polarity of right and wrong. In the hierarchical model, it becomes a power struggle. As might seem obvious, the Satir model does not advocate this approach to resolving conflict within, between, nor among people.
2. *Denial as a solution.* Even though differences exist, people using denial, either verbally or nonverbally, have decided to avoid the differences. For example, people never share or discuss their religious or political views because of potential disagreements or conflict. They withhold their views and might, instead, withdraw from each other and avoid intimacy and closeness.
3. *Compromise as a solution.* When people compromise, both parties give in and both win and lose as they choose something that possibly neither wants, but both feel they can accept. It is sometimes a 50/50 settlement. Very often, in therapy, this level of dealing with differences is the beginning of reconnecting with each other.
4. *Resolution as an answer.* At this level of dealing with differences, both parties win. The resolution usually takes place at a deeper level of connectedness, at the level of yearnings. Here, people accept each other, both with positive intentions and good will. Often, resolving major differences needs a third party to help the individuals work through some of the disappointments, anger, fear and hurt that might be lingering.
5. *Growth as an outcome.* Finally, when we look at how differences help people grow, we find that through understanding, acceptance, and risk-taking, clients can learn to incorporate some of their differences into their lives. Here, I usually share an example with my

clients of some aesthetic differences between my wife and me. "I liked opera and she liked ballet. Now, we both like opera and ballet." In therapy, differences often trigger the survival needs and, therefore, differences become a life/death issue between couples or among family members.

The Family-of-Origin System

The Satir model puts a great deal of emphasis on family-of-origin work. The major shift over the years has been away from using the family map (genogram) as a way of connecting with one's parents as adult peers. The current emphasis is on resolving the negative impact of one's internal experience in the family of origin and reclaiming the resources one has received from one's family of origin. Family maps are very important in family reconstructions, one of Satir's most well known therapeutic vehicles for change. Now, they are often used in individual and family therapy sessions, as well. The family maps might look very much like they did when Satir used them. The processing of them seems to have evolved into something very different.

Working with an adult individual, we usually do a family map of the client's family of origin. The map includes two major time frames: the factual present and the perceptual past. For therapeutic purposes, it seems advisable to do the factual present first, and then follow it with the perceptual past.

The factual present portion of the family-of-origin map includes the following:

1. Father and mother's name
2. Their birth dates and birthplaces
3. Their current ages or ages at death
4. The date of their marriage and of their separation/divorce, if applicable.
5. Their religious affiliations, if any.
6. Their occupations
7. Their education
8. Their ethnic backgrounds
9. Their hobbies and interests
10. Any illnesses, infirmaries, or disabilities

We then add the same information for each of the children in the family including, of course, the client. The client is a child in the family-of-origin map, regardless of age.

We also include the deaths of any siblings, any miscarriages and abortions, if applicable. A stage I present, factual family-of-origin map is illustrated in Figure 1.2.

Figure 1.2

Stage I: Present Factual Family-of-Origin Map

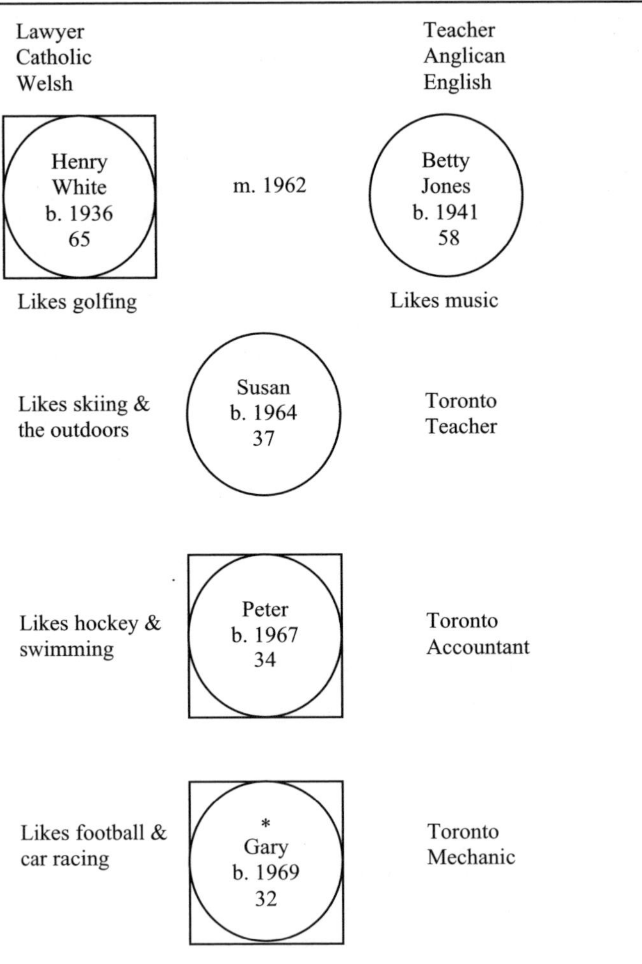

As you look at the factual, present family-of-origin map, you can see the structure of the map drawing. Children are placed in a vertical line instead of the more common horizontal line. Women are identified with circles; men are shown with squares around circles.

Once this factual present portion of the family-of-origin map is completed, we ask our clients to go back in time, preferably before the age of 18, and relax to give us some experiential data. We want two aspects of their experience. One is to give each member of their family, including themselves, two or three positive adjectives and two or three negative adjectives as they recall their childhood/adolescent experience of their family. During the early Satir model practice, as indicated in Satir and associates (1991), we only asked for three adjectives for each family member. We found that people who placate, who try to please others, often only gave positive adjectives. People who blame often gave negative adjectives. As we know that all people have both positive and negative aspects of themselves, we now ask for both.

The second aspect of the client's childhood experience we access is the way that people in the family behaved in relationship to each other under times of stress or considerable disagreement. This description of relationships under stress is, of course, a generalization of how they remember childhood family experiences.

We give the client a code with four possibilities:

1. A solid, thick line often indicates an enmeshed relationship between two family members.
2. A wavy or jagged line indicates a stormy, turbulent, or hostile relationship under stress.
3. A solid, thin line indicates a normal, accepting relationship, even under stress.
4. A broken line indicates a distant, negative, or indifferent relationship under stress.

Of course, other possibilities exist, but we find that these four types of relationships are usually enough to capture the picture of how most people relate under stress.

Family maps become useful once we start our therapy and find some emotional experiences that do not make sense in the client's present circumstances and which have not yet been resolved from childhood experiences. They are also helpful to assist clients to go inside themselves or when we suspect that some impacts of the past are interfering with present living.

If no specific event or context is generating the negative impacts which the client is experiencing, we use a wide net to explore the impact of many areas. For example, we might explore the impact on the client of the family member relationships, the adjectives of each family member, the survival stances of each family member under stress, any illnesses that family members had, any losses that the family had, any other significant events family members had, and so forth.

Figure 1.3

Stage I and II: Present Factual & Perceptual Past Family-of-Origin Map

Gary White's Family

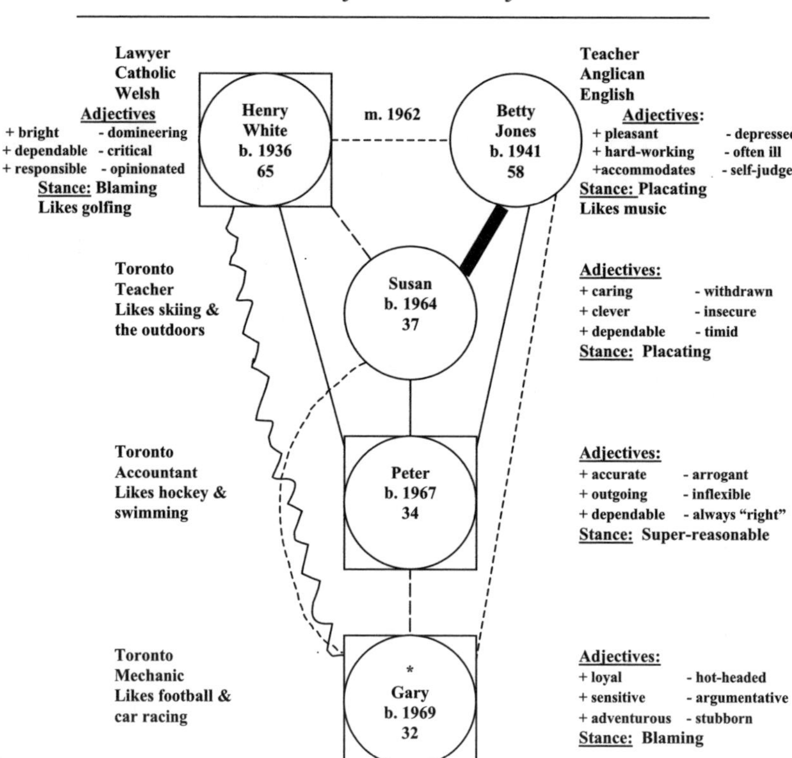

The purpose is to reduce the negative impact these matters had or still have on the individual in terms of influencing, affecting, or controlling his or her behavior, feelings, perceptions, expectations, yearnings, or experience of their deeper Self. More optimistically, sometimes these negative impacts can be transformed into positive resources.

When dealing with families, the most common use of family maps is to have the factual and perceptual stage both in the present context. The map often becomes slightly more complex because each family member might have different perceptions of themselves and of the others in the family. Sometimes a more common picture evolves when people have worked through some serious differences of perceptions and expectations. Nevertheless, differences need to be acceptable in a healthy, growing family.

The Survival Coping Stances

In earlier times, while Satir was still at the Mental Research Institute, her approach was considered to be a communication model. At that time, she placed a lot of emphasis on people interacting with each other in a "straight" manner. After observing a large number of families interacting, or communicating, she formulated some basic behavior into patterns that she called "survival stances." No matter how rough or difficult the experience people had in their family of origin, they would find a way to cope and survive. In order to show how people experienced themselves in these patterns, Satir sculpted, or externalized, the internal experience of family members. Out of this developed her well-known coping stances, which she referred to as 1) placating, 2) blaming, 3) super-reasonable, and 4) irrelevant. Much can be said about these stances. Excellent background reading material can be found in The New Peoplemaking (1988) by Virginia Satir.

Coping stances are modes of surviving under emotional stress. They are not personality categories. Most people have one major coping stance that they use when they are under stress. Many people actually use all four coping stances depending on the circumstances and relationships in which they find themselves. For example, a person might placate at work and blame at home and act irrelevant with friends at a party.

Assuming that most readers know these aspects of the Satir model, little will be said about the characteristics of each coping stance. More information can be found in Satir et al. (1991).

What is important here is how these stances help us therapeutically. Once we assess our clients, even if it is just an observation of how they talk about their problem, we might be able to identify their coping stance. Knowing the coping stance, we will know how to connect with them in their internal process. Making contact with the client is an important concept and requirement for Satir-model therapy. While other models talk about building rapport, Satir emphasized making contact. By seeing each client in terms of an Iceberg Metaphor and immediately appraising the client's likely coping stance, the therapist can use the following ways to make deeper and faster contact.

Clients who use the placating stance as their way of coping under stress can easily be reached through their feelings. Clients like this are often depressed, see themselves as victims, and feel helpless and hopeless. By relating to the client through their feelings, rapport is built and therapy can begin.

Clients who use the blaming stance as their way of coping under stress can easily be reached through their expectations. The therapist focuses on what the client wants instead of how he feels. By doing this, rapport can be built quickly and easily.

Clients who use the super-reasonable stance as their way of coping under stress can easily be reached through their perceptions. These clients seem to be in their heads, rational, reasonable, logical, factual, and poorly connected with their feelings. To engage these clients beyond their super-reasonable stance, the therapist might first explore their body reactions and their expectations before they can connect with their feelings.

Clients who use the irrelevant stance as their way of coping with stress are difficult to reach. Body sensations, touch, and physical activities such as going for a walk with them are three ways to start making contact with people who use the irrelevant stance. I often start working with them in terms of their context. In that moment of time, that usually means having them explore their immediate surroundings, namely my office. Inviting them to comment on the space, the furniture, the colors, and the office contents helps them to settle down, build some boundaries, and build some trust. This seems to work especially well with ADHD (Attention Deficit Hyperactive Disorder) clients who would be considered to be using the irrelevant stance in the Satir model.

Knowing your clients' stances and using the Iceberg Metaphor will greatly reduce the time needed to make contact with them. Once contact has been made and you have entered the client's internal system, the whole Iceberg, the whole person, becomes available to the therapist to help bring about change.

Let us now look at a simple outline that would show the general aspects of a Satir-model therapeutic session in point form.

1. The therapist prepares himself or herself. We find it important that the therapist prepares him- or herself internally as well as preparing externally. That includes centering oneself, focusing one's energy on the client, becoming prepared to receiving and accepting the client.
2. As the client enters the office, the therapist makes contact with the client. At first, a few social interactions might help. Contact suggests a connection with the clients that is focused on hearing and accepting clients in their present state of operation. Contact is very important in the Satir model. Assessing the clients' coping stances during this time and communicating within the component of the Iceberg Metaphor, as stated elsewhere, would increase the speed and depth of the contact.
3. Once some contact is made, the therapist is ready to listen to the problem. "What brings you here today? What would you like to look at today? What are we going to work on today?" might be questions that will begin the clients' sharing of their problems. Many clients seem ready and able to respond to these or similar questions, but most want to tell the therapist what is "wrong" with them or some other member of the family. Their focus is to tell the problem. The question for the therapist is how much of the story do the clients tell before the therapist starts asking questions that will take the clients inside of themselves? Most therapists, in our experience, not only allow the clients to tell their story, but actually encourage it by asking more content questions than process questions, thereby continuing the talk therapy mode. What the Satir model encourages is to keep the story short and use it as part of the context within which to do therapy.
4. Once there is a general sense of what is happening to the client or clients, the therapist starts the process of helping the client formulate the problem into some positively directional goals for each part of the internal process. These include goals for feeling, perception, expectations, yearnings, and, finally, goals for behavior. Goal setting is a joint effort between therapist and client, but it includes goals for the whole person, not just behavior or cognition. As the therapy proceeds, goals often change into deeper or more hidden areas of the client's experience.

5. Sometimes, clients are out of touch with their inner self, or are confused, depressed, or extremely angry. What is needed then is some effort by therapist and client to explore the internal functions of the client. Some time and effort is needed for the clients to experience themselves, to increase their awareness of themselves, and to accept what they surface before they can realistically set positively directional goals. Some clients need to do some work on a major impact of an event before they can set positively directional goals. If there is a serious block keeping the client from looking ahead, often some work needs to take place before such positive movement happens. Nevertheless, the Satir model encourages early positive goal setting to avoid pathologizing the client and/or the therapy focus.
6. Once the goal setting starts, and it is hoped still during the first session, the client is asked to make a commitment to working on making changes. Are you willing to work on achieving that goal?"

   "Is that something you are willing to work on?"

   "Will that goal help you to change your reaction?

   "Are you ready to commit to working on that goal?
7. Often therapists seem to assume that clients are committed to change when they are only willing to talk about it, or, worse, they expect the therapist to do the work for them.
8. The major task in the Satir model is working on change. This is best achieved when the process is experiential. The therapist takes an active part in taking the clients into their internal experience and works on helping the clients to change the negative impact of their many experiences. Again, the meta-goals are for the clients to experience higher self-esteem, to be better choice makers, to be more responsible (especially internally), and to be more congruent. Changes in the areas of feelings, perceptions, expectations, yearnings, and behavior are the basic therapeutic areas of work. The rest of the process is person-specific; it is driven by the yearnings and positively directional goals of the client, not just the problem.
9. Anchoring changes is also an important aspect of change therapy. This important therapeutic process includes accepting the change, internalizing the change, making room for the change in the different parts of the internal process (the Iceberg Metaphor), and integrating the change. Anchoring change takes place throughout the session whenever some shift, some new insight, some therapeutic movement, or some internal healing has taken place. Of course, at the end of the session, anchoring any work of the client is important.

10. Before the session ends, the therapist, with some input from the client or the family, gives homework designed to put into practice the changes that were worked on or achieved during the therapy session. Homework, according to the Satir model, is usually focused on internal change instead of the old behavioral activity like going for a walk or taking a bubble bath. Early examples of homework might include:
    - Monitoring one's feelings
    - Tracking one's expectations
    - Surfacing one's perceptions (beliefs)
    - Connecting with one's yearnings
    - Becoming aware of how feelings and perceptions interact
    - Becoming aware of how feelings and expectations interact

    Of course, later on much of the homework is focused on changing what no longer fits and making room for more congruence.
11. With a short summary of the work achieved, the session comes to an end.

The above gives the reader a short description of what most sessions today are like using the Satir model. The main focus is on achieving positively directional internal goals first. Many of the clients who come to therapists who are using the Satir model present us with problems such as couples' relationships, family relationships, suicide, sexual abuse, family violence, depression, obsessive-compulsive disorder, post-traumatic stress disorder, bipolar disorder, dissociative personality disorder, anxiety disorder, and the many other common or typical difficulties.

We do acknowledge clients' problems, their symptoms and their struggles, but we want to focus first on the client, on the person, and not get lost in the "problem" or "symptom." We want to have clients tap and connect with their own life energy and allow that life energy, or life force, to become their own center of being. Then they will have access to all of the rewards and responsibilities possible at their own level of competence.

Conclusion

The Satir model is situated within the experiential/humanistic tradition of therapy with a strong existential flavor. During the last few years of Virginia Satir's life, she added more of a spiritual component to her therapy. Her personal mandala, mentioned elsewhere, indicates this as well.

The spiritual aspect of people has continued to expand in the Satir model and now is an important aspect of the therapist's growth and part of the therapeutic process. The main focus is on change towards greater wholeness, more harmony, greater responsibility and, ultimately, a fuller life.

References

Damasio, A. (1999). *The feeling of what happens.* New York: Harcourt Brace and Company.

Le Doux, J. (1996). *The emotional brain.* New York: Simon & Schuster.

Pert, C. (1996). *Molecules of emotion.* New York: Scribner.

Satir, V. (1988). *The new peoplemaking.* Palo Alto, CA: Science and Behavior Books.

Satir, V., Banmen, J., Gerber, J., & Gomori, M. (1991). *The Satir model: Family therapy and beyond.* Palo Alto, CA: Science and Behavior Books.

2

The Positive Psychology of Virginia Satir

Lenley Lewis and John Banmen

For too long we have been caught in the morass of "pathology" and have forgotten that growth is possible at any age, given the proper context.
— Virginia Satir (1964)

Virginia Satir was an innovative family therapist and a forerunner of positive psychology. Her methods continue to be developed, studied, and applied today, nearly two decades after her death in 1988. In 2002, the international journal *Contemporary Family Therapy* devoted an entire volume to Satir's work, which is the basis for this book. Avanta, the Virginia Satir Network, is publishing *Applications of the Satir Model,* which addresses the model's use in individual, family, and organizational contexts (Banmen, 2006).

Virginia Satir's work is most often referred to as the Satir Model (Banmen, 2002; Satir et al., 1991) and sometimes the Satir Process (Loeschen, 2002). More recently, it is known as Satir Transformational Systemic Therapy (Banmen, 2002). By any name, Satir's therapeutic system is compatible with and complementary to those of positive psychology as championed by Seligman (1998, 2005) and eastern-inspired positive approaches that have emerged in growing numbers over the last decades (Linehan, 1991; Epstein, 1995; Germer et al., 2005). Taken together, Satir, positive psychology, and adaptations of ancient eastern psychology, or Abhidharma (Goleman, 1991; Bhikku, 2005) give us a more comprehensive positive psychology that attends to the dynamics of transformation, spiritual matters, amelioration, maturation, and self-fulfillment.

In the last decade, positive psychology has emerged as an increasingly influential trend in psychological research and treatment. It is commonplace to observe that modern psychology, founded on a medical model fixed on pathology, has neglected the study of positive emotions, virtues, and strengths. How do these qualities promote resilience and recovery from negative events and states? How can we help people in whom negative thoughts and emotions predominate, such as those with depression, personality disorders, post–traumatic stress disorder, and anxiety? How can psychotherapy prevent mental illnesses and antisocial behaviors from developing or recurring, or both? Is the personhood, or self, of the therapist key to the success of psychotherapy, or can equally good results arise with a combination of psychoeducation and cognitive behavioral techniques deliverable by anyone with a modicum of training (or even self-administered)? Finally, in what ways can we help clients, as Satir did, to connect with the ability to direct their energies toward both maturation and transformation, or toward what Ryff and Singer (2000) called "interpersonal flourishing"?

Martin Seligman and Barbara Fredrickson, along with Ryff and Singer, are among a growing number who believe that positive psychology can enhance our ability to understand and treat mental illness and promote mental health: the amelioration and maturation part of the goal outlined earlier. Seligman's work has focused on optimism, happiness, and learning to live a pleasant, engaged, and meaningful life (Seligman, 1998, 2002, 2003, 2005). The "meaningful life" aspect of Seligman's positive psychology addresses transformation as Satir viewed it: change toward greater wholeness, harmony, and responsibility in relation to self, others, and context (Satir, 1964, p. 91).

Fredrickson (2003) has demonstrated ways in which positive emotions help us to use all of our mental capacities more fully and effectively (also Fredrickson & Jonner, 2002, Fredrickson & Branigan, 2005).

Her formulations, too, explain how truly transformative, qualitative psychological change occurs. Seligman, Fredrickson, and many others are contributing to a growing body of literature on strengths-based and positive approaches. We broaden this list by adding the "positive psychologists" inspired by Abhidharma to incorporate mindful awareness practices: Linehan, 1993a; Hayes, 2005; Germer et al., 2005). Included, in addition, are practitioners of Satir's methods, which predate and prefigure many elements of both Seligman's and Abhidharma-inspired approaches to positive psychology.

The literature and research make a compelling case for a turn toward a more psychoeducational, strengths-based approach to psychotherapy, one that aims not simply to alleviate suffering, but also to prevent recurrence of maladaptive patterns and foster ongoing growth through transformation of one's relationship to suffering (Lewis, 2006). Satir and Abhidharma bring to these goals an explicit recognition of innate sanity and goodness, a recognition of self as process, and an emphasis on acceptance and the capacity for growth and change across the lifespan. These approaches also bring practical methods which, like Seligman's gratitude visits and daily lists, may prevent recurrence of problems and promote lasting change. A growing body of scientific and experiential evidence suggests that such behavioral and mental practices or methods change not only brain chemistry but also brain structure and function over the long term (Cullen, 2006; Siegel, 1999).

In many ways, Satir's approach prefigured key aspects of positive psychology as conceptualized and practiced today. Satir died in 1988, but her followers and students continue to teach and use the Satir Model in schools, clinics, and private practices worldwide. It has become particularly influential in Asia and is enjoying a resurgence in the United States, Canada, and Europe (Satir, Banmen, Gerber & Gomori, 1991; Cheung & Chan, 2002; Banmen, 2006). The model's popularity in Asia may be due, at least in part, to the many parallels between Satir's approach and Abhidharma, whose rise in the west has already helped usher in a more complete positive psychology. Many empirically supported therapies now incorporate meditative practices (Linehan, 1993a, b; Hayes & Smith, 2005; Germer et al., 2005), as Satir did more than forty years ago (Banmen & Gerber, 1985; Banmen, 2002, 2003).

To greater or lesser degrees, the Satir approach, positive psychology, and Abhidharma-influenced psychotherapy share six key elements:

1. Therapy appeals to and builds on strengths and virtues.
2. Therapy prevents recurrence of maladaptive patterns.
3. Therapy fosters a shift in focus from content to process.
4. Therapy includes psychoeducation to enhance plasticity, the capacity for unlearning negative patterns, and ongoing learning throughout life.
5. Therapy presumes that the capacity for change and the ability to grow and thrive, not just survive, is always available.
6. Therapy can be brief *and* transformational.

This chapter is organized into four main parts: Satir's Place in the History of Psychology, Satir as Forerunner and Promoter of Positive Psychology, Therapeutic Qualities and Methods, and Current Applications and Future Directions. The chapter concludes by suggesting that our ability to relieve suffering is enhanced by a new synthesis of (1) positive psychology (as defined mainly by Seligman, 2005), (2) Abhidharma and mindfulness-based approaches, and (3) wholistic/humanistic approaches exemplified by Satir.

Satir's Place in the History of Psychology

Satir was born in 1916 and came of age in the Freudian era. She trained first as a teacher, then as a social worker at the University of Chicago in the late 1940s. Her childhood was spent in rural Wisconsin as one of five children of an alcoholic father and Christian Scientist mother. Her parents' match was apparently not the happiest. At age five, Satir experienced a nearly fatal consequence of their nearly habitual, but mostly unexpressed, disagreement as she lay on the living room couch in excruciating pain from a ruptured appendix. For nearly two days, her father did nothing to oppose her mother's steadfast refusal of medical treatment until, alarmed at his daughter's obvious deterioration, he scooped her up and took her to the hospital. Satir later reported that she thought, "When I grow up, I'm going to become a detective on parents," so baffled was she by her parent's unspoken disagreement and inaction (personal communication by Sandy Novak to L. Lewis, November 12, 2005).

It comes as no surprise that, along with Don Jackson, Jay Haley, Carl Whitaker, Murray Bowen, Salvador Minuchin, Nathan Ackerman, and John Elderkin Bell, Satir later became a chief architect and great proponent/practitioner of family therapy (Banmen, 2002). Nor is it surprising that she came to place so much emphasis on congruent (i.e., authentic and accurate) communication, so much so that her approach was "mapped" by Bandler and Grinder (1976) and used later as partial foundation for Neurolinguistic Programming (NLP). Satir felt that NLP was too formulaic and lacked emphasis on empowering the client (Baldwin, 2000).

What is somewhat more surprising is that Satir departed so radically from her traditional psychoanalytic training to develop a new approach to psychotherapy, one that incorporated a systemic, process-focused approach, a belief in innate goodness and capacity for self-healing, and a deeply spiritual (as opposed to religious) view of all life as sacred. She retained the psychoanalytic view that we develop defensive strategies very early on that can harden into lifelong dysfunctional patterns. She called these "coping" or "survival" strategies or stances.

Instead of focusing mainly on the past, Satir, like some of those who employ the principles of positive psychology today, looked at the individual's embeddedness in ever-widening and ever-changing contexts (relationships), from family to community to nation to world and universe. She was very comfortable moving back and forth from intra- to interpsychic processes. In fact, she viewed them as an inseparable, integrated whole. Unlike many positive psychologists, however, Satir left plenty of room to explore the inner conflicts people often experience as a result of mismatches or misconceptions that carry over from past experience and beliefs.

Seligman, for example, describes how a discussion of attachment theory and styles may benefit severely depressed clients in individual therapy, but for the most part he ignores developmental family history and the resulting inner conflicts to which Satir paid close attention, even though she believed, "The problem isn't the problem, the coping is the problem" (Satir et al., 1991). She saw the distortions of connectedness that arise in childhood as the origin of habitual coping patterns that obscure inborn self-worth and self-efficacy. By dealing with those distortions in the present, individuals could become more aware and congruent: better able to relate to self, other, and context (Satir, 1964; Satir et al., 1991; Banmen, 2002).

Satir shared with other humanistic psychologists a belief in the worth of each individual and a wholistic approach to growth, but she went farther. She believed in innate goodness, health, or sanity that could not be destroyed and which could always be tapped, no matter how deeply buried under layers of "copings"— a fundamental view of Abhidharma but not most western psychologies (Goleman, 1991; Trungpa, 2005; Germer, 2006). Satir said, "The whole of the therapeutic process must be aimed at opening the healing potential within the client" (Baldwin & Satir, 1983, p. 25). Western psychology, even when "positive," tends to view individuals as needing amelioration.

Satir, like the Zen master Suzuki Roshi, could warmly convey the seemingly paradoxical truth that, "You're all perfect just as you are, *and you could use a little work*" (Suzuki, 2000). How we are at any moment could not be otherwise, given all the causes and conditions that led to that moment. How we are also contains all we need to grow. Once that is recognized, appreciated, and accepted without hanging on or pushing away, one is free to move on, or in the term Epstein borrowed from Winnicott, to "go on being" (Epstein, 2001).

Thus, Satir came early to a relational, interdependent perspective and a belief in innate sanity that resembles both ancient Buddhist Abhidharma and the burgeoning number of contemporary Buddhist-influenced approaches to psychotherapy (Goleman, 1991; Epstein, 1995; Germer et al., 2005). Epstein's definition of self as "unique relational process" is the one we use in this chapter (Epstein, 1995). It is very close to Satir's "understanding self." It may be helpful to understand this view better by looking at it through the eyes of perhaps the world's foremost practitioner and scholar of Abhidharma, the Dalai Lama (1997):

> . . . when we talk about the notion of self in Buddhism, it is important to bear in mind that there are different degrees or types. . . . some types are not only to be cultivated but also to be reinforced and enhanced. For instance, in order to . . . benefit of all beings, one needs a very strong sense of confidence, which is based upon a sense of commitment and courage. This requires a strong sense of self. Unless one has that identity or sense of self, one will not be able to develop the confidence and courage to strongly seek this aim. In addition, the doctrine of Buddha-nature gives us a lot of encouragement and confidence because we realize that there is this potential within us which will allow us to attain the perfection that we are seeking.
>
> — the Dalai Lama

This view is akin to Satir's belief in self-worth as fundamental. Abhidharma also emphasizes the ever-present possibility of accessing innate sanity by seeing how "self" and "reality" are created moment to moment by our changing thoughts, with which we mistakenly identify as "self." Satir knew this intuitively and taught it in various ways to her clients.

As Satir did, a more complete positive psychology views all life as a sacred manifestation of energy, and knows that each individual is capable of tapping into the wellspring of innate healing which the Dalai Lama calls "Buddha-nature," wisdom infused with compassion. This key tenet of Abhidharma (Goleman, 1991) corresponds to what Satir called "Being" or the "I Am" (Banmen, 2002). Satir and Abhidharma emphasize an ongoing process of and capacity for transformational growth, i.e., qualitatively different from previous relational patterns, not just more or less of particular behaviors, thoughts, or feelings. Systems theory called this process second-order change (von Bertalanffy, 1968).

Satir adopted a systems approach based in part on the work of von Bertalanffy and Korzybski's general semantics (1935, 1994), both of which reflect key elements of Abhidharma, including interdependence and impermanence, or recognizing that change is constant and the whole is greater than and different from the sum of its parts, all of which influence each other. Korzybski coined the term, "The map is not the territory," a view echoed and enlarged in Satir's therapeutic adage, "The problem is not the problem; the coping is the problem."

The incorporation of systems theory evolved during her work as director of training at the Mental Research Institute (MRI) in Palo Alto, California from 1959 to 1966. MRI included Gregory Bateson, Don Jackson, Jay Haley, Jules Riskin, and others (Banmen, 2002). Prior to joining MRI, Satir worked in private practice in the early 1950s, and then helped to set up the family therapy training program for residents at the Illinois State Psychiatric Institute, where one of her students was Ivan Boszormenyi-Nagy. He later became a respected and influential family therapist and theorist (Nichols & Schwarz, 2001).

With Satir's emphases on ongoing experiential growth, communication, and choice and responsibility, she cannot be classified simply as a systemic therapist. She left MRI in 1966 to become the director of training for the newly formed Esalen Institute at Big Sur, California, a hotbed of creative approaches to growth and change, including the encounter movement.

In later years, Satir traveled extensively nationally and internationally to lead workshops and therapeutic training for therapists. She and her students (exemplified by the authors in this volume) continued to develop methods for incorporating her nurturing, directive approach to families into brief therapeutic growth workshops and brief therapy with individuals. Satir also held month-long training programs for large groups of therapists from 1970 until her death in 1987. Then and now, these programs came through the Avanta Network, founded to promote her work.

Satir argued that therapy is more art than science, and that love and faith in innate healing capacity are more important than skills and techniques. She did not discount techniques, however, and was the innovator of many, such as sculpting coping stances, exploring the self mandala of mind–body interplay, family reconstruction, here-and-now explorations of bodily states, and Temperature Reading. These are still used widely in individual and family therapy and organizational training (Banmen, 2002).

Through her travels and training workshops, Satir hoped to promote world peace through what she called “peace within, peace between, and peace among,” a belief some criticized and found naïve. Salvador Minuchin, who once criticized the “softer” Satir style, recently said, “I’ve moved . . . to a softer style, in which I use humor, acceptance, support, suggestion, and seduction on behalf of the same goals that I once reached with a sharper style” (Sykes Wylie, 2005, p. 50). It is also interesting to note that we have now learned that females most often manage stress not via the typical male “fight-or-flight” response, but via a “tend and befriend” response (Taylor et al., 2000), which resembles Satir’s positive, directive, and nurturant approach to therapy.

Satir is still acknowledged as one of the giants of therapeutic practice and innovation. Her model was refined and described by her, her senior students, and more recently (1991), her colleagues Banmen, Gerber, and Gomori in *The Satir Model: Family Therapy and Beyond.* In individual, couples, and family therapy, practitioners continue to apply her methods, such as exploring the iceberg and personal mandala, sculpting coping stances, and family reconstruction. They also use them in classrooms, police departments, addictions treatment, and organizational development contexts in many countries throughout the world, as Carl Sayles describes in a subsequent chapter. As acceptance and mindfulness, wholistic, somatic, and alternative approaches and positive psychology gain ground, and as cognitive-behavioral therapies find greater success by incorporating a strengths-based approach, we can profitably revisit Satir’s work to re-evaluate her contributions for ways to enhance positive psychology.

Satir as Forerunner and Promoter of Positive Psychology

Martin Seligman is widely viewed as both founder and popularizer of the science of positive psychology, which started, by his reckoning, in 1998, when he was the newly elected president of the American Psychological Association (Seligman, 1998, 2005). It should be noted, however, that Satir used the basic principles of positive psychology, such as a focus on health and strengths and recognizing the importance of positive experience, engagement, meaning, and self-worth in her clinical work long before 1998. In fact, many of the core principles of positive psychology, including some not specifically addressed by Seligman, Fredrickson, or others, were firmly in place in Satir's work by 1964, when she published *Conjoint Family Therapy*. Satir's work set the stage, and perhaps the standard, for Seligman's development of positive psychology.

For example, Satir focused on health and strengths, not illness. She saw dysfunctions as misguided solutions: ways or means of coping or surviving that contain the seeds of transformation and growth. Clients cannot see this, but the therapist can, and can lend hope and strength to clients as they learn to access their own innate positive resources, make choices, and take responsibility based on the exercise of their undistorted strengths and creativity, the deepest of which is the capacity to give and receive love (Satir, 1964).

Satir believed in focusing on the problem or "story line" only to the degree that it enabled process to emerge—the habitual patterns of relating that would change in the therapeutic relationship. Seligman's story line engagingly describes how *his* positive psychology began with a personal epiphany prompted by his then five-year-old daughter, to whom he had spoken sharply while he worked and she played in their garden. She responded by asking if he remembered how he had told her she was whiny when she was four, and asked whether he had noticed she had not been whiny in the weeks since turning five. He reflected, then acknowledged she had changed. She said she had just decided not to be that way any more, and added that if *she* could choose not to be whiny, *he* could choose not to be grumpy.

Seligman had been vaguely dissatisfied with his well-known work in the field of prevention, and with psychology overall. He said his exchange with his little daughter led him to see that his success until then was not because of his ability to identify what is weak or wrong, but in spite of it (Seligman, 2005). A wholistic psychologist like Satir, or one influenced by eastern thought, might reframe this: Seligman had his realization not in spite of anything but because of everything. We need our weaknesses *and* our strengths; confusion dawns as wisdom.

Prompted by his daughter, Seligman concluded that if all we do is try to correct, or even prevent, weaknesses, as psychology tried to do for its first century (and as Seligman and most of us have done in child-rearing), "you can only go from minus five to zero" (Seligman, 2005). Seligman thought that was not good enough. He enlisted helpers, and embarked on a systematic project to figure out how to go to plus five or more instead of from minus five (dysfunction) to baseline, or zero (Freud's much quoted "ordinary unhappiness"). His intent was not to replace the disease or "remediation" model, but to supplement it with an enhancement model that would identify and build on positive emotional engagement and meaning to build a psychology that was "good enough" (Seligman, 2005).

This emphasis on "plus five," not baseline or deficits, is similar to Satir's insistence that a key role of the therapist is to promote ongoing positive growth and change to help the individual connect with positive thoughts and feelings associated with self-esteem and self-worth at all levels of what she called "The Iceberg" (see the graphic depiction of the Iceberg metaphor in Banmen's subsequent chapter). Visible above the waterline are actions, behaviors, and the spoken word; a vaster territory of "interior" or unspoken aspects lies beneath. This territory includes habitual coping patterns, feelings, beliefs, expectations, yearnings, and a desire and capacity for engagement and a fundamental connectedness at the deepest level of being, the level at which the individual has maximum connection with self, other, and context. This is the level of "Self" or "Being" or "I Am," to use three of the terms Satir used to describe the essence of personhood (Banmen, 2002).

Satir's work was also formed by her belief in universal human qualities that are embodied and expressed uniquely within each individual. This belief enabled her to work effectively across cultures. In 1998, Seligman and his colleagues began their search for universal human virtues and strengths. They identified 24 of these, which they grouped into six universal classes or clusters: wisdom and knowledge, courage, love and humanity, justice, moderation, and spirituality. These are exhaustively described and compared cross-culturally in what Seligman calls "the un-DSM," an 800-plus–page volume called *Character Strengths and Virtues: A Handbook and Classification* (Peterson & Seligman, 2005).

Of these, those most strongly linked to happiness are the "interpersonal virtues," those linked not so much to wisdom or achievement but to the well-being of one's fellows. "As a professor, I don't like this," Seligman confessed, "but the cerebral virtues, curiosity, love of learning, are less strongly tied to happiness than interpersonal virtues like kindness, gratitude and capacity for love" (Wallis, 2005). Satir encouraged the development of empathy, especially for one's parents, which she fostered through family reconstruction, an intensive brief-therapy model (see the later chapter by Taylor and Beaudry).

For more than two millennia, the world's religious traditions have taught the primacy of fellow-feeling for lasting happiness. Abhidharma teaches numerous kinds of mindful awareness, concentration, and analytical types of meditation as ways to develop the interpersonal virtues as well as ways of observing the mind to reduce emotional reactivity and identifying one's self with one's thoughts. Psychotherapy has incorporated some of these (Germer et al., 2005). All of the foregoing remind us of Satir's insistence, dating back nearly fifty years, on congruence: integrating all aspects of the person with ever-widening contexts of family, community, country, world, and the mysterious web of the universe in infinite connection. Satir can thus be seen as an avatar of both positive psychology and the growing incorporation of Abhidharma into western psychology. She did so using two main theoretical constructs: the Iceberg Metaphor and coping (or survival) stances. These stances represent four ways of behaving under stress, which restrict our full range as human beings—our ability to be congruent (see Banmen's subsequent chapter).

In Seligman's moments of communication, connection, and realization in the garden with his daughter, he experienced was what Satir called congruence—with himself, with his present context and the past inherent in it, and with other: his daughter. He recognized his daughter was able to correct herself. Abhidharma calls this innate sanity (Trungpa, 2005); Satir called it "beyond coping," that is, beyond the reactive self, or "the I Am"—the I Am that knows it somehow includes All (Banmen, 2002).

What Seligman's daughter needed from him, he realized, was not correction but encouragement in naming and developing positive qualities. For Satir, another key role of the therapist was to "label assets" and to reframe negatives so the strengths and seeds for change hidden within complaints could emerge (Satir, 1964). A very vivid example of Satir's reframing of experience, not just words, is given in Russ Haber's article, in which he describes her work with a family attempting to break a cycle of violence and abuse. Satir showed the family how to use both nurturance and boundary setting to do so, beginning by making contact with a brutalized youngster still able to use his hands to express affection.

The interaction between Seligman and his daughter obviously led to growth for both of them. This illustrates a key concept of Satir's systems approach and of Buddhist psychology: that self is ever-changing and relational, not static and unchanging, and that any positive growth builds a greater capacity for positive change in much the way Fredrickson's "broaden and build" model postulates (Fredrickson, 2003). Process takes precedence over content as a focus of therapy. In 1964, Satir wrote, "The process . . . is the relationship, here and now" (1964, p.189).

Seligman and his colleagues defined three components of happiness: the positive emotions of pleasure, engagement (involvement with family and friends, work, and interests), and meaning (using one's signature strengths to serve something larger than oneself). Of the three, they found that hedonic pleasure is least important to lasting happiness and life satisfaction; engagement and meaning are much more important (Seligman, 2002, 2005). Hedonic pleasure alone has little correlation with life satisfaction anywhere on the globe. Seligman found that the happiest people have all three components, and their level of life satisfaction is greater than the sum of the three (Seligman, 2005).

In Satir's systemic view, awareness and integration of all levels of a person's Iceberg permits emergence of a whole larger than the sum of its parts: an individual capable of congruence with self, other, and context. Satir believed that such integrated experience promotes ongoing and exponential positive growth. One of her early suggestions was that therapists ask family members what each could do to bring pleasure to other family members (1964). This intervention nourishes all three of Seligman's happiness components at once, although it focuses on the most important one, meaningful interaction with something larger than self.

Because of the already mentioned exponential effect and ongoing capacity for growth, one person's "optimal" is another's minimal, and no optimal state can be posited for all. The aim for Satir was qualitative change: not just more or less of some behavior or thinking, but an experiential, transformational shift. That kind of change arises from a connection with innate sanity, the "being" level of the Iceberg. People gain access to that experience, Satir believed, when they integrate their behavior, feelings, cognitions, beliefs, expectations, and yearnings. This integration allows entry to the spiritual, being level. One may wish to compare the universal spiritual dimension in the Satir-based Congruence Scale with the life satisfaction and signature skills self-tests on Seligman's web site, authentichappiness.com. Seligman's tests tend to focus somewhat more on the intra- and interpersonal dimensions, although the Congruence Scale are also includes them (see the ensuing chapter by Lee).

Therapeutic Qualities and Methods

Seligman and his collaborators aimed to develop a *science* of positive psychology. Peterson and Seligman's (2005) *Character Strengths and Virtues* thus includes definitions, paradigmatic examples, measures, genetic concordances, sex ratios, correlates, and enabling and disabling conditions and interventions that have been validated through research for all twenty-four of the qualities they identified as universally valued human characteristics (Peterson & Seligman, 2005). Buddhism, too, according to the Dalai Lama and others, is an empirical science of the mind aimed at increasing well being for all, as well as an educational system for training the mind. Abhidharma lists and classifies wholesome qualities in a way similar to the work of Seligman (Goleman, 1991).

Through examination of the mind through various strategies, including visualization, mindfulness, concentration, and analysis, Buddhism developed a list of six wholesome qualities important to the well-being of self and others, along with recommendations for how to cultivate them (Goleman, 1991). They are the *paramitas*, the transcendent qualities, and they bear a striking resemblance to the six clusters identified by Peterson and Seligman (2005). The six paramitas are translated and described somewhat differently by various scholars, but Goleman lists them as: generosity, self-discipline (or moderation), patience (or courage, fortitude), energetic enthusiasm, stability and clarity of mind, and wisdom or insight into the causes and nature of suffering (1991, p. 97). Satir has given us a contemporary model of how to apply the transcendent qualities therapeutically through the skillful use of relational self (Baldwin, 2000).

It must be emphasized that use of self, as Satir conceived it, meant aware and congruent use of personhood in context, including the therapist's interaction with each client and the core beliefs the therapist brings to the therapeutic encounter (Baldwin & Satir, 1987). Satir said (p. 26):

> The whole therapeutic process must be aimed at opening up the 'healing' potential within the client . . . . This clearly brings in the spiritual dimension. People already have what they need to grow . . . if I believe that human beings are sacred, then . . . I can help them live up to their own sacredness.
>
> — Virginia Satir

The core beliefs that underlie the Satir Model are: (1) self-worth is primary, (2) nurturance is the way to effect growth, (3) awareness is the first step toward change, (4) acceptance of self and others is healing, and (5) change is always possible.

As in Buddhist Abhidharma, Satir believed that people have *inborn* goodness and creative qualities such as imagination, creativity, the ability to perceive accurately, to feel and express genuine emotion, and to choose with courage. Any of these can become blocked or distorted by familial and social rules, according to her, resulting in decreased self-worth or self-esteem. *Self-esteem* is how people experience themselves internally and in relationship, not just how they feel emotionally. For Satir, self-worth affects behavior more than any other factor, and it is influenced by how connected people are with their innate health or sanity or, in Satir's term, their *being*. When self-worth is distorted or low, people have problems and act out. When it is high, Satir believed that symptomatic behaviors extinguish themselves (Loeschen, 2002). So self-worth is inextricably linked to congruence, just as it is in Abhidharma.

Satir saw change as coming from the inside out, rather than outside in (see the subsequent chapter by Innes). In systems/process views such as Abhidharma's and Satir's, the "unique relational process" that is the self can accommodate the unknown as well as the known and the negative and uncomfortable aspects of one's relational process as well as the positive. As Satir's colleague Michele Baldwin observed, "Scientific inquiry looks for certainty, instructions, and specificity, when in fact the self as process makes no sense unless you accept that its effectiveness is positively correlated with openness and imprecision" (Baldwin & Satir, 1987, xxi). Sometimes this entails not just flow, but the ability to "not know"—allowing for chaotic unfolding in the here and now: what Daniel Stern called *sloppiness* so that "*now moments*"—the healing ones—can emerge (Stern, 2004). Satir talked about the creative power of chaos and presence in the here and now in the therapeutic process as early as 1964, noting that the experience of chaos disrupts old systemic patterns and motivates change via heightened awareness (Satir, 1964).

The first step in Satir's model of therapy, therefore, was to prepare her *self* to make genuine contact, centering herself and preparing to focus her entire attention and energy on receiving and accepting the client (see the subsequent chapters by Banmen and Lum et al..; Baldwin & Satir, 1987). She then connected with each individual's personhood, conveying respect for his or her *being* so that the client could experience that for him- or herself. Satir made contact using her own well-developed qualities and skills (as opposed to mere techniques), and this *integration of cognition*, *emotion*, *conation*, and *chosen behavior* was what she referred to as the therapist's congruent use of self.

It has often been observed, by Satir and others, that therapists gain therapeutic effectiveness and grow both personally and professionally while serving clients, blurring distinctions between helped and helper. Seligman's garden vignette with his daughter illustrates this mutuality of benefit quite clearly. Coaches, too, know that players get better the more they are aware of and attuned and committed to the larger-than-self world of the team and the setting.

The therapist's skillful use of the congruent, relational process self (i.e., in tune with self, other, and context) is one of Satir's greatest contributions to therapy, one in danger of being lost in self-therapies based on manuals or the web or both. Even Seligman, who extols the virtues of web-based, "no-hands" (i.e., no one-on-one relationship) interventions for mild to moderate depression, emphasizes that the more severe the illness, the greater the need for therapeutically skilled one-on-one intervention (Seligman, 2005).

We believe this means a therapist skilled in *use of self* as well as techniques, in keeping with the well-known findings of Hubble, Duncan & Miller (1999) about the therapeutic relationship's primary significance. Germer (2006) notes that when therapists themselves have problems, they do not usually go to behaviorists known for their skills, but to therapists known for qualities of warmth and acceptance. He emphasizes, as Satir did, that kindness and genuine (congruent) warmth must precede, accompany, and inform the therapist's actions, because whatever the theoretical orientation, these are the qualities associated with effectiveness.

Once Satir made contact with clients, she went on to hear the client's problem, all the while assessing coping and communication styles. She validated people's efforts, pain, individuality, feelings, wants, and points of view. Acknowledging these mattered not only for increasing their self-esteem but also for increasing their ability to choose and their capacity for change. For example, she might build hope and ask clients to express their hopes out loud. Some of the most important skills she used to validate people are: appreciating, reassuring, affirming, and clarifying, all of which add up to accepting where and who each client is in the moment. She modeled for them the kind of "moment-to-moment awareness with non-judging acceptance" that Abhidharma-influenced therapies advocate as the paradoxical gate to inside–out transformational change (Germer et al., 2005, p.3).

Goal-setting as an active process between therapist and client also starts as early as possible in Satir-model therapy, preferably within the first session (Banmen, 2002). However, if a client was too angry, confused, or depressed to do so , Satir allowed additional time for exploration and self-experience, using her understanding of people's coping stances to connect with their internal process at various levels of the Iceberg (see the subsequent chapter by Banmen). For example, with someone assuming a super-reasonable stance, she might first explore his or her bodily reactions and expectations to enable that person to access feelings more readily. (Banmen's later chapter describes ways to approach clients at their present levels of coping.)

When we strengthen our ability to relate in ways that promote our own and others' ongoing growth and full use of self, we naturally look for ways to convey that. Therapy and psychoeducation aimed at increasing this full use of self is one way. Later in this book, Innes characterizes Satir's method as a "therapeutically oriented educational process." Another way is to integrate mindful awareness practices into therapy. Satir used guided meditations, centering, and here-and-now body scans to enhance aware experiencing and self-integration (Banmen, 2003).

In Satir's process, once she established trust and engagement by making genuine contact, she moved toward change by helping clients heighten awareness. Some heightening of awareness already takes place through making genuine contact and validating. That process is enhanced through interventions such as mapping, educating, shifting from content to process, identifying dysfunctional process, sculpting, and exploring. Therapists can do this using family maps, manipulation of coping stances, and exploring the Iceberg to expose feelings, beliefs, expectations, yearnings, and the interactions among them (elaborated in the ensuing Banmen chapter). We argue that this sort of exploration with a client is a kind of meditation *à deux*. Siegel's observation that the psychotherapeutic relationship reshapes the brain, encouraging more integrated function over time, suggests this may be the case. Brain scans of meditators show similar integration of function (Cullen, 2006).

Another hallmark of Satir's process is promoting acceptance of self and others in the moment as a key to healing, growth, and change. In recent years, numerous therapies have been developed to help clients learn to accept themselves and their circumstances, such as Linehan's (1993a) Dialectical Behavioral Therapy (DBT) and Hayes' Acceptance and Commitment Therapy (Hayes & Smith, 2005). It is important to understand that for Satir, as for Linehan and for Hayes, acceptance does not mean resignation, passivity, or acquiesce to the unacceptable. It means being able to see clearly, then move from content to process: "to meet them[selves] at their capacity for growth" (Haber, 2002). Some of the therapeutic skills Satir used to foster acceptance were reflecting, normalizing, personalizing, contracting, bridging, and reframing (Loeschen, 2002).

After facilitating greater awareness and acceptance, and after goal setting, Satir focused on making changes. She characterized this as a learning process, and she knew that unlearning was harder than learning anew. Satir allied herself with the part(s) of the individual, couple, family, or group that desired growth and uncovered and reduced the need for employing habitual coping styles so that intentional change could occur. She did so by selectively challenging, modeling, guiding, and encouraging rule breaking and face- to-face dialogue (Loeschen, 2002). Satir was a very directive therapist who believed accepting clients where they are is just the beginning of the change process., As positive, strengths-based, and brief therapies do, she also used homework exercises to anchor change, to build self-esteem and self-efficacy, and to generalize change (see the subsequent chapter by Banmen).

Because change is difficult to maintain and takes repeated practice, Satir reinforced changes to increase the likelihood of (1) continued development over time, a built-in protection from relapse, and (2) generalization of changes in thinking and experiencing to new situations and settings. In each phase of the therapeutic process, she reinforced the changes made in the previous phase and constantly reformulated positively directional goals. She also used imagery and guided meditations to anchor change (Banmen, 2003), techniques that brain research suggests help anchor new learning and modulate emotional and intra- and interpersonal process (Siegel, 1999; Blakeslee, 2006).

Current Applications and Future Directions

In 1967, in her preface to the revised edition of *Conjoint Family Therapy*, Satir wrote,

> I have been interested to see an evolution in the practice of medicine, in which the idea of empowering the patient has brought medicine "back" to the idea that patients can heal themselves. I am also pleased to see the development of personal responsibility in health. One of the most important things is that we have . . . substituted the growth model for the medical model in psychotherapy.

— Virginia Satir

Satir's approach to therapy was goal directed and time limited, just as most strengths-based and positive approaches are today. It is also transformational, aiming toward not just more or less of something the client wants, but "to fundamentally alter the patient's stance in relation to emotional experience" (Lewis, 2006, in press). Such shifts can promote lasting change and build prevention into therapy by promoting resilience. Satir would call this developing congruence. Mindfulness-based cognitive therapy, for example, has been shown to reduce the risk of recurrence of depression (Segal et al., 2002).

Abhidharma, too, emphasizes a fundamental, accessible shift in the experience of emotion, which it classifies together with thoughts, intentions, constructs, perceptions, and sensations as "mental events" in a way similar to Satir's listing thoughts, beliefs, assumptions, and ideas together with feelings and feelings about feelings in the "underwater" levels of the Iceberg. If we realize that our thoughts create our feelings and experience, rather than the other way around, we can learn to tolerate negative feelings until they shift, as they will on their own, given mindful awareness and acceptance rather than pushing away. We can have our change *and* be ourselves if we allow "self" to go on being rather than striving to change (Germer, 2006). As Satir said, "When I am in touch with the unknown in me, my presence is healing and helpful" (Baldwin & Satir, 1987, p. 36).

Satir taught us that our problems are not the problem we think they are; our habitual, unconscious ways of coping are. Abhidharma tells us we are not *who* we think we are; we are constantly changing relational processes that can choose and learn, given the proper context, just as Satir insisted. New approaches that merge positive psychology with mindful awareness are promising ways of creating "the proper context" for innate health to emerge, especially in the hands of therapists skilled in use of relational self (including not knowing and the ability to use whatever arises in the moment), as Satir assuredly was.

One such approach is a merger of Linehan's DBT, which includes mindful awareness practice, with mentalizing (awareness of one's own and others' mental states and processes) and some aspects of positive psychology which is now being used at the Menninger Clinic at Baylor University School of Medicine (Lewis in Allen & Fonagy, 2006). Many others could be cited. The advantage of such mergers is that they recognize the adaptive value of both positive and negative emotions, and they aim to help clients not simply to modulate negative emotion but to cultivate positive emotion and "maintain an optimum balance of cognition and emotion" that makes sense of raw bodily experience. One component of Linehan's DBT model which Lewis believes may promote increased capacity for mentalizing is the GIVE interpersonal effectiveness module (Lewis, 2006). It is a way to train relational self in process. *G* stands for gentleness: no attacks, threats, or judgmental moralizing. *I* stands for interest: listening, not interrupting, making eye contact, and so on. *V* stands for validating: acknowledging one's understanding and appreciation of the other's position. *E* signifies an easy manner that incorporates humor and light-heartedness (Linehan, 1993b). These can readily be seen as "signature strengths" of Satir's use of self in therapy (Satir et al., 1991; Baldwin & Satir, 1987; Lum, 2002). We believe they may promote second-order, transformational change that builds resilience and helps prevent relapse.

Fredrickson suggests that the experience of prosocial feelings engendered by such practices "elevates" individuals by broadening and building capacity to experience positive emotion and to respond to others in such skillful ways as Linehan's GIVE module describes (Fredrickson & Branigan 2005). Haidt's (2000) research found that the experience of elevation can be induced in the laboratory by showing inspirational videos, such as the life of Mother Teresa. His findings thus relate to the previously cited research on mirror neurons, Blakeslee's so-called "cells that read minds" and the correlation of increased integration of brain function with mindful awareness and other elevated states, such as compassion and reverence (Cullen, 2006; Haidt, 2000; Blakeslee, 2006). These efforts remind us of Satir's emphasis on empathy and congruence, and her use of the body and sculpting to promote new learning more rapidly.

It appears that the combination of mindfully *witnessing* a skillful therapist's (such as Satir) mindfully *experiencing* the "corrective" interaction, and mindfully mentalizing (particularly the process of creating meaning out of the raw experience of interaction) work together to build capacity for interpersonal flourishing. The transformational change or lifelong plasticity that psychotherapy seeks to promote is best facilitated through these kinds of integration of emotion, cognition, conation (motivation and directed intention), and behavior in relationship that Satir, almost alone among therapists of her era, demonstrated to us so well decades ago. This is evident in videos of Satir at work (available from www.avanta.net). From both positive psychology research, such as Seligman's and Ryff's scales, and from neurosciences research, such as EEG, MRI, and CAT scan studies, many tools now provide evidence of what works best for various sorts of mental suffering. Random assignment studies are another tool than be used to conduct the research into Satir's methods for which Satir practitioners are calling (Innes, 2002).

Seligman has said, "the *zeit* is really *geisting*" on Positive Psychology (Seligman, 2005). Many projects are under way in addition to Seligman's and Fredrickson's. Other therapies gaining attention include Mindfulness-Based Stress Reduction (Kabat-Zinn, 2005), Mindfulness-Based Cognitive Behavioral Therapy for depression (Segal et al., 2002), Acceptance and Commitment Therapy (Hayes & Smith 2005), Innate Health/Health Realization (Sedgeman, 2005; Capuzzi & Gross, 2003), DBT (Linehan, 1993a), Mentalizing (Allen & Fonagy, 2006), and ongoing refinement of Satir's work through training centers throughout the world (Banmen et al., 2006).

Conclusion

Whatever the theoretical orientation, our ability to alleviate suffering and promote transformational change does depend on relationship (Hubble et al., 1999)., Whatever the method employed, that is, clients' perceptions about the therapist's empathic understanding or warmth play a big rolein developing those qualities themselves. Empathy and compassion are qualities that lead to lasting happiness (Germer et al., 2005; Seligman, 2005; Bhikku, 2005). As we have seen, the therapist's ability to relate with warmth and empathy is a key element of the Satir model.

Satir was practical and eclectic, willing to use whatever worked to enhance self-esteem and congruence. Given the depth and breadth of human diversity, there is plenty of room—and need for a multiplicity of approaches at any given time. As described in the later chapter by Cheung and Chan, Satir integrated intellect and intuition to bridge east and west and help others achieve "peace within, peace between, and peace among." What the *zeit* seems to be *geisting* on now is a belief, like Satir's, in innate health and the capacity of each individual to connect with ever-widening and constantly changing contexts through mindful relationship. A true pioneer, Satir instinctively and distinctively tied the common threads of Abhidharma and positive psychology together long before other practitioners began to develop similar approaches.

Those interested in positive psychology and applications of Abhidharma to psychotherapy are likely to find much that resonates and inspires in the positive psychology of Virginia Satir. She is a skillful guide whose methods are being studied and taught by a new generation of therapists. Close examination of her work richly rewards those who aspire, as Satir did, to promote peace within individuals, between family members and friends, and among diverse members of the world community.

References

Allen, J. G. & Fonagy, P. (Eds.) (2006). *Handbook of mentalization-based treatment.* Chichester, U.K.: Wiley.

Baldwin, M. (Ed.) (2000). *The use of self in therapy. 2nd ed.* New York: Haworth Press.

Baldwin, M. & Satir, V. (1987). *The use of self in therapy.* Binghamton, NY: Haworth Press.

Bandler, R.; Grinder, J.; & Satir, V. (1976). *Changing with families.* Palo Alto, CA: Science and Behavior Books.

Banmen, J. (2002). The Satir model: Yesterday and today. *Contemporary Family Therapy, 24,* 7–22.

Banmen, J. (Ed). (2003). *Meditations of Virginia Satir.* Seattle, WA: Avanta, the Virginia Satir Network.

Banmen, J. (Ed). (2006, in press). *Applications of the Satir growth model.* Seattle, WA: Avanta, the Virginia Satir Network.

Banmen, J. & Gerber, J. (Eds.) (1985). *Virginia Satir: Meditations and inspirations.* Berkeley, CA: Celestial Arts.

Bhikku, T. (2005). The karma of happiness. *Shambhala Sun, 14,* 44–49, 99–104.

Blakeslee, S. (2006). Cells that read minds. *New York Times.* January 10, 2006, D1, D4.

Capuzzi, D. & Gross, D. (2003). Health realization. In *Counseling and Psychotherapy.* Columbus, OH: Merrill Prentice Hall.

Chadwick, D. (2001). *To shine one corner of the world.* New York: Broadway Books.

Cheung, G. & Chan, C. (2002) The Satir model and cultural sensitivity: A Hong Kong reflection. *Contemporary Family Therapy, 24,* 1, 199–215.

Cullen, L. T. (2006). How to get smarter, one breath at a time. *Time.* January 10, 2006.

Dalai Lama. (1997). *Healing anger: The power of patience from a Buddhist perspective.* Ithaca, NY: Snow Lion.

Epstein, M. (1995). *Thoughts without a thinker.* New York: Basic Books.

Epstein, M. (2001). *Going on being.* New York: Broadway Books.

Fredrickson, B. L. (2003). The value of positive emotions. *American Scientist, 91*, 330–35.

Fredrickson, B. L. & Branigan, C. (2005). Positive emotions broaden the scope of attention and thought–action repertoires. *Cognition and Emotion, 19*, 313–33.

Fredrickson, B. L. & Joiner, T. (2002). Positive emotions trigger an upward spiral toward emotional well-being. *Psychological Science, 13*, 172–75.

Germer, C. (2006). You gotta have heart. *Psychotherapy Networker, 30*, 54–60.

Germer, C., Siegel, R., & Fulton, P. (Eds.) (2005). *Mindfulness and psychotherapy*. New York: Guilford Press.

Goleman, D. (1991). In H. Benson, H. Gardner, D. Goleman, & R. Thurman (Eds.), *MindScience: An east–west dialogue*. Somerville, MA: Wisdom Publications.

Haber, Russ (2002). Virginia Satir: An integrated, humanistic approach. *Contemporary Family Therapy, 24*, 23–34.

Haidt, J. (2000). The positive emotion of elevation. *Prevention & Treatment, 3* (March 7), 3.

Hayes, S. C. & Smith, S. (2005). *Get out of your mind and into your life: The new acceptance and commitment therapy*. Oakland, CA: New Harbinger Publications.

Hubble, M. A. Duncan, B. L. & Miller, S.D. (1999). *The heart and soul of change: What works in therapy*. New York: American Psychological Association.

Innes, M. (2002). Satir's therapeutically oriented educational process: A critical appreciation. *Contemporary Family Therapy, 24*, 35–56.

Kabat-Zinn, J. (2005). *Coming to our senses*. New York: Hyperion.

Korzybski, A. (1935; 5th ed. 1994). *Science and sanity: An introduction to non-Aristotelian systems and general semantics*. New York: Institute of General Semantics.

Lee, B. K. Development of a congruence scale based on the Satir model. *Contemporary Family Therapy, 24*, 217–39.

Lewis, L. (2006, in press). Enhancing mentalizing capacity through dialectical behavior skills training and positive psychology. In Allen, J. G. & Fonagy, P. (Eds), *Handbook of mentalization-based treatment*. Chichester, UK: Wiley.

Linehan, M. M. (1991). In L. Lewis (2006, in press). Enhancing mentalizing capacity through dialectical behavior skills training and positive psychology. In J. G. Allen & P. Fonagy (Eds.), *Handbook of mentalization-based treatment*. Chichester, UK: Wiley.

Linehan, M. M. (1993a). *Cognitive-behavioral treatment of borderline personality disorder*. New York: Guilford Press.

Linehan, M. M. (1993b). *Skills training manual for treating borderline personality disorder*. New York: Guilford Press.

Loeschen, S. (2002). *The Satir process*. Fountain Valley, CA: Halcyon Publishing.

Nichols, M. & Schwartz, R. (2001). *Family therapy: Concepts and methods*. Boston: Allyn & Bacon.

Peterson, C. & Seligman, M.E. P. (2005). *Character strengths and virtues: A handbook and classification.* London: Oxford University Press.

Ryff, C. D. & Singer, B. (2000). Interpersonal flourishing: A positive health agenda for the new millennium. Personality and Social Psychology Review, 4 (1), 31–44.

Satir, V. (1964, 1967, rev.). *Conjoint family therapy.* Palo Alto, CA: Science and Behavior Books.

Satir, V. (1988). *The new peoplemaking.* Palo Alto, CA: Science and Behavior Books.

Satir, V. & Baldwin, M. (1983). *Satir step by step.* Palo Alto, CA: Science and Behavior Books.

Satir, V., Banmen, J., Gerber, J., & Gomori, M. (1991). *The Satir model: Family therapy and beyond.* Palo Alto, CA: Science and Behavior Books.

Sedgeman, J. (2005). Health realization/innate health: can a quiet mind and positive feeling state be accessible over the lifespan without stress-relief techniques? *Medical Science Monitor 11* (12), HY1–6.

Segal, Z. V., Williams, M. G., & Teasdale, J. D. (2002). *Mindfulness-based cognitive therapy for depression: A new approach to preventing relapse.* New York: Guilford Press.

Seligman, M. E. P. (1998). President's column: Building human strength: Psychology's forgotten mission. *APA Monitor, 29* (1), 2.

Seligman, M. E. P. (2002). *Authentic happiness.* New York: Simon and Schuster.

Seligman, M. E. P. (2003). The past and future of positive psychology, foreword in C. L. Keyes & J. Haidt (Eds.), *Positive psychology and the life well-lived.* Washington, DC: American Psychological Association.

Seligman, M. E. P. (2005). *The science of positive psychology.* Address to the Evolution of Psychotherapy Conference, December 7–11, 2005, Anaheim, CA.

Siegel, D. (1999). *The developing mind: How relationships and the brain interact to shape who we are.* New York: Guilford Press

Stern, D. (2004). *The present moment in psychotherapy and everyday life.* New York: W. W. Norton.

Suzuki, R. (2001). In D. Chadwick, *To shine one corner of the world*, p. 3. New York: Broadway Books.

Sykes Wylie, M. (2005). Maestro of the consulting room. *Psychotherapy Networker*, 29, 40–50.

Taylor, S. E., Klein, L. C., Lewis, B. P., Gruenewald, T. L., Gurung, R. A. R, & Updegraff, J. A. (2000). Biobehavioral responses to stress in females: Tend-and-befriend, not fight-or-flight. *Psychological Review*, 107, 429–41.

Trungpa, C. (2005). Th*e sanity we are born with.* Boston: Shambhala.

von Bertalanffy, L. (1968). *General systems theory.* New York: George Braziller.

Wallis, C. (2005) The new science of happiness. *Time.* January 17, 2005

3

Satir's Therapeutically Oriented Educational Process:

A Critical Appreciation

Max Innes

At the outset, I think it important to state my point of view; my bias, as some might say. I never met Virginia Satir. I know her work through her writings, the writings of those who have adopted and developed her approach, videotapes of her clinical demonstrations, and the teachings of one of her close colleagues, John Banmen. While I appreciate much that I have learned from the Satir model, and although I incorporate aspects of the approach in my clinical work, I do not regard myself as a follower of the model. Rather, I see myself as an eclectic family therapist drawing from many of the traditional and current family therapy approaches, reaching toward an integrative theory and practice.

Like Virginia Satir, I began my career in education. Unlike Satir, I came to practice family therapy relatively late in my career, bringing to it a "sociological imagination" (Mills, 1959). Like Satir, I became excited by a humanistic perspective that taught that we had the potential to become masters of our own destiny. Unlike Satir, I came to question the extent to which we can control our lives within the context of the larger society: the structural entity that we are a part of, that supports us, that shapes us, that we maintain, and that we collectively sometimes change. As one social commentator put it, “Men [humans] make their own history, but they do not make it just as they please; they do not make it under circumstances chosen by themselves, but under circumstances directly encountered, given and transmitted from the past” (Marx, 1885, p. 97).

As Satir passionately believed and taught, we can and do make changes in our lives. However, as I see it, the process must not just be “inside–out” but also “outside–in” if it is to be significant and lasting. By “inside–out,” I mean motivating a person in such a way that his or her internal process becomes more transparent and consequently more susceptible to change of his or her own making. By “outside–in,” I mean the process of becoming aware of and addressing factors external to the individual that are likely to support or hinder change. Without knowledge of these factors, our efforts toward change will be poorly grounded and sometimes ineffective. Satir, as I interpret her, was a master of encouraging the first process; she paid less attention to the second in her clinical work with families.

In what follows, I focus primarily on conceptual matters related to the Satir model as they pertain to family therapy. The relation of theory to method and practice is the least developed part of the Satir model. Because those with busy clinical practices do not usually regard theoretical issues as a priority, I begin by making my case for the importance of theory and its significance for the Satir model. Theory in family therapy is about how we believe what we do (methods) and how we do it (therapeutic process) affect those with whom we work (outcome). Unless we have some way of explaining what we do, it is difficult to think, talk about, and plan our work. Without an account of how theory relates to method and practice, it is also difficult to pass on what we learn, other than through personal example.

Satir’s personal example was one of a charismatic, gifted clinician. Following the personal example of a master is effective in dance and martial arts but less helpful in family therapy. If I wish to be able to learn or communicate effectively about what I do in family therapy and how I do it, I must have a good grasp of how methods and therapeutic process relate to outcome. I need some sort of a map to guide me during the process and I need to know which route to follow, when to approach from this direction, when from the other, and where and when to stop and make turns along the way.

To talk to colleagues who do not share my point of view, I must also have some idea of how my ideas relate to other areas of knowledge about human behavior and change. Furthermore, when I work as a family therapist, if I am to appreciate the perspectives of those who visit me to talk about their lives, I must know what assumptions are being made about humans, their behavior, and the social world. When a model expresses these components as an integrated set of principles, we have what I consider to be a theory of family therapy.

Overview of the Satir Model

In this overview, I set out what I see to be the essential, conceptual characteristics of the Satir model. I have drawn on a number of sources: Satir & Baldwin (1983); Satir & Banmen (1984); Satir, Banmen, Gerber, & Gomori (1991); Nichols & Schwartz (2001); as well as Satir (1972, 1988).

The Satir model, like any other approach to understanding and changing human behavior, is grounded in a particular worldview. A worldview is like a lens thorough which one views the world, a conceptual framework that orders and interprets sensations and experience. Worldviews are supported by presuppositions that answer fundamental questions about the field of inquiry. Although not all approaches to human behavior openly state their presuppositions, all worldviews rely on a number of specific presuppositions (for an example of a theory of psychotherapy that states its presuppositions clearly, see Breunlin, Schwartz, & MacKune-Karrer, 1998).

Winter (1992), who has studied Satir's work carefully, suggests that the Satir model is based on common principles that are recognizable in three "foundational assumptions" or presuppositions:

1. An emphasis on systemic process
2. A particular conceptualization of humanity
3. A specific view on change and learning

In Figure 3.1, The Satir Model, I have organized what I take to be the Satir model's major components, including Winter's "foundational assumptions," under four categories: presuppositions, basic constructs, therapeutic process, and methods. This graphic representation indicates how the parts relate to the whole and provides a reference point for the discussion to follow.

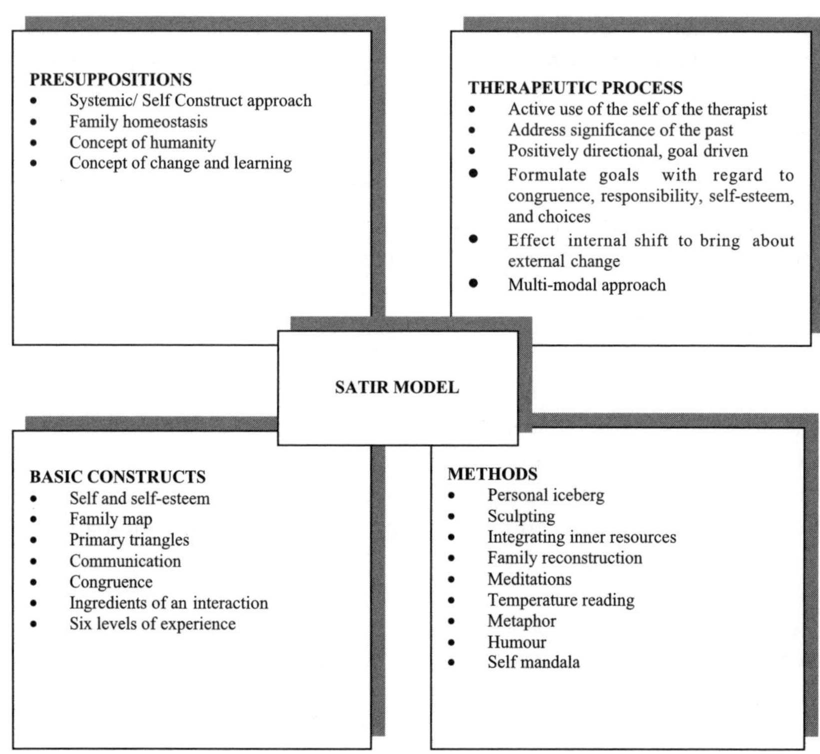

Figure 3.1

The Satir Model

I then focus on the Satir model's presuppositions and basic constructs. While I have already alluded to the way in which presuppositions and basic constructs relate to therapeutic process and methods, I have not specifically described the components of the latter two categories (for an account of Satir's therapeutic process and methods, see Satir, Banmen, Gerber & Gomori, 1991).

Presuppositions

Systemic/Self construct approach. Satir, when talking of change, often used the analogy of a seed and its growth, an organic system. In spite of her attention to personal choice, interaction, and human creativity, she emphasized this organic-systems model as a fundamental aspect of her approach. Like a non-human organic system, the parts of a human system—whether family, communal, or societal—interrelate and are isomorphic.

Isomorphism, a mathematical term borrowed by systems theorists, refers to a relationship between two complex structures that have corresponding parts which play similar roles in their respective structures (Simon, Stierlin & Wynne, 1985). For example, a young teen bargaining with his father for more money for his allowance is isomorphic with his mother and father arguing about money matters, which is, in turn, isomorphic with our entrepreneurial market society.

Rather than viewing them in a linear manner, a systemic framework explains events as arising from a complex set of interactions among multiple variables evolving over time. A system, expressed in the typical systems language of the time (Satir & Baldwin, 1983, p. 191), occurs where:

> . . . every part is related to the other parts in a way such that a change in one brings about a change in all the others. Indeed, in the family, everyone and everything impacts and is impacted by every one person, event and thing. Thus, in assessing the family, it is important to understand the multiple stimuli and multiple effects at work within the given family system.

While systems theory has gone through a number of transitions in the last twenty-five years (see Nichols & Schwartz, 2001, pp. 103–22), the importance of understanding multiple stimuli and effects as they affect the family remains central.

Family homeostasis. The concept of homeostasis, which was central to Satir's thinking about the family as a system (Satir & Baldwin, 1983), was a way of understanding families that Satir had come to appreciate during her time with the Mental Research Institute (Jackson, 1959). Referring to the tendency of living organisms and some mechanical systems to seek a dynamic balance in fluctuating conditions, early family-systems theorists suggested that a similar process was evident in families. This process, which they called *family homeostasis*, revealed itself in the complementary behavior of family members and in the repetitious, circular, and predictable patterns of communication among them.

Satir used the concept of family homeostasis to demonstrate how individual behaviors and relationships within the family maintain some sense of balance in managing the numerous factors that affect the family. For example, when a child is born, the family system must readjust. The mother and father must attend to the new activity of childcare and must cope with the experience of being less available to one another. Considerable temporary conflict may arise within the relationship. One parent may protest about the other parent's not finding enough time to devote to the infant's care. Meanwhile, the other parent may protest that his or her partner is no longer attentive.

In a model that has an underlying assumption about the process of family homeostasis, these conflicts represent the healthy attempts of family members to attend to imbalances that exist within a member or the system. Difficulties (*dysfunction* in functionalist terms or *pathology* in medical terms) arise when these healthy attempts to adjust are blocked or prove to be irresolvable. Considerable balancing and unbalancing is likely to take place before the system reaches a new state of equilibrium. In time, this new equilibrium will be unsettled and new changes will take place, requiring new adaptations.

A systems perspective acknowledges the inherent self-organizing principle of organisms. This perspective views the family as a system within itself and, at the same time, a system in relationship with other systems. The principles governing the family system are evident in the habitual patterns, rules for behavior, and communication styles that various family members use in their relationships with each other. Members use these patterns, rules, and styles both to maintain and restore balance to the family system.

Satir recognized that to understand the system, the patterns, rules, and styles of communicating were much more important than the subject matter. Focusing on the subject matter or event (the content) that stresses a family system and threatens homeostasis is likely to result in power struggles and prevents addressing the underlying conflicts. If, instead, the focus is on how people manage the problem (the process), resolving that problem is more likely. This focus on the process generalizes to solving other issues. Consequently, Satir focused on the process or manner in which problems occur and are sustained, rather than the problem itself.

Humanity. Fundamental to all Satir's work is the conviction in the potential for goodness and wholeness of all human beings. In keeping with the traditional concepts of good and evil, Satir identified and contrasts two perspectives on human nature: hierarchical and organic.

According to Satir, one, the hierarchical, must be overcome; the other, the organic, must be promoted.

The hierarchical perspective, according to the Satir model, views humanity as weak-natured and "inherently bad" (Satir & Baldwin, 1983, p. 165). To control this weakness, a hierarchy exists through which acceptable standards are maintained. The members of this hierarchy's elite provide leadership and act—in their opinion—for the good of all. They promote their standards through reward and punishment. This sort of human organization creates roles based on dominance and subordination. People gain acknowledgment according to their conformity to standards set by the elite. Individuality is not encouraged.

Because the hierarchy socializes people to follow rules of the elite, they take on prescribed roles. As a result, people have few options in life: they act in keeping with the characteristics of their socialized roles.

Defining people and their relationships in this way has many consequences. People in a subordinate role experience a range of self-defeating feelings and behaviors, including hopelessness, despair, rebellion, guilt, and fear. Action is frozen or becomes reactionary.

In spite of appearances to the contrary, prescribed roles and responsibilities also limit members of the elite: they too are governed by tradition. The hierarchical perspective explains noncompliant responses as the elite's failure to socialize people to behave according to the established norms. Such circumstances often lead to blame and faultfinding.

Change is rare since noncompliant behavior constitutes a threat to the status quo. To maintain the existing order, people expend considerable energy, both personal and social, resisting change.

The organic perspective, as Satir used the term in relation to human systems, defines people in terms of their unique characteristics. Acting in their social context, individuals have the potential for goodness and wholeness. She believed that irrespective of personal difficulties, individuals and families have the potential to change and possess the necessary resources for health. Organic systems encourage individual differences, and human relations are based on a mutual recognition of them. People take an interest in self-knowledge and self-development.

From the organic perspective, change is natural and inevitable in nurturing contexts, which recognize and promote choice. Defining people in terms of their individuality instead of in terms of roles and rules places importance on creativity, the process of relationship, and mutual agreement.

Seen this way, atrophy quickly erodes the significance of power and its accompanying relationships of dominance and subordination. An egalitarian system creates the conditions for hopefulness, acceptance, openness, an orientation toward growth, and a realization of potential.

Satir, in her consideration of the dynamics influencing individuals at the macro-social level (hierarchical and organic perspectives), showed a grasp of the importance of the interaction between the individual and society. However, depicting hierarchical relationship in a negative light and organic relationship in a positive light is obfuscation. Both coexist in contemporary society. In undermining the hierarchical perspective ("bad") and championing the organic perspective ("good"), she overlooked the ongoing struggle between two structural components of industrial society. One group struggles to retain a traditional, elitist social order while the other attempts to transform the social order. One needs to acknowledge and address the ongoing struggle between those who maintain the traditional, elitist perspective and those who represent an emerging, egalitarian perspective. Choosing sides does not bring about change. As Satir showed so often in her clinical work, it is not a matter of either/or. Rather, it is a matter of accepting what is present and, when change is desirable, working toward a new state.

Transferring this to the discussion of Satir's conceptualization of humanity, in matters of social change, it is more productive to acknowledge the existence and present inevitability of both the hierarchical perspective (and its structural consequences) and the alternative organic perspective (and its structural possibilities) and act accordingly.

Change and learning. Change, according to the organic perspective, is a natural, ongoing process that enhances the growth and development of the organism and its relationship to the environment. Central to Satir's belief about human characteristics and her approach to therapy is her certainty that people can change and grow, and do so by learning new ways of thinking, feeling, acting, and relating. Change is fostered in the process of creating and fostering new responses to enable people to experience the world differently. Satir taught that when people become aware of their resources, they seek change and actively search for new learning and alternative contexts that promote healthy growth. According to the Satir model, change occurs on several levels.

The process of learning and changing necessitates the willingness and ability to acquire new awareness at a cognitive, emotional level as well as at a visionary and intentional level. When someone integrates these awarenesses, that person has changed by acquiring a new experience that questions the old, regardless of the original motivation for change (Satir & Baldwin 1983).

Satir referred to intentional change as the process of transformation and atrophy. Her experience was that when new learnings are added to old learnings, and new responses are attempted, they gradually, if they are appropriate, take the place of the old learnings and responses. The old ways atrophy and become obsolete. For example, if a mother and her adolescent daughter have grown apart, and both wish to change their relationship so that they become closer, the transformation process might look something like the following. The mother and daughter, with guidance to draw attention to their internal processes, might talk about their sadness about the past and their hopes for the future, and then agree to try something different from their normal routine. This might be having a cup of tea together at the same time every afternoon. Without dwelling on their previous distance and without rushing to manufacture a new closeness, the mother and daughter have an opportunity to learn to relate differently: they can begin to address their unmet expectations and share their hopes. As they learn to relate differently, new possibilities become apparent. In their new daily routine, the relationship gradually changes, the old way fades, and a new way evolves: the possibility exists for change within and change between them.

Basic Constructs. Several fundamental concepts integrate the underlying assumptions of the Satir model outlined above:

1. Self—the individual's experience of self
2. Self-esteem—the value individuals ascribe to themselves
3. Primary Triangle—the formative unit of family relationship
4. Communication—the manner in which people interact
5. Six Levels of Experience—the elemental levels of experience common to human interaction

Self. Satir referred to the self as the nucleus or innermost structure, the "I am" of every individual. She viewed the self metaphorically as a *mandala*, an Eastern concept symbolizing totality or wholeness. Satir used the *self mandala* to characterize the eight facets of mind–body interplay: physical, intellectual, emotional, sensual, interactional, nutritional, contextual, and spiritual (see Satir et al., 1991). The dynamic interplay of these elements constitutes the whole self.

Self-esteem. Self-esteem is "the ability to value one's self and to treat oneself with dignity, love, and reality" (Satir, 1988, p. 22). Those following the Satir approach (Satir et al., 1991, p. 19). suggest that we all come into a world with intrinsic and equal worth. So the question of self-esteem is not whether we have it, but how we manifest it. Self-esteem is always inside us, struggling to be recognized, acknowledged and validated.

Satir recognized that, especially in the first five years of life, one's family of origin, extended family, and significant others, together with additional influences, significantly affect one's sense of self. Both low self-esteem and high self-esteem are products of one's formative experience. However, Satir maintained an optimistic perspective, believing that everyone could develop high self-esteem. Differences in feelings of self-worth become most apparent during periods of crisis and adversity. Those with high self-esteem tend to utilize their resources well, recognize and welcome change, balance the self's eight facets and, in this way, resolve difficulties. Satir believed that such skills could be taught and learned by anyone who made a commitment to do so.

Primary Triangle. The major source of early learning is the *primary triangle*, composed of mother, father, and child. In the course of living with family members, especially parents, the child first experiences and learns about meaningful relationships, principles of closeness and distance, and inclusion and exclusion. The child also learns a set of family rules, which may assist or hinder his or her development. Furthermore, the child becomes aware of different styles of communication and behavior.

To survive, the child must be able to recognize congruent behavior and adapt to incongruent behavior within the family. *Congruent behavior*, in the Satir model, occurs when a person communicates and acts with balanced attention to self, other people, and their context.

Although primary triangles are the contexts we first enter and in which we mature, they are not always nurturing. Nurturing triangles, which may be within or outside the family, encourage an atmosphere of respect, honesty, responsibility, and cooperation. Because they uphold the importance of self-worth, learning, support, and growth, they hold the potential for change.

Communication. Because Satir's work relied so heavily on various aspects of communication, writers often referred to it as a communications approach. Satir did recognize the complexity of communication. In what she termed the "six ingredients of an interaction," she drew attention to the components of perception and conceptualization that are present for each person participating in an interaction. The "ingredients of an interaction" are (Satir et al., 1991):

1. Perception—what one sees or hears or so forth
2. Conception—the meaning of the perception to that individual
3. Primary affect—the feeling evoked by that conception

4. Secondary affect—the feeling about the primary affect (for example, being ashamed of feeling frightened)
5. Defenses—the learned response to uncomfortable situations (for example, showing anger when frightened)
6. Rules for commenting and acting, and the action that ensues from this process

Satir, in keeping with her systemic stance, went beyond viewing an interaction as communication between two or more people. She also took account of context, the setting in which an interaction occurs. Thus, any interaction comprises three components: self, other, and context. These are most readily apparent in Satir's well known "survival (coping) stances" —placating, blaming, being super-reasonable, and irrelevant—in which one or more of the components becomes accentuated at the expense of others.

Drawing from Murray Bowen's terminology (Bowen, 1976), congruence is the goal of a fully differentiated individual. It results when the forces of self, other, and context are in balance (Satir et al., 1991). In its recognition of the significance of context, the Satir model had the potential to situate itself in a larger macro-perspective. However, in the predominant focus on self-esteem and micro-interactions of the moment, Satir never explored the impact of context beyond its negative influence in the super-reasonable and irrelevant survival stances. Context is presumed to be in harmony with self and other in the state of congruence. Little has been written about context, the structural component of human interaction, by Satir and those who have adopted her approach.

Context includes all those factors that might impinge on an interaction, such as political-economic conditions, ethnicity, gender, class, religion, and minority status, to mention the more obvious. Satir had little to say about the influence of such factors because she presented her ideas as universal principles. Her concept of change is grounded in the ability of the individual, with congruent assistance, to pull him- or herself up by the bootstraps, so to speak. Satir attended most to internal process, least to the significance of context.

Without doubt, if change is to occur, the individual or persons wishing to make change must be committed to the process: internal change must take place. However, just as there needs to be a balance among self, other, and context, if a person is to realize congruence, so there must be balance in the process of change. If change is to be optimal and long lasting, this includes attention to internal process, the interaction of self and other, and the significance of context.

Six levels of experience. Satir identified six levels of human experience:

1. Behavior
2. Coping
3. Perceptions
4. Feelings
5. Unmet expectations
6. Longings

In the Satir model, these six levels of experience underlie the clinical method known as entering the *personal iceberg,* a way of engaging the client in inner process work (Satir et al., 1991).

To illustrate these levels in everyday life, let me introduce the following example. I sometimes work with teenagers whose *behavior* is angry. They swear, treat furniture (and sometimes people) roughly, and generally conduct themselves in such a way that a prudent observer would give them a wide berth.

Most of them have experienced considerable trauma in their lives, in their families, in their communities, and in the school setting. Many have experienced anger, in their homes, on the street, and even in school as the way adults and peers deal with frustration. All this illustrates *coping.*

In their *perception*, anger is a way of surviving because most people avoid angry encounters. Anger is not the only feeling these young people experience. Most, if one has the time to listen and earn their trust, say that they have been treated unfairly by adults and that their *feelings* include being uncared for, ignored, pushed around, and generally disrespected.

While many of these young people come from loving homes, they usually go through a time when one or both parents are not available to them. Not always receiving the care or attention they feel entitled to or believe they deserve, they have *unmet expectations.*

Some share their secrets—such as feeling ignored, unlovable, unworthy, or bad—and reveal their *longings*—to be accepted, recognized, and loved. Identifying these levels and gaining access to the experiences associated with them are the beginning of inner process work.

The Satir model's fundamental constructs (self and self-esteem, primary triangle, communication, and the six levels of human experience) are a readily understandable set of concepts from which to explore human action and interaction. They are also an effective basis from which to plan interventions designed to bring about change. Satir's understanding of these constructs allowed her to develop and practice a rich variety of therapeutic interventions.

Locating Satir within the History of Ideas

From the perspective of classical philosophy, the Satir model is most closely aligned with idealism, which suggests that the external material world is either constructed by or dependent upon the mind. More specifically, the approaches known today as constructivism and social constructivism are descriptive of the Satir approach. Satir's belief in the potential of the individual to find internal reserves to overcome difficulties and make significant changes in their lives suggests individuals constructing their own realities: *constructivism*. Her awareness of the significance of the shaping influences of the family and of family interactions across generations suggests individuals constructing their realities in association with others: *social constructivism*. While acknowledging the importance of others, Satir emphasizes the individual's importance in the change process. Primary to her model is her belief in internal process and in the ability of individuals to overcome their difficulties and make significant change in the course of empathetic interaction.

Humanism is also an underpinning of the Satir model. Briefly, humanism arose during the Renaissance as an attempt to reintegrate humans into the world of history and nature, an attempt to counter the deterministic order inherited from the Middle Ages. Humanism is a philosophy that recognizes the value and dignity of humans, and human nature and its interests; and regards humanity as a measure against which to evaluate all else. A major theme in this perspective regards the freedom that humans may choose to exercise in their interactions with each other, society, and nature.

Satir developed her ideas at a time when the deterministic tenets of behaviorism and psychoanalytic theory, on the one hand, and medical psychiatry, on the other, were the accepted canons of the day. Like the Renaissance thinkers, Satir wanted to challenge the notion that previous external or internal factors limited humans in some way. Clearly, freedom of choice is an integral part of the Satir objective of enabling humans to be congruent: "I own me, and therefore, I can engineer me" (Satir 1988, p. 29).

Satir's Methods and Current Trends

Several aspects of the Satir model are apparent in recent developments in psychotherapy. For example, in clinical settings, "internal family systems therapy" (Schwartz, 1995) has systematized, taught, and applied a version of the technique Satir called a "Parts Party." This arose out of a recognized need to bring a person's self back into the family system. Satir, throughout her career, emphasized the importance of parts of the self as they related to the family system.

Another example illustrating the relevance of Satir's work to current developments involve the Family Reconstruction and "sculpting" processes she employed to help individuals free themselves from trauma and abuse in family history. The power for change that Satir recognized in these techniques has been rediscovered in a revised form known as "family constellations," exemplified in the work of Hellinger and his associates (Hellinger, Weber & Beaumont, 1998).

Yet another of Satir's trademarks, her emphasis on sensitivity and feeling-expression, is apparent, and has been shown to be effective, in research and clinical work with "emotionally focused couples therapy" (Greenberg & Johnson, 1985, 1986, 1988).

The 1990s saw increasing interest in the role of religion and spirituality (Brothers, 1992; Aponte, 1994; Walsh, 1999). While the majority of her colleagues avoided any consideration of spirituality in their clinical work, Satir addressed the issue in her workshops, her writing, and her therapy. She regarded spirituality as an essential part of the therapeutic context because it is "our connection to the universe and is basic to our existence" (Satir, 1988, p. 344). Satir described therapy as spirituality in action: "I consider the first step in any change is to contact the spirit. Then together we can clear the way to release the energy for going toward health" (p. 340). Satir approved of the work of Alcoholic Anonymous and reminded us that their work rests on the conviction that "when individuals face their higher power, their life force is called upon and their healing begins" (p. 338).

Long before the current trend to look for the best in different approaches to family therapy, and the accompanying effort to build cross-disciplinary and cross-theoretical models, Satir had embraced the pragmatism of eclecticism. As she put it, "My recommendation is that we free ourselves to look anywhere and use what seems to fit. This makes each of us a continually growing entity" (Satir, 1983 p. ix). In short, many features of the Satir model are contemporary.

Critique of the Satir Approach

Virginia Satir did not apply herself to the formality of linking theory, method, and practice. She was unlike Murray Bowen (1976), who determinedly formulated a theory of human behavior and family systems and which then supported his approach to clinical practice; and unlike Salvador Minuchin, who established an integrated methodology, a body of family therapy techniques that drew from systems theory, structural functionalism (Parsons, 1955), and family development. Instead, she wrote about what worked in her experience. She was well read, and well informed of developments in the field throughout her professional life. Also, she could communicate the models, methods, and processes she used in her work with families. Rather than setting down her ideas about theory and practice in a formal manner, however, her life's work suggests that she was more committed to working with people in therapy and in training, and in spreading the word of the human potential movement and all that is associated with it.

Her writings in *Conjoint Family Therapy* (Satir, 1964) are a collection of notes and essays about her work, which speak loudly about process and method but whisper only occasionally about the principles and theoretical assumptions on underlying her work. She never spelled out those assumptions and threads of connection between the many parts of her work's rich body of techniques. In *Peoplemaking* and *The New Peoplemaking*, she did more than any other pioneer in the family therapy movement to set her ideas before the public: As Minuchin put it, "No one has transcended better than Virginia Satir the problem of taking family therapy to the public" (1988).

What she wrote in *The New Peoplemaking* (Satir, 1988) was clearly articulated, psychoeducational information for the layperson. It was also a clear statement of her belief about family structure and the dynamics of the family. Furthermore, in this book, Satir outlined the precept "peace within, peace between, and peace among (p. 368)," which she hoped would be the guiding principle of her legacy.

The previous edition, *Peoplemaking* (1972), was a self-contained statement about the family through the eyes of Virginia Satir, which drew on what she had learned from others and from her work with families.

In spite of these significant accomplishments, no one, to date, has systematized the presuppositions and theoretical framework underlying Satir's methods and techniques, showing the relationship between theory and practice. Perhaps, like Whitaker (1976), one might wish to claim that "all theories are destructive." However, it may be significant that in the absence of theory, neither Whitaker nor Satir established a distinctive school that has been passed on to the mainstream of family therapy. Instead, they have both been included within a general approach known as Experiential Family Therapy (Nichols & Schwartz, 2001).

Satir's vision was global: "A new evolution in mankind is afoot. All people who are working toward becoming more fully human will be bridges to that new time. We are the transition people" (Satir, 1988, p.xi). However, although her vision is global, and her analysis systemic, her beliefs about change are individualistic:

> My basic message has been and is that a strong link exists between life in the family and the kind of adults that the family's children become. Since individuals make up society, it seems very important that we develop the strongest and most congruent people possible. It all starts in the family. In time, having congruent people at the helm will change the character of our society (Satir, 1988).

In spite of her knowledge of interactions in families, and in spite of her knowledge of systemic principles, Satir suggests an individualist, unidirectional model of societal change: congruent people in powerful positions will change society. If this individualistic ideal of leadership was ever applicable, it ended with the complexity of modern industrial society. Systemic principles suggest that individual, family, group, and societal change is multi-causal and interactional. Arguing that the family influences the individual who, in turn, if he or she is able to become congruent, will change society is a big leap. Unless one ignores the considerable body of evidence of such disciplines as anthropology, sociology, and political economy, it is impossible to overlook the ever-present and sometimes overpowering impact of societal influences. Willing that congruent individuals will make a difference will not change the effect of societal influences.

Satir's stance of methodological individualism is all the more surprising in light of her knowledge of systemic principles and her acknowledgement of societal influences: "The Industrial Revolution profoundly affected the modern family, relieving mates of many burdens, yet also placing many extra strains upon them" (Satir & Baldwin, 1983, p. 29). As Satir suggests, individuals learn and act in social circumstances. As I see it, individuals will only change these circumstances if they are cognizant of the social influences that affect them, and are able to act accordingly. People must not only be congruent, they must also be socially and politically astute, and able to act in concert if they are to change the social conditions that shape family and individuals. The picture of people of the future, "brought up in nurturing families, living in a nurturing world" (Satir & Baldwin, 1983, p.385) is an optimistic view. It will take more than high self-esteem and congruent behavior to enter such a future. In the meantime, at an interpersonal level, optimism is one place to start.

Systems theory teaches us that change is multifaceted: no single cause is sufficient to explain a particular problem, no single intervention will lead to long-term change in human behavior. If this basic tenet of systems theory is accepted (and it was by Satir) high self-esteem by itself will not be enough to overcome the inertia of others, and the other perspectives, practices, and structures that go to make up the context of the social environment.

Congruent behavior (that is, acting in harmony with one's own principles, with regard for other(s) and context) is clearly where change must begin. In the words attributed to Rabbi Hillel, "If I am not for myself, who will be for me?" As Hillel continues, "If I am for myself alone, what am I? If not now, when?" Valuing oneself is not enough. High self esteem and congruent behavior will not bring about the sort of change suggested by "peace within, peace between, peace among." For this sort of change to be possible the change process itself must be multifaceted.

An example may help to illustrate the point as it applies to the therapeutic context. A young woman who is not so different from one that anyone working with adolescents might recognize meets the criteria for being clinically depressed. Various events in her life have resulted in her feeling that life has dealt her harshly, that she has never received the affection she needs from her parents. She compares herself unfavorably with her siblings. She presents as anxious, lacking in self-confidence, and quick to despair. At times of despair she turns to drugs (alcohol, marijuana, cocaine). She has low self-esteem, in terms of the Satir model. This same young woman is intelligent, open to addressing her problems, and willing to make changes in her life. Her mother has experienced depression and is as willing as her daughter to address the issues and work toward a future that would lead to her daughter's happiness. In spite of these hopeful factors likely to support change, and in spite of well-intentioned individual and family therapy, the young woman is trapped increasingly in a damaging cyclical pattern. She feels despair, reaches out for help from friends and family, finds that the help she receives (for example, drugs from friends, sympathy or "pull yourself together" from family) is not what she needs, becomes increasingly hopeless and suicidal, and is admitted to a hospital. In the hospital she recognizes the full significance of her difficulties and makes a commitment to change. When discharged from the hospital she has the best intentions to make sure that things are different this time. In time, the young woman experiences emotional pain, more than she believes she can stand, and it is probable that, without new interventions, the cycle will unfold in much the same way. It usually takes more than inner process work aimed at raising self-esteem to break such a pattern.

More intrusive interventions may have to be used if the above cycle of emotional pain and substance abuse is to be broken. For lasting change to occur it is likely that a number of carefully planned and integrated interventions will have to be in place. She will need to attend a detoxification treatment program, live in a new environment where the old friends, coping mechanisms, and destructive patterns cannot so easily be repeated, and receive an intensive re-education program to assist her to change her taken-for-granted ideas and lifestyle to replace the old ways. After such an away-from-home-and-community program has been completed, the young woman will need to be prepared for return to her home and community (or in some cases situated elsewhere) and supported to continue her new lifestyle when she returns.

Such interventions clearly reach beyond inner process work, beyond individual-therapist and family-therapist clinical process. A micro-structural element has been introduced: in Satir model terms, a change in context has been introduced to affect self and relations with others. In the new social context the taken-for-granted social norms of the young person have been challenged and, if the process is successful, some will have been replaced. This is a multifaceted process—"outside in" as well as "inside out."

Recognition that there needs to be change at the level of context, as well as at the level of self and self–other interaction, for a young person to be able to break free of a harmful, cyclical lifestyle problem takes one beyond the micro-structural level of family and community. At the macro-structural level, there are social, political, economic, and cultural factors that need to be considered if social problems such as substance abuse are to be effectively addressed. While these concerns may be regarded by some as beyond the scope of psychotherapy and family therapy, they are worthy of consideration if our intentions are meant to be more that attempts to assuage the injuries of contemporary industrial society. If we want to think of ourselves as healers, we need more than individual treatment methodologies. In more colloquial terms, it is not effective to treat disease with Band-aids. A systems perspective that claims to address contemporary psycho-social issues needs to grapple with ways of moving between the internal systems perspective applicable to the individual, the micro-systems perspective of the family and community, and the macro-systems perspective of the socio-cultural and political economic structure. To attempt to integrate these systems and apply them to clinical practice is an ambitious undertaking. To attempt less, and claim that any one element will lead to individual change, and through individual change eventually to societal change is to undermine the potential of systems theory and its clinical application to psycho-social problems.

There is no doubt that in her work, Satir moved easily between the intrapsychic world of individuals and the interpersonal world of the family. She was also able to see the life of the individual and the family in a historical context. She clearly demonstrated her skill in working with these two levels, once evident in her workshops and still observable in her demonstration videotapes. Satir worked hard to teach what she had learned and the skills she had acquired. She saw her followers as the leaders of a transitional movement that would lead to an enlightened future: "peace within, peace between, peace among." Many were introduced to Satir's work and were deeply affected by it. Yet, in spite of many followers throughout the world, and a book that has sold well over 700,000 copies and been translated into more than 12 foreign languages, the Satir model has yet to be accepted into the mainstream of family therapy. In spite of Satir's training sessions throughout the world, and several excellent books outlining the techniques of the approach, there is little evidence of a recognizable school representing the Satir model. Instead, there are fragmented groups throughout North America who all practice their own interpretation of the Satir approach. Satir talked and wrote about her work in a non-technical language. Consequently, the Satir model may have appeared too folksy for a new approach to psychotherapy that had to prove itself in the same arena as the medical-technical world of psychologists and psychiatrists.

Another reason may have been that Satir's clinical work and training had a visionary quality about it. She was charismatic in both roles. Her charisma encouraged both therapists and those interested in personal development to follow her ideas and training. Her ideas and methods were commonsensical and appeared deceptively simple to apply. Many, with varying degrees of success, tried to do what she did and taught. Those who became aware of just how much took place in Satir's deceptively straightforward interventions discovered that trying to copy her frequently did not work. It was difficult for most to emulate Satir because, apart from a few basic constructs, there was no way of understanding the principles on which her clinical work was based. Therapists following Satir's work attempted to do what she did. But without her charisma, and without the principles of practice from which to formulate their own approach, their outcomes have been less convincing.

Conclusion

Satir (1988, p. 1) reports that, at the age of five years, she decided that when she grew up she would be a "children's detective on parents." In her perceptive, careful, yet probing approach to clinical work she certainly fulfilled her childhood fantasy. However, she left a legacy of greater depth than a Sherlock Holmes or a Hercule Poirot. She was an independent thinker and clinician who had the courage to pursue new directions in the face of criticism. During her time with the Mental Research Institute (MRI) in the early 1960s Satir was immersed in the concepts of functionalism and cybernetics, the basic concepts of the early family therapy movement. While she accepted some systemic principles (especially those of natural systems), she took on few of the MRI characteristics that produced the strategic therapy of Haley, Watzlawick, and Weakland. Instead, she brought a sensitive, caring, optimistic approach to her work that emphasized the inner strength of individuals and families. Satir encouraged all she worked with to access this strength and use it to address difficulties.

I will let Virginia Satir have the last words. The following passage speaks to the strengths and the optimism of her work. It also indicates her belief in the power of the individual. From her position of "inside–out," she suggests that, with courage and high self-esteem, people can determine their own destinies and create a global "family of the future." As I have previously commented, I believe this "inside–out" optimism must be tempered with the pragmatism of "outside–in" influences. Only then will we be sufficiently aware to be able to remove the constraints that prevent us from realizing new futures. And so to the last words:

> Let us remember that old, traditional, entrenched, familiar attitudes die hard. We need to have patience and, at the same time, be bold enough to take our courage and move forward. We can be prompted by our compassion and intelligence. . . . As we move closer to achieving individual self-worth, the family will be strengthened. In turn, this will produce a more mature society, in which people can have many creative ways to enjoy their lives, making them meaningful as well as socially and personally responsible (Satir, 1988, p. 385)

References

Aponte, H. (1994). *Bread and spirit:* Therapy with the new poor. New York: Norton.

Bowen, M. (1976). *Family therapy in clinical practice.* New York: Jason Aronson.

Brothers, B. J. (Ed.) (1992). Spr*ituality and couples: Heart and soul in the therapy process.* New York: Haworth Press.

Breunlin, D. C., Schwartz, R. C., & MacKune-Karrer, B. (1988). *Metaframeworks: Transcending the models of family therapy.* San Francisco: Jossey-Bass.

Greenberg, L. S., & Johnson, S. M. (1988). *Emotionally focused therapy for couples.* New York: Guilford Press.

Hellinger, B., Weber, G., & Beaumont, H. (1998). *Love's hidden symmetry: What makes love work in relationships.* Phoenix, AZ: Zeig, Tucker & Co.

Jackson, D. Family interaction, family homeostasis, and some implications for conjoint family psychotherapy. In J. Masserman (Ed.), (1959), *Individual and family dynamics* (pp. 122–41). New York: Grune & Stratton.

Kniskern, D. P. (Ed.). *From psyche to system: The evolving therapy of Carl Whitaker* (pp. 317–29). New York: Guilford Press.

Marx, K. (1885). The eighteenth brumaire of Louis Bonaparte. In K. Marx & F. Engels, *Selected works* (pp. 95–180). London: Lawrence & Wishart.

Mills, C. W. (1959). T*he sociological imagination.* New York: Oxford University Press.

Minuchin, S. (1988). Comment on cover of V. Satir, T*he new peoplemaking.* Palo Alto, CA: Science & Behavior Books.

Nichols, M.P., & Schwartz, R.C. (2001). *Family therapy: Concepts and methods.* Boston: Allyn & Bacon.

Parsons, T. & Bales, R. F. (1955). *Family, socialization, and interaction process.* Glencoe: IL: Free Press.

Satir, V. (1964). *Conjoint family therapy.* Palo Alto: Science & Behavior Books.

Satir, V. (1972). *Peoplemaking.* Palo Alto, CA: Science & Behavior Books.

Satir, V. (1988). *The new peoplemaking.* Palo Alto, CA: Science & Behavior Books.

Satir, V., & Baldwin, M. (1983). *Satir step by step.* Palo Alto, CA: Science & Behavior Books.

Satir, V., & Banmen, J. (1983). V*irginia Satir verbatim, 1984.* North Delta, BC: Delta Psychological Associates, Inc.

Satir, V., Banmen, J., Gerber, J., & Gomori, M, (1991). *The Satir model: Family therapy and beyond.* Palo Alto, CA: Science and Behavior Books.

Schwartz, R. C. (1995). *Internal family systems therapy.* New York: Guilford Press.

Simon, F. B., Stierlin H., & Wynne, L. C. (1985). *The language of family therapy: A systemic vocabulary and sourcebook.* New York: Family Process Press.

Walsh, F. (Ed.) (1999). *Spirituality in families and family therapy.* New York: Guilford Press.

Whitaker, C. (1976). The hindrance of theory in clinical work. In P. J. Guerin (Ed.), *Family therapy: Theory and practice* (pp. 154–64). New York: Gardner Press.

Winter, J. E. (1992). *Satir process model: Theoretical foundation.* In family research project: Outcome study of Bowen, Haley, and Satir. Unpublished manuscript. Richmond, VA: Family Research Project.

4

Congruence in Satir's Model: Its Spiritual and Religious Significance

Bonnie K. Lee

Although Virginia Satir's (1916–1988) place as a pioneer and major figure in family therapy is well established (Becvar & Becvar, 1996; Goldenberg & Goldenberg, 1996; Guerin & Chabot, 1997; Hoffman, 1981; Luepnitz, 1988; Nichols & Schwartz, 1998; Sprenkle, Keeney & Sutton, 1982), a number of authors have noted the undervaluation of Satir's contribution and her marginal status in the field of family therapy (Duhl, 1989; Luepnitz, 1988; McGoldrick, 1989; Schwartz, 2000). Satir's success has been cited mostly in historical terms and attributed to her personal "warmth," "artistry," and "charisma" as a clinician rather than in terms of any substantive theoretical contribution (Guerin & Chabot, 1997; Nichols & Schwartz, 1998; Schwartz, 2000). Those most familiar with Satir's work saw her as a "visionary" whose contributions have global and spiritual significance (Brothers, 1991; Duhl, 1989; Loeschen, 1998; Satir, Banmen, Gerber & Gomori, 1991). However, the case for the spiritual significance of Satir's contribution remained to be articulated and characterized systematically and philosophically.

One reason that Satir's model has not been subjected to critical analysis and appraisal for its ideas and theory is that she chose the route of experiential workshops to teach her model. This she did for important reasons which would be subject of another discussion (Lee, 2001). Representations of Satir's work in family therapy textbooks are thereby limited mainly to her early typology of family "communication stances" (Becvar & Becvar, 1996; Goldenberg & Goldenberg, 1996), whereas Satir's integrative, systemic understanding of the person and the elaboration of her construct of congruence in the 1970s and 1980s have not yet been adequately explicated as centrally important to her model. Satir's references to human beings as "sacred," "unique manifestations of life" and "miracles" (Banmen, 2003; Satir, 1987; Satir, 1988) resonated more with religious than scientific discourse which seemed to have put her out of step with the trend in the field of family therapy in the 1970s (Pittman, 1989). However, the *Zeitgeist* that marks the opening of the 21st century is ostensibly more hospitable to inquiries into religion and spirituality than the 1970s and 1980s. In this contemporary climate of resurging interest in religion and spirituality, it is timely to rethink the relevance of Satir's model in terms of its spiritual and religious significance.

The purpose of this chapter is to bring to the fore the coherent philosophy of religious and spiritual significance underlying Satir's work which revolves around her key concept of congruence, a key concept in her model that has not been elaborated fully in the literature on Satir. The meaning of Satir's congruence will be articulated in terms of the goal of the religious quest as explicated by Paul Tillich, preeminent theologian of the 20th century. A comparative analysis of Satir's understanding of congruence pivotal to her therapeutic goal and Tillich's philosophy of religion will be drawn. The purpose of this analysis is to illuminate the religious and spiritual significance of Satir's model in its vision of healing and restoration of humanity's wholeness manifested as reconnection with self, others, and one's spiritual essence.

Defining Religion and Spirituality

Words mutate in their meanings and connotations over time. "Religion" and "spirituality" are words whose meanings have been in flux in recent years (Zinnbauer et al., 1997). Therefore it is important to begin with a clarification of these terms as used in this chapter.

Etymologically, the word "religion" comes from the Latin root *ligare*, meaning "to bind" or "to connect." Spirituality derives from the Latin words *spiritus* meaning "breath." In contemporary usage, the word "religion" is generally associated with institutional beliefs and practices, whereas spirituality is understood in individual and experiential terms, such as in relating to a higher power (Wulff, 1997; Zinnbauer et al., 1997). Although "spirituality" is part and parcel of "religion" in some usage, a disjunction between "spirituality" and "religion" is implied in others (Wulff, 1997; Zinnbauer et al., 1997). More polarized definitions of "spirituality" and "religion" are reportedly found among those who tend to have a negative view of organized religion, and for whom the word "religion" carries distinct authoritarian and institutional overtones (Zinnbauer et al., 1997).

For the purposes of this article, the term "religious" will be used with a meaning that goes beyond its narrower, institutional connotations in contemporary usage. "Religious" will be used with a broadband, multidimensional meaning that is inclusive of the personal, interpersonal, communal, and spiritual. The spiritual is therefore a subset of the religious. At the risk of going against the current linguistic and conceptual trend that favours the word "spiritual" with its more positive, private, and individualistic connotations and a contrasting narrow understanding of "religious" with its restrictively mundane and institutional meanings, this article uses the word "religious" intentionally to enlarge our understanding of "religiosity" and "religion" as a multifaceted phenomenon that embraces both personal and interpersonal, material and spiritual, vertical and horizontal, earthbound and transcendent dimensions.Thus this article attempts to restore to an understanding of "religiosity" its complex, systemic interconnections and connotations.

Satir's Model and Tillich's Philosophy of Religion

Paul Tillich (1886–1965), German-American philosopher and theologian, is recognized as one of 20th century's most influential theologians (Livingston & Fiorenza, 2000). In systematic fashion, Tillich demonstrates in philosophical terms humanity's existential "ultimate concern" which in the end is the substance of the religious quest. Tillich regards psychotherapists as contemporary theology's "allies" in exploring the character of existence in all its manifestations (Tillich, 1957). In turn, humanistic and existential psychologies recognized Tillich's contributions. Humanistic psychotherapist, Carl Rogers, finds Tillich's ideas congenial to the discoveries of modern humanistic psychology at many points (Rogers, 1970). Existential psychotherapist, Rollo May, both contributed to and drew from Tillich's existential understanding of anxiety in his framework of existential analysis (May, 1967).

All psychotherapies carry implicit assumptions about human nature and the human condition. The hallmark of Satir's model is the explicit primacy it places on health, spirit, and human potential as the starting point of healing. This positive orientation suggests a compatibility with Tillich's essentialist philosophy in its affirmation of a positive, intrinsic order and structure implied in human nature that is not arbitrary, but potential and creative (Tillich, 1961). The essentialist pole in the essential–existential tension is often overlooked in the formulations of existential therapies, although order and structure to human nature are implied in the goals of humanistic and existential therapies. Tillich's essentialist philosophical theology offers a "philosophical matrix" for psychotherapy that takes into account not only existential principles, but the implicit reference to a larger essentialist framework implied in existential propositions (Tillich, 1961). Therefore it seems that comparing key dimensions of congruence in Satir's model with Tillich's philosophical and ontological categories can cast into relief the religious significance and meaning of Satir's healing model.

The Human Condition

This section explores how Tillich and Satir saw the human condition.

Tillich: Estrangement and Essentialization

According to Tillich, human existence is marked by estrangement: estrangement from ourselves, from each other, and from the mystery and depth of our being (Tillich, 1948). However, Tillich argues that estrangement implies a prior state of ontological unity from which existence is estranged (Tillich, 1959, 1961). Tillich describes the human condition as one of fragmentation and distortion deriving from the separation of humanity's essence and existence. Separation of existence from what one is essentially manifests as existential "anxiety" (Tillich, 1952). Salvation, the goal of religion, stems from the Latin root *salus* or *salvus*, which means "to heal" or "to make whole" (Tillich, 1959). The philosophical term Tillich uses for this process of "making whole" fragmented and separated parts that originally belong together is essentialization (Tillich, 1963). Thus salvation is the process of essentialization, of reuniting essence with existence. The religious quest for salvation is the process of *religare*, "rebinding," or restoring humanity to its true essence in its vital dimensions. A purposeful dynamic, or *telos*, is at work in human nature aiming towards the reunification of the essential and existential, although this reunification is necessarily partial and fragmentary and falls short of its complete fulfillment in history (Tillich, 1963).

Satir: Disharmony and Health

When there is a blockage of innate human resources and energies, and the potential health of the human being is untapped or inaccessible, symptoms result (Satir, 1986). If ill health is blocked-up energy and disharmony in the human system, then health means a harmonious interplay between all levels within a person intrapsychically, between a person and others interpersonally, and contact with one's deep resources spiritually. Satir recognizes in each person a "positive life energy" that seeks to manifest itself in a life-giving direction (King, 1989, p. 32). Her therapeutic enterprise is based on looking beyond symptom and pathology to activate a person's propensity toward health, which means in the first place to make contact with a person's spirit or essence:

> The question for me was never whether they had spirits, but how I could contact them. That is what I set out to do. My means of making contact was my own congruent communication and the modeling that went with it. It was as though I saw through the inner core of each being, seeing the shining light of the spirit trapped in a thick black cylinder of limitation and self-rejection. My effort was to enable the person to see what I saw; then together, we could turn the dark cylinder into a large, lighted screen and build new possibilities. I consider the first step in any change is to contact the spirit. Then together we can clear the way to release the energy for going toward health (Satir, 1988, pp. 340–41).

Contacting a person's spirit or essence is central to Satir's therapeutic work. Satir believes that people are "basically good" and she aims to bring out the possibilities and resources within the self and its potential for growth (Satir et al., 1991). Satir's essentialism is thus revealed in her affirmation of humanity's spiritual nature and its goodness, and the human potential for growth. To Satir, humanity's essential nature is dynamic. Dynamic metaphors and references abound in Satir's descriptions as she speaks of growth as "life force revealing itself" (Satir 1988, p. 334), of life coming from "a power much greater than our own" (Satir, 1988, p. 336), and of our having a "pipeline" to universal intelligence and wisdom. Restoration of health consists of making contact with an energy underlying existence and bringing the multiple dimensions of the human being into alignment and harmony with this dynamic source.

Tillich's and Satir's Essentialism

Both Tillich and Satir operate out of an essentialist framework that affirms an underlying order, norm and structure to human nature.

Satir is clear on this point (Satir et al., 1991, p. 221):

> The universe is orderly. We as human beings operate that way, too. We cannot always see the order of our humanness, because we do not look or we do not look with open eyes. To find that order was important to me. I knew it was there somewhere. For me, the basis of that order is the Life Force.

Likewise, Tillich maintains an essence intrinsic to humanity. Essence means the nature, the pattern, the norm — that which makes a thing what it truly is (Tillich, 1951, 1959). Hence separation from one's essential nature results in existential anxiety, guilt, and suffering. Similarly, Satir views symptoms as frustrated attempts to express health that has been blocked, covered up, or put out of reach to the person. The main therapeutic task is therefore to help a person rechannel bottled-up energy into useful and productive purposes (Satir, 1986).

Congruence: The Goal of Satir's Model

Congruence is a core construct in Satir's model (Davis, McLendon, Freeman, Loberg, et al., 1996; Loeschen, 1998; Satir et al., 1991). Congruence began as a motif in her early work with communication, and eventually became the organizing principle and the goal of her therapeutic system. How this construct of congruence has evolved is set out as follows (Satir et al., 1991):

1. In the 1950s, congruence referred to the awareness, acknowledgment and acceptance of feelings and their expression in a nonreactive manner. Congruence characterizes communication that is "straight" when a single, unambiguous message is conveyed verbally and nonverbally.
2. In the 1960s, congruence was seen as a state of wholeness, inner-centredness, and self-acceptance corresponding to high self-esteem.
3. In the 1980s, Satir began more explicitly to speak of a third level of congruence in relation to the realm of spirituality and universality as connecting with "universal life force" that creates and supports growth in humans and other natural forms.

These progressive formulations of congruence capture the state of wholeness, awareness, openness at the interpersonal, intrapsychic and universal spiritual dimensions of the human being. Beyond a conceptual level, congruence for Satir has energetic and physiological manifestations noted in body relaxation, skin colour, breathing patterns, and as the unobstructed flow and manifestation of one's life force (Loeschen,

1998; Satir et al., 1991). Therefore, congruence according to Satir is not merely a concept, but a bodily, wholistic experience of energy flow that accompanies a systemic openness of the person in multiple dimensions.

To summarize, congruence is a state of awareness, acceptance, and openness manifested as a harmonious flow of life energy through all levels and experiential dimensions of a person at a given moment. The goal of therapeutic change is to transform the flow of a person's energy from a blocked, dysfunctional pattern to a more open, free, and healthy pattern. The goal of healing is greater congruence (Satir, 1986; Satir et al., 1991). In a state of congruence, a person has greatest access to one's own resources. Congruence in Satir's model can be understood more specifically in terms of Satir's description of the human being in its key dimensions.

Three Key Human Dimensions: The Iceberg Metaphor

The Iceberg (Figure 4.1) is one of Satir's chief metaphors to illustrate the various layers that make up the human being. In this representation, the person is viewed as a multidimensional system. A system is defined as "a set of actions, reactions, and interactions among a set of essential variables that develop an order and a sequence to accomplish an outcome" (Satir, 1986, p. 287). In other words, a system is an interactive set of variables and dimensions that exert influence on one another leading to an outcome that is more than the sum of its parts. In a system, the change in one part or dimension is related to change in the other dimensions. Behaviour and communication represent only the tip of the Iceberg in the multilayered totality of personality. The author further conceptualizes Satir's Iceberg as three dimensions: the interpersonal, intrapsychic, and universal-spiritual. These dimensions are related in systemic fashion such that the change in one element is related to changes in the other elements. Congruence is the harmonious interaction of these key dimensions within a person. Each of these key dimensions will now be elaborated in greater detail.

Interpersonal Dimension

Satir's five communication stances depicting the interpersonal dimension are the best known aspect of her model. For communication to be congruent, Satir postulates that the three components of self, other, and context have to be honoured and represented. The four stances of blaming, placating, super-reasonable (computing), and irrelevant (distracting) represent an imbalance of self, other, and context in a communication

(Satir, 1988; Satir et al., 1991). These communication stances are also known as "survival stances" learned by children in their family systems in order to gain love and acceptance. Blaming protects one's self-worth at the expense of other. Placating involves the surrendering of self to other. Super-reasonable communication discounts both self and other, paying attention only to context. Irrelevant communication abdicates from self, other, and context. Congruent communication, or straight communication, reflects a match between verbal and nonverbal messages, and a consonance in word, affect and meaning. Congruence is a choice at a conscious level based on awareness, acknowledgment, and acceptance of self, other, and context (Satir et al., 1991).

Figure 4.1

The Iceberg: Three Dimensions of the Satir Model
(adapted from Satir, Banmen *et al.*, 1991)

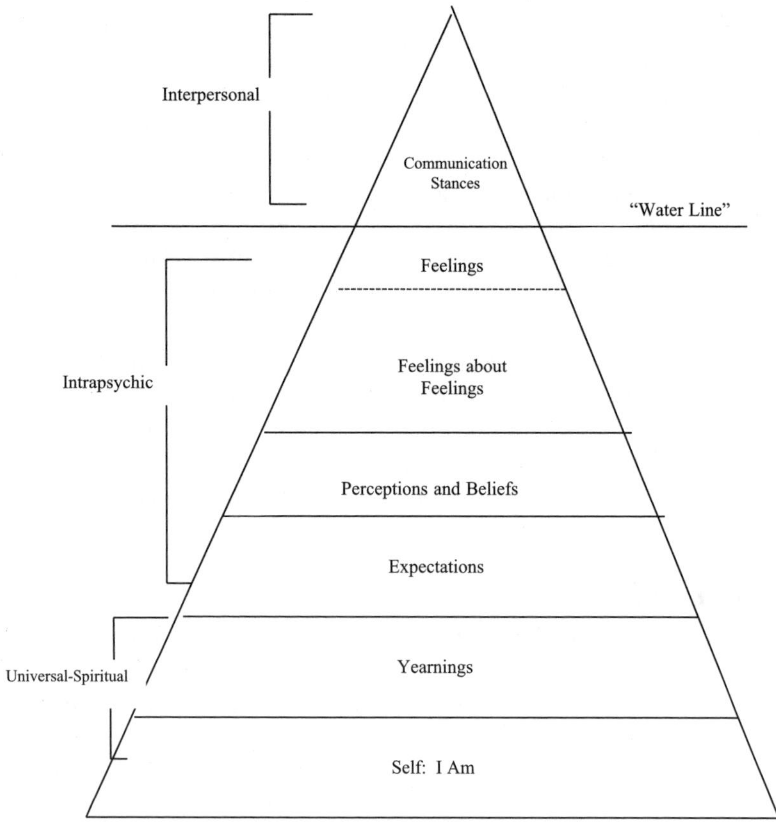

Intrapsychic Dimension

The intrapsychic dimension is constituted by a set of internal events that give rise to behaviour and communication. According to Satir, these internal events consist of feelings, feelings about one's feelings, perceptions and beliefs, and expectations. Typed as an experiential model of therapy, Satir's orientation has been commonly understood as working primarily with emotions (Nichols & Schwartz, 1998), a view which fails to recognize the integrative multidimensionality of Satir's model in its maturity. In its later development, Satir's model is an integrative model that challenges, unblocks, and transforms multiple internal variables including perceptions, beliefs, feelings, feelings about feelings, and expectations that impede the flow of one's life energy (Loeschen, 1998; Satir et al., 1991). To transform these intrapsychic constructs, they are first exposed through verbal exploration and "sculpting," a means of externalizing through enactments of internal constructs. Perceptions, feelings, and unmet expectations from the past are brought into awareness, experientially worked through, and new choices are made. When a new perception, a new feeling, a new expectation is added, a new coping pattern emerges that allows for greater congruence (Satir et al., 1991). For example, a father who adjusts his inordinately high expectations about his son is able to feel more warmly towards his son and form a closer relationship with him. This in turn affects their communication and the son's behaviour. Hence a shift in expectations can alter feelings and perceptions in the intrapsychic dimension, leading to a shift in the interpersonal dimension.

Universal-Spiritual Dimension

The last two strata of the Iceberg, namely human yearnings and what Satir calls the Self, or the "I Am," constitute the universal-spiritual dimension of the person. Yearnings consist of the universal human longing to be loved, accepted, validated and confirmed (Satir et al., 1991). Yearnings are universal to human beings and reflect essential human needs and aspirations. To be congruent with our yearnings is to acknowledge and accept our humanity. What is also universal to human beings is the human connection to a dynamic spiritual base which Satir calls the universal "life force." As spirituality assumed increasing prominence in Satir's system in the 1980s, Satir spoke of congruence as harmony with one's Self, life energy, spirituality or God (Banmen, 2003; Satir et al., 1991). Yearnings and connection with a universal life force constitute the universal-spiritual dimension of Satir's Iceberg model of the human person.

Congruence

Congruence is a phenomenon that can be facilitated or impeded by each of the three dimensions described above. In other words, the interpersonal, intrapsychic, and universal-spiritual dimensions are interrelated and interactive. To move a system towards higher congruence, Satir's therapeutic interventions aim at "second-level" deep structural change rather than just surface behavioural change in the three dimensions (Satir et al., 1991). This involves changing a person's expectations, perceptions, feelings, and the acknowledgment of one's yearnings, and becoming reconnected to one's life force or life energy.

Congruence as the goal of Satir's model brings elements in the interpersonal, intrapsychic, and universal-spiritual dimensions into an integrative, harmonious relationship. The establishment of an integrative, harmonious relationship of elements in these three central dimensions parallels the process of essentialization described by Tillich as the reunification of ontological polarities and the goal of the religious quest.

Congruence: Universal-Spiritual Dimension

Again, this section compares the views of Tillich and Satir.

Tillich: Essential Goodness and the Divine Ground of Being

Tillich begins his theology with the affirmation of a creation that is good. In counterpoint to existential being, Tillich places priority on the goodness of essential being. Essence is the hidden potential that seeks to be realized in existence. Despite the destructive distortion of existence, the power from the essence of being urges irrepressibly to shine through.

Furthermore, in its essence, humanity is rooted in the "creative ground of the divine life" (Tillich, 1951, p. 256). Hence, in its essence, humanity participates in the divine. The divine is envisioned as the depth dimension of humanity, the "depth" in human life which "gives substance, ultimate meaning, judgment, and creative courage to all functions of the human spirit" (Tillich, 1959, p. 9). Tillich argues that it is this prior experiential participation in the divine or spiritual ground that makes it possible for humanity to raise the question of "God" and sparks the quest for wholeness (Tillich, 1959). Therefore, Tillich's understanding of religiosity is rooted in his premise of divine immanence native to humanity. God is not "out there," but in humanity. Religiosity for Tillich is not an intellectual assent to a set of propositions or content about God. Rather, religiosity is an existential quest involving the whole of personality for the reconnecting experience with one's divine "ground" and essence of being (Tillich, 1957, 1959).

Satir: Essence, Spirit and Universal Human Yearnings

In her theory and practice, Satir makes an important distinction between a person's "behavior" that was learned as a coping response to a specific situation in the past for the sake of survival, and the "essence" of a person, which is "perfect and pure" (Banmen & Banmen, 1991, p. 22; Satir, 1986). Satir affirms that people are essentially good and that dysfunctional behavior comes from "woundings" when something in the human being is denied, projected, ignored, or distorted (Satir, 1986). Satir believes in the human ability to grow from an inner core of strength and motivation (Satir et al., 1991). In the later stages of her work, Satir arrives at the conclusion that human essence is in the final analysis "spiritual" (Banmen, 2003). Satir describes human beings as "spiritual beings in human form," and as "divine in our origins" (Satir, 1988, pp. 336, 338). Grounded in her belief that spirituality is "our connection to the universe" and is "basic to our existence," Satir's healing work concentrates on finding ways to affirm and nourish the spirit.

Having a "reverence of life' and "learning to love the spirit unconditionally" are the cornerstones of her therapeutic approach (Satir, 1988, pp. 334, 338). To regard human beings as "sacred" (Satir, 1987, p. 24) means to respect, cherish, and value human beings for their intrinsic worth. Satir believes that contact with one's life force gives one the impetus to change (Simon, 1989). Hence her therapeutic manoeuvers aim at accessing the power and potential of humanity's "higher nature" and "spirit" as the basis for change (Satir, 1988, p. 383). Satir speaks of the human person as a "manifestation of life." Growth is the "life force revealing itself, a manifestation of spirit" (Satir, 1988, p. 334). Providing the optimal context for nurturing growth, nourishing our relationship with our life force to release the inner "healing potential" (Satir, 1987, p. 24) is central to Satir's approach to healing (Banmen, 2003; Satir, 1988).

Satir's view represents a depth humanism that has an essentialist base which differs from therapeutic models such as behaviorism, which subscribes to the sufficiency of external control that uses reward and punishment, and classical psychoanalysis, which focuses on instinctual drives. In the contemporary family therapy context, social constructionism has been proposed as a theoretical base for Satir's work (Cheung, 1997). However, in light of Satir's belief in the "essence" and spiritual nature of humanity as the fundamental premise in her therapeutic system, social construction can only be seen as that which supports or hinders the intrinsic creative dynamism within humanity, and hence is secondary to and at the service of or detrimental to essential humanity. A human core with spiritual roots expressed in universal human yearnings propels the growth and healing process. This philosophical position differs from the relativistic assumptions of constructionism that gives primary salience to socially constructed narratives, and differs from constructivism based on the relativistic claims of arbitrary subjective preferences. Examination of Satir's implicit philosophy reveals that the source of her widely admired therapeutic success derives from her faith in the human spirit and the intrinsic human potential for healing.

Satir believes that the "life force" could be called by many names (Satir, 1988). The naming of the life force is less important to Satir than the ways in which one could make contact with it and experience it within oneself. Using evocative words and imagery, Satir attempts in her meditations to help people open up to their own spirit and to be in contact with a universal spirit dimension (Banmen,2003). Satir believes that human beings possess an "inborn spiritual base and sacredness" (Satir et al., 1991, p. 14). The aim of her work is to create a context to transform previous limited copings and internal constructs to enable people to live out of an inner source of strength and validation as unique manifestations of the universal life force.

Satir identifies "yearnings" that are universal among human beings. Yearnings include the longing to love oneself, to love others, to be loved by others, to be accepted, validated and confirmed (Satir et al., 1991). When a child's yearnings are satisfied, the child will thrive, develop high self-esteem, a harmonious sense of self and the ability to cope with stressful situations (Satir et al., 1991). Yearnings point to that which the person seeks in order to thrive. They point to the potential natural human order that has yet to be realized. Satir validates human yearnings and encourages their expression. She believes that acknowledgment rather than denial or suppression of one's yearnings gives the opportunity for their being actualized (Satir et al., 1991).

Instead of focusing on problems, Satir's approach is to tap into human yearnings and their energy to provide the motivations and actions for change in a positive direction (Satir et al., 1991). For example, instead of finding out more about a client's depression and what family members are depressed, Satir asks how the client would like to feel and suggests that together they can put all their energies into working toward that positive state of being for which the client yearns (Satir, 1998, Tape 1). Through affirmation of strengths and resources and tapping into positive expectations and yearnings, Satir opens up hope, motivation, and energy for change. The process of transformation includes helping people to become aware of, acknowledge, and accept their yearnings, which Satir believes is a basic process of connecting with a person's inner core or life force (Satir et al., 1991).

Summary

Both Tillich and Satir subscribe to a universal in humanity's ontological structure that precedes and supercedes cultural and historical conditioning. They point to a solution of the human predicament from a source within humanity itself, made possible by a reconnection with a power from within that can be released as a healing and transformative potential. Dysfunction, pain and suffering found in existence are expressions of humanity's deep yearnings for a lost state of wholeness. Human suffering and pathological symptoms are consequences of the disruptions and violation of an essential order. For both Tillich and Satir, the distortions of existence and pathology are set against a larger, positive, spiritual, essentialist potential that presses for its own actualization and manifestation in existence. Hence, Tillich's theology and Satir's therapeutic philosophy are eminently hopeful. Both hold the position that humanity's essential nature participates in a spiritual dimension that is immanent to humanity. "Recognizing the power of spirit is what healing, living, and spirituality are all about," states Satir toward the end of her career (Satir, 1988, p. 338).

Congruence: Interpersonal Dimension

According to Tillich, a person as a centred self develops out of relatedness to other selves. The person as a fully developed individual self is impossible without other fully developed selves (Tillich, 1951). Participation, to be a part of community, is essential to full individualization (Tillich, 1951). Ontologically, according to Tillich, individualization and participation, to be a self and to be related to others, are interdependent (Tillich, 1951). However, in the state of existential estrangement, these interdependent elements that formed an original dynamic unity become separated from each other (Tillich, 1957). Solipsistic self-affirmation poses the threat of loneliness in which connections with others are lost. On the other hand, in seeking acceptance by the group and drawing support and energy to exist by being part of a collective separates one from oneself. The tension is manifested in many psychological and sociological problems, Tillich observes, and for this reason reconciling the tension between self-relatedness and other-relatedness is "a very important subject for research for depth psychology and depth sociology" (Tillich, 1951, p. 199).

Satir: Self and Other

In her early work on communication, Satir discovered that when people do not feel good about themselves, or have low self-worth, under conditions of stress, they resort to ways of communication that either elevate oneself over the other, or depreciate oneself in deference to the other, or leave both self and other out of the picture. From these observations, Satir developed her well-known communication stances discussed earlier in relation to the interpersonal dimension in the Iceberg. Each stance represents a missing piece of self, other, or context in a given communication. Most notable among these four stances of blaming, placating, super-reasonable, and irrelevant are the first two. In the blaming stance, only the self counts but not the other. It represents a domineering or condescending position that is often hostile, angry, and threatening towards the other. Assuming a blaming stance gives a person a sense of power, but it hides a lonely and vulnerable self within. The placating stance disregards one's own feelings of worth and hands one's power over to someone else. It keeps peace at the expense of self-worth and self-respect. The placating person is usually apologetic, helpless, and begging. Both super-reasonable and irrelevant stances are nonpersonal stances where self and other are dismissed. These four stances are seen as incongruent because they represent the absence of self, other, or both or context thus compromising the fullness of congruent relating.

The four communication stances are developed in childhood as ways to meet existential survival needs. These are a child's needs to gain love, acceptance, and belonging. Hence, they are also known as "survival stances." Satir notes differences in breathing patterns, body tensions and postures that accompany these different stances. Thus these communication stances have effects on the person and others at physical, physiological, and emotional levels.

To hold both self and other in balance in relationship so that both self and other are acknowledged and allowed to exist fully, one needs a secure sense of self, or high self-worth. In her work, Satir challenges family rules, beliefs, and expectations that maintain a low sense of one's worth. She uses meditations to mediate one's sense of connectedness to one's intrinsic spiritual and essential worth. One's sense of worth also reflects the extent to which one accepts one's humanity, with one's human yearnings and fallibility. A secure sense of self makes possible congruence in communication, when both self and other are present and valued. Congruent communication validates both self and other.

Summary

Tillich and Satir identify a paradox in human nature: we are fundamentally alone and set apart from others, yet are inescapably in the world with others and attain a sense of self only in relation to others. Under conditions of existence, these two poles of the paradox are strained and we are compelled to resolve the tension by gravitating to one pole or the other. Congruence reflects the essential nature of being where the polarities of individualization and participation are united. Blaming and placating stances in communication are transcended in an interpersonal congruence that honours both self and other.

Congruence: Intrapsychic Dimension

Human freedom is "finite freedom" as all the potentialities that constitute one's freedom are limited by one's destiny (Tillich, 1957). Destiny refers to the limits and necessity imposed on existence by virtue of heredity, biology, history, and society (Tillich, 1957). Destiny and freedom are distinct but not separated, in tension but not in conflict in essential being (Tillich, 1957). One depends on the other to be meaningful. Destiny without freedom is fate—meaningless and mechanical necessity. Freedom without destiny falls into arbitrariness and unrelatedness, as what one chooses is purely the whim of the subject, unrelated to the destiny of the total person who acts. Freedom separated from the awareness of one's destiny is compromised by internal compulsions that condition one's acts and decisions, and parts of self overtake the centre, truncated from other parts. Thus, finite freedom falls under biological and psychological necessities without the awareness of the subject (Tillich, 1957). True freedom is found in the "creative act" in which a person can act centrally and centredly to deliberate and decide with awareness of the impinging contingencies of destiny (Tillich, 1957). Essentialization is the optimization of freedom in the context of one's destiny.

Satir: Compulsion and Choice

Satir recognizes that human beings are often limited in their range of present options for coping with life because of learning developed as a specific response to a context in the past (Satir, 1986). Compulsion results from a lack of awareness of past events that influence us in the present. The impact of past experience is often manifested in our automatic and often charged reactions to events in the present. Healing consists of becoming aware of how our learnings from the past influence our present reactions, and claiming for ourselves the power to choose a better way to respond based on the knowledge available to us as mature adults. Many past learnings consisting of feelings, feelings about one's feelings, perceptions, expectations, coping, and communication may be at the root of our limitations today. Problem creation and resolution lie in our interpretation and framing of the situation and our chosen response to it. To exercise the choice of how to respond rather than to react to situations is an important goal in healing (Satir et al., 1991). Many of Satir's therapeutic vehicles for change aim at "de-enmeshment," that is, to separate people's past-contaminated material, which conditioned them, from their experience of the present. De-enmeshment is a process of appropriating the past and its influences to free up resources and choices for the present and the future:

> Growing up does not necessarily reduce the impact of the our childhood rules and relationships. The present is the only dimension we live in physically, but when the past contaminates the present, Satir knew, we continue repeating old patterns. One goal of therapy is to change this contamination to illumination: to use the past to see and live in the present more fully. This helps us move from being compelled to being able to cope, and from coping to recognizing our choices and our freedom (Satir et al. 1991, p. 221).

Most notable of Satir's vehicles to separate a person from the limitations of past learnings is *family reconstruction*. The process of family reconstruction externalizes internalized constructs from the past so that new perceptions and choices can be made. The impact of old learnings in childhood "prevent us from defining ourselves holistically because they keep us focused in the past and using the incomplete perceptions we had as children" (Satir et al., 1991, p. 221). We carry the constructs of our families inside us and it is the interpretation of these earlier experiences that need changing to free up new perceptions and ways of being. Family reconstruction aims at second-order change that involves an internal structural change and transformation of energy. Negative energy transforms into positive energy at the level of feelings, perceptions, and expectations when we no longer strain to suppress or defend against past pains and disappointments. Energy used in suppression and denial can then be released to meet current needs and desires. Simultaneous with reworking one's learnings from the past is the emphasis on being conscious of one's life energy, freedom, choices and inner resources that come from the Self (Satir et al., 1991, p. 233). In doing so, one's history that shaped one's destiny is brought into consciousness and its negative effects transformed.

Challenging and discarding the chains of limiting human constructions, both external and internal, is one part of healing. Yet another part involves a connection with one's deep "wisdom" as emergent knowledge of life's movement that can be accessed through one's bodily sense, or what Satir refers to as the "wisdom box," situated two inches below the navel (Banmen, 2003). The interiorly directed emergent or becoming character of existence is central to humanistic and existentially oriented therapies (Greenberg & Rice, 1998). Satir regards each person as a life energy that seeks to be manifested into the world, energy that is drawn to connections with other beings (Banmen, 2003). Thus, freedom has two aspects: freedom from the past and its conditioning effects, and freedom to become what one essentially is within the frame of one's destiny.

Summary

Tillich's understanding of salvation as the restoration of the unity between one's destiny and freedom parallels Satir's congruence as compulsions give way in the exercise of choice. Freedom that is compromised by internal compulsions is enlarged as a conscious, deliberating, deciding self chooses to act with awareness, in line with one's essence and life force. The past is not negated, cut off, or denied, but its influence on one's intrapsychic functioning is brought to awareness and its impact transformed. Satir's congruence thus parallels Tillich's essentialization as the optimization of freedom through the acceptance and integration of one's destiny.

The Human and Religious Quests: A Systems Perspective

Satir's view of the person as a multidimensional system, which she depicted in the Iceberg metaphor and the Mandala with its eight interactive components of the Self (Satir, 1986; Satir et al., 1991), is remarkably similar to Tillich's understanding of the person as a "multidimensional unity" (Tillich, 1963). In their views, the person is a complex interrelation of many parts, as opposed to a hierarchy of disjointed parts. The multidimensional view respects the autonomy of each contributing element, while remaining mindful of the interrelationship among the elements, and how the elements affect one another in the system. A systems understanding of personality avoids reductionism that gives primacy to one part to explain away or subsume another part. Hence the spirit is not superior to matter, or the intellect superior to emotions. A "centre" of awareness, deliberation and decision orchestrates the relations of the parts, not imperially, but by attending to and in consultation with what each part indicates. Therefore, the whole depends on a "centred self" that is the seat of consciousness (Tillich, 1963) which converses with and manages the various parts of personality.

In a systems framework, any partial view that privileges one dimension over another leading to the denigration of other dimensions runs the risk of upsetting an essential balance, the basis of health in the system. A systems view of the person shakes up many established categories that have been dichotomized and separated from each other, such as body and spirit, human and divine, secular and religious, historical and eternal. A systemic, multidimensional view of life affirms the interpenetration and interrelation between the material and spiritual dimensions. Put differently, human beings are seen not only seeking salvation in a spiritual dimension, but spiritual beings seeking salvation in a human, historical dimension.

Healing, Congruence, and Wholeness

Healing ushers in a new creation, a new reality of being where the structures of destruction are broken (Tillich, 1955). The New Being is the new reality of humanity in history, made possible by an "event" of radical "acceptance of the unacceptable" (Tillich, 1996, p. 53). The New Being makes actual what is potential, and is the undistorted manifestation of the essential being within the conditions of existence. Hence, the fruit of salvation, for Tillich, does not lie only in a supernatural future or eternity, but is realized, albeit in fragmentary fashion, in the midst of history and human existence. As such, the New Being represents the living manifestation of humanity's "essential truth" as the integration with self, with each other and with the depth of one's being, a "manifestation of the divine" in the world (Tillich, 1996, p. 51).

Congruence reconnects and brings into harmony elements in the intrapsychic, interpersonal and universal-spiritual dimensions of the person. Elements and dimensions of the human being that have been separated are brought into awareness and integration, or "made whole," which harks back to the original meaning of "healing," and "salvation." Elements that have been disrupted are restored and brought into proper relations with one another.

The Human and Religious Quest

As noted at the outset, the scope and coherence of Satir's vision and its spiritual and religious significance have not been sufficiently recognized or amply articulated. Tillich's philosophical theology supplies a lens that magnifies the underlying ontological assumptions and salvific nature of Satir's vision, at the same time that Satir's model gives flesh and historical specifications to Tillich's vision of the religious quest. The religious quest and the human quest are seen to coincide in a life lived in increasing alignment and flow in its three principal relationships with self, other, and the spirit or divine. In Tillich's vision, the religious quest is not merely spiritual, but material and historical, as in Satir's vision, the human quest is at once personal, historical, and spiritual. Religiosity is a multidimensional quest that seeks to restore personal, interpersonal and spiritual dimensions to an interactive and interdependent unity. Congruence, in Satir's model, as reconnection with one's self and one's origins, with others, and with the spiritual essence of being is therefore simultaneously a rehumanization and religious process.

REFERENCES

Banmen, J (Ed.). (2003). *Meditations of Virginia Satir.* Seattle, WA: Avanta, the Virginia Satir Network.

Becvar, D. S. & Becvar, R. (1996). *Family therapy: A systemic integration.* 3rd ed.. Toronto: Allyn and Bacon.

Brothers, B. J. (Ed.). (1991). *Virginia Satir: Foundational ideas.* New York: Haworth Press.

Cheung, M. (1997). Social construction theory and the Satir Model: Toward a synthesis. *American Journal of Family Therapy,* 25 (4), 331–43.

Davis, B., McLendon, J., Freeman, M., Hill, N., Loberg, J., Lester. T. & Huber, C. (1996). Satir and congruence: A response. In B. J. Brothers (Ed.), *Couples and the Tao of congruence* (pp. 143–59). New York: Haworth Press.

Duhl, B. (1989). Virginia Satir: In Memoriam. *Journal of Marital and Family Therapy,* 15 (2), 109–110.

Goldenberg, I. & Goldenberg, H. (1996). *Family therapy: An overview.* 4th ed. Pacific Grove, CA: Brooks/Cole.

Greenberg, L. & Rice, L. (1998). Humanistic approaches to psychotherapy. In P. L. Wachtel & S. Messer (Eds.), *Theories of psychotherapy: Origins and evolution* (pp. 97–129). Washington D.C.: American Psychological Association.

Guerin, P. & Chabot. D. R. (1997). Development of family systems theory. In P. L. Wachtel & S. B. Messer (Eds.), *Theories of psychotherapy: Origins and evolution* (pp. 181–221). Washington DC: American Psychological Association.

Hoffman, L. (1981). *Foundations of family therapy.* New York: Basic Books.

King, L. (1989). Virginia Satir. In *Women of power* (pp. 11–40). Berkeley, CA: Celestial Arts.

Lee, B. K. (2001). *The religious significance of the Satir model: Philosophical, ritual, and empirical perspectives.* Doctoral dissertation. University of Ottawa, Canada.

Livingston, J. & Fiorenza, F. S. (2000). *Modern Christian thought.* Vol. 2. Upper Saddle River, NJ: Prentice Hall.

Loeschen, S. (1998). *Systematic training in the skills of Virginia Satir.* Pacific Grove, CA: Brooks/Cole.

Luepnitz, D. A. (1988). *The family interpreted: Feminist theory in clinical practice.* New York: Basic Books.

May, R. (1973). *Paulus.* New York: Harper and Row.

McGoldrick, M. (1989). Remembering Virginia. *Family Therapy Networker, January/February, 13(1),* 33–34.

Nichols, M. & Schwartz, R. (1998). *Family therapy: Concepts and methods.* 4th ed. Toronto: Allyn and Bacon.

Pittman, F. (1989). Remembering Virginia. *Family Therapy Networker, January/ February, 13(1),* 34–35.

Rogers, C. (1970). Paul Tillich and Carl Rogers: A dialogue. In *Carl Rogers on tape.* Atlanta, GA: Bell and Howell. Audiocassette.

Satir, V. (1964/1967/1983). *Conjoint family therapy.* 3rd ed.. Palo Alto, CA: Science and Behavior Books.

Satir, V. (1970). *Self-esteem.* Berkeley, CA: Celestial Arts.

Satir, V. (1972). *Peoplemaking. Palo Alto: Science and Behavior Books.*

Satir, V. (1976). *Making contact.* Berkeley, CA: Celestial Arts.

Satir, V. (1978). *Your many faces.* Berkeley, CA: Celestial Arts.

Satir, V. (1986). A partial portrait of a family therapist in process. In C. Fishman & B. Rosman (Eds.), *Evolving models for family change* (pp. 278–93). New York: Guilford Press.

Satir, V. (1987). The therapist story. In M. Baldwin & V. Satir (Eds.), *The use of self in therapy* (pp. 17–25). New York: Haworth Press.

Satir, V. (1988). *The new peoplemaking.* Palo Alto, CA: Science and Behavior Books.

Satir, V. (1998). *Satir family series* (Tapes 1–9). Burien, WA: Avanta.Videocassettes with transcript and study guide.

Satir, V., Banmen, J., Gerber, J. & Gomori, M. (1991). *The Satir model: Family therapy and beyond.* Palo Alto, CA: Science and Behavior Books.

Schwartz, R. (2000). Psychotherapy as a spiritual practice. In F. Walsh (Ed.), *Spiritual resources in family therapy* (pp. 223–39). New York: Guilford Press.

Simon, R. (1989). Reaching out to life: An interview with Virginia Satir. *Family Therapy Networker*, 13 (1), 36–43.

Sprenkle, D., Keeney, B. & Sutton, P. (1982). Theorists who influence clinical members of AAMFT: A research note. *Journal of Marital and Family Therapy*, 8 (3), 367–69.

Tillich, P. (1948).You are accepted. In P. Tillich, *The shaking of the foundations*, (pp. 153–63). New York: Charles Scribner's Sons.

Tillich, P. (1951/1965). *Systematic theology*. Vol. 1. Chicago: University of Chicago Press.

Tillich, P. (1952). *The courage to be.* New Haven, CT: Yale University Press.

Tillich, P. (1955). *The new being.* New York: Charles Scribner's Sons.

Tillich, P. (1956). *The eternal now.* New York: Charles Scribner's Sons.

Tillich, P. (1957). *Systematic theology.* Vol. 2. Chicago: University of Chicago Press.

Tillich, P. (1959). *Theology of culture*. New York: Oxford Free Press.

Tillich, P. (1961). Existentialism and psychotherapy. *Review of Existential Psychology and Psychiatry*, 1, 8–16.

Tillich, P. (1963). *Systematic theology.* Vol. 3. Chicago: University of Chicago Press.

Tillich, P. (1967). *On the boundary.* London: Collins.

Tillich, P. (1996). *The irrelevance and relevance of the Christian message*. Cleveland, OH: Pilgrim Press.

Walsh, F. (Ed.). (2000). *Spiritual resources in family therapy.* New York: Guilford Press.

Wulff, D. (1997). *Psychology of religion: Classic and contemporary.* 2nd ed. New York: Wiley and Sons.

Zinnbauer, B., Pargament, K., Cole, B., Rye, M., Butter, E., Belavich, T., Hipp, K., Scott, A. & Kadar, F. (1997). Religion and Spirituality: Unfuzzying the fuzzy. *Journal for the Scientific Study of Religion,* 36 (4), 549–64.

5

The Family Reconstruction Process and Its Evolution to Date:

Virginia Satir's Transformational Process

Gilles Beaudry

The purpose of this chapter is to present both the family reconstruction process (Satir's transformational process) and an overview of its evolution to date. The family reconstruction process has already had a wide influence on generations of therapists up to this time. The influence has continued to spread with the new developments since Satir's death in 1988. The classical version of family reconstruction, in which Satir first emphasized connecting with self and personal growth through deeper understanding of the patterns learned in the family of origin, was quite a lengthy process. A shorter version of the classical approach which puts more emphasis on the transformational process has been developed. Today, the emphasis is more on "briefer-shorter," and we are learning to do more of what she was doing in a shorter time.

The first section will introduce the Satir model and describe how she developed the classical family reconstruction approach as a vehicle for change. The sameness and the differences in the classical approach and the shorter version will be discussed in the second section. Along with the development of a shorter version goes the development of the importance of the personal iceberg metaphor, a gestalt which integrates the theoretical ideas of Satir's philosophy and practice.

The Satir Model: Family Reconstruction

The Satir model is a process model, a process of family therapy in which the therapist and the family join forces to promote wellness among the family members. The heart of the model process consists of all those interactions and transactions, translated into methods and procedures, which move the individuals in the family, and the family system itself, from a symptomatic base to wellness.

In the 1960s, her powerful process, called family reconstruction, began emerging. Looking for ways to "externalize internal processes," she developed her particular style of using role-playing. In it, one relives formative experiences that were influenced by three or more generations of his or her family of origin (Satir, Banmen, Gerber, & Gomori, 1991).

Assumptions Underlying Family Reconstruction

The first assumption in this model is that people are geared toward growth. The second assumption is that all human beings have within them all of the resources they need to flourish or that they have had contact with someone who can model those resources for them. The third assumption is that everyone and everything is affected by, and affects, everyone and everything in the system. The fourth assumption is that therapy is a process which takes place between persons in a positive and health-promoting context to accomplish a positive change. The therapist is to lead by initiating and teaching the health-promoting process in the family, but is not to take charge of the persons involved (Horne & Ohlsen, 1982).

Emphases in Famly Reconstruction

The model stresses enhancement and validation of self-esteem. In this process model the family rules are revised as guidelines for living, defensive communication patterns are identified, and congruent communication is taught as an important step in achieving personal freedom. Family mapping and family life-fact chronologies are often used to identify patterns that help create low self-esteem so that more life-giving patterns might be developed. In both the classical form of family reconstruction and the shorter version (developed after 1988), family maps, chronologies, the wheel of influence, and role play are used.

The Satir model highlights the importance of making contact, being emotionally honest, communicating clearly, and creating new possibilities. The ability of the therapist to use metaphor, reframing, drama, humor, and personal touch in the therapy process is emphasized. The model helps to bring past patterns to life in the present, either by having families develop maps (genograms) and life-fact chronologies or by creating a group process in which family patterns and experiences can be simulated and reconstructed (Satir et al., 1991).

Family reconstruction enables the family member designated the Star to explore significant events in three generations of family life. This telling of the Star's life is more than a mere recounting of chronological events; it includes the tragedies and triumphs, the losses and victories. By participating in a group simulation of three generations of family life, the Star is able to make sense out of past experiences that would otherwise continue to mystify him or her. The experience of reenacting and observing significant life events in a group process often gives the Star a new starting point and the opportunity to interrupt old and entrenched family patterns in favor of more useful processes (Corey, 2001). The reconstruction begins in the present to establish the characters and issues of the Star's current life (that involve both the past and the present) and their associated catharses. It ends with a return to the present and a celebration (Wegscheider-Cruce 1994).

Family reconstruction helps clients move beyond both the behaviour or content level and their coping patterns to clarify their internal and interpersonal processes. This enables them to refocus on their yearnings, to deal with their expectations in a realistic way by reframing their perceptions and working through their feelings. In this manner they are able to integrate themselves and become more congruent. They are also helped to become reintegrated into the historical and psychological matrix of their own family of origin. It provides a way for a person to see himself or herself and their parents with new eyes, seeing the present and the future with a new perspective and new possibilities.

This major vehicle for change has the objective of connecting with one's parents and their personhood to reveal the sources of old learning, thus paving the way to finding one's own personhood and is a multi-level spiritual experience. It includes both therapeutic intervention and personal growth. Family reconstruction attempts to guide clients to unlock dysfunctional patterns stemming from their families of origin. The process blends elements of Gestalt therapy, guided fantasy, hypnosis, role playing, and family sculpting (physically moulding family members into characteristic poses representing one family member's view of family relationships). Family rcconstruction is a process that takes family members through certain fixed stages of their lives. By role playing their family's multigeneration drama, members have an opportunity to reclaim their roots and in the process perhaps view old perception in a new light, thereby changing entrenched perceptions, feelings, and beliefs (Nerin 1989). The Star can now achieve peace and reconciliation with estranged family members (if not in external reality at least within his or her own heart) and be released from developmental stuck points by resolving unfinished business. Thus childhood learning can be transformed.

Family mapping and family life-fact chronologies are often used to begin accessing the internal perceptions of an individual family member. Information is collected on three generations in order to truly understand the foundations of the life behaviour of a single individual. Based on the information gathered, the therapist assists the individual to externalize his or her perceptions of self and others by sculpting patterns of communication and/or significant events in the family. Role play is used to make the family patterns and events dynamic and to surface the deeper feelings and meanings still connected to them. The individual and therapist then resculpt or reconstruct past patterns and events. By creating new possibilities together, using old resources in new ways and transforming past liabilities into present and future resources, the therapist enables the individual to take new responsibility for his or her own life. As the individual learns that he/she is able to change the impact of past events on his or her life, self-esteem rises. Relearning is also fostered in triadic groups that mimic the structure of the original triad of mother, father and child. In the context of the triad, old sculpts and communication patterns arise naturally for identification. Similarly, the triad provides the opportunity for practicing new, self-nurturing behaviours and new group behaviours such as cooperation rather than competition.

The reconstruction deals with important ideas such as the triumph of the human spirit, the survival of people despite tremendous tragedy or against great odds, and the potential for recovery to win out over disease. The unconditional regard for all human beings and their right to self-actualize is an idea basic to all forms of reconstruction.

Classical Family Reconstruction

Classical family reconstruction was done in a large group (of 15 to hundreds of people) and took one to three days. The schedule for a reconstruction can only be approximate. For any number of reasons, the sequence of events within a reconstruction may take a different order with any given Star and/or Guide. Certain sections may be short in one reconstruction and long in another. The reconstruction event allows one person to reexperience his or her past, take a look at the present, and make plans for how things can be in the future. Therapeutic methods will allow the Star to move beyond thoughts, feelings, and behaviours that are self-defeating in order to heal. In this way the Star will be able to see new choices in life. In the context of this process, the star experiences the reconstruction process, and others may participate as witnesses (audience) or role players and thus have an opportunity to "role play" to get in tune with the particular family member they will portray.

Classical family reconstruction usually follows a four-act format: sculpting the family of origin; sculpting the families of origin of the Star's mother and father; sculpting the Star's parents' meeting, courting, and wedding; and resculpting the Star's family of origin. Dramatizing the dynamics of the family's last three generations gives the Star a chance to achieve the personal and universal goals identified at the origin of the process.

The Shorter Version of Family Reconstruction

A shorter version of family reconstruction has developed since 1988. It is sometimes called critical impact reconstruction because in this version the Guide works more with a critical impact of the events/issues or on unmet expectations. This version is much shorter; lasting about two to three hours as compared to a one- to three day reconstruction with Satir. Although it can be done in a short time and at various intervals in the Star's life, reconstruction is still based on the classical format and orientation.

In the shorter version a great deal of the work is with what we can call the current family; i.e., in working with present-day situations. Current families can also include ex-spouses and others who may not be living with the star at present, but who retain strong emotional involvement whether positive or negative. In the current family we can see the present problems, the present "stuck points," the area of pain today, what current relationships need to be explored, and so on. Current families can also include a work-related family that is the persons with whom one works.

The first part of the work is to identify current issues, and then to use the reconstruction vehicle to find out why a person stays stuck, to understand what happened, thereby reaching points of forgiveness, understanding, and letting go that allow growth and transformation to happen. The reconstruction process helps to surface strengths and resources for healing, change and growth and teaches the client how to use them (Satir et al., 1991).

Our observation is that the reconstruction helps to heal current pain, reawaken old dreams, and to give the Star permission to develop new dreams. The Satir model reminds us that to heal and to grow requires two processes that have to be accomplished: one is unlearning, and the other is learning. Since the set of meanings, rules, coping strategies, and ways of communicating are learned in childhood, rather than inherited, a person can transform these elements into a new set of meanings, rules, ways of coping, and communicating. Growth comes as we realize that the only way to run our life is to give up fighting for complete control and to let our life unfold.

The shorter reconstruction focuses on making specific major changes. A change in one major area may precipitate other relevant changes. This process usually transforms an automatic survival pattern or it may address a traumatic experience that needs healing at the level of the self Becoming more fully human includes expressing and transforming the pain we felt, and still feel, from what happened in the past (Satir et al., 1991). New eyes see old situations in a new framework, especially in relation to the self. It is a way to regain and acknowledge our wholeness. This shorter version can be used with many issues such as the sudden death of a significant other, a traumatic, violent, or tragic experience, repressed anger, rage, and so on (Satir et al., 1991).

The Work of the Guide

In the shorter version of family reconstruction the Guide takes the following steps:

1. The Guide makes contact with the Star's outer and inner world. As Satir stated, By exploring the Star's inner and outer experiences, the Guide enhances and helps the Star to cope in new ways. Focusing on process to bring about change in a systemic approach is often considered Satir's major therapeutic contribution (Satir et al., 1991).

2. The Guide also uses the coping stances and the family map to assess psychological constraints, stuck places, patterns, dynamics, resources, strengths, and willingness to change, bringing them into the therapeutic change process. The Guide works not only from family maps, but from a map of human wholeness. As noted, the Guide may also incorporate other vehicles for change including sculpting, metaphors, mandala, and others.
3. The Guide views the process as a fluid ever-changing energy that can move a client (Star) toward a positive goal through key interventions, keeping the focus not on the client's stories, but on the impact of these stories on the internal process. The internal change must come from process, the Satir model acknowledges that people's present experiences are often affected by memories of the past. In exploring these impacts with the Star, the Guide is able to facilitate new perceptions and internal acceptance of past events.
4. In the process the Guide then works on change at the levels of feelings, perceptions, and expectations to assist the Star to satisfy yearnings and to live in the self. The process is mostly experiential, facilitating internal change. This is how more emphasis can be put on helping to heal the impact of the past. The Guide then helps the Star integrate and anchor changes at all levels of the iceberg (described below). This requires the Guide to be very active, congruent, creative, and intuitive.
5. The Guide does not take the Star where the Guide wants to go, but leads the Star along his or her own path of discovery and growth. The Guide offers opportunities and directions to lead the Star to new places (Wegsheider-Cruse, 1994), guiding the action, but following the feelings of the Star in so doing. To bring about the kind of reconciliation, forgiveness, and healing necessary for the Star, the Guide has to have done his or her own healing beforehand. Having healed his or her own past and current relationships and family issues, the Guide can be empowered so that the needs of the Star are the primary focus. The Guide must become a talented detective watching for clues and signs, not letting things go unnoticed. The Guide has to have enough confidence to be able, as Satir would say, to follow an instinct and not always need the facts. Why dig for all the facts when a hunch would work just as well?
6. Listening to the presenting problem(s), the Guide formulates positive directional goals with four therapeutic meta-goals: congruence, responsibility, self-esteem, and choices.

Intended Effects of the Shorter Reconciliation Approach

The shorter family reconciliation approach is intended to help the Star:

1. To raise his or her sense of self-esteem. Self-esteem is one's own judgement or belief or feelings about one's own value. Satir used to say, "The job of the therapist is to help people have stars in their eyes—to truly feel their own value." In the Satir model, the level of a person's self-worth is the most important factor affecting behavior. It is the crucial factor in terms of what happens inside and between people. The higher one's self-worth, the more wholesome the coping. In the reconstruction the Star experiences high self-worth and thus is more able to behave in more mature, productive and loving ways. The Star is able to see himself or herself as worthwhile even when he or she does make mistakes. The Star is now more able to take risks, to choose and maintain supportive relationships.
2. To become a better choice maker. We all have the ability to choose. In the reconstruction the Star is encouraged to consider at least three choices and is empowered to be his or her own choice maker.
3. To become responsible. A great part of growing up is gaining the wisdom and ability to be responsible for oneself. We especially need to develop trust and respect in our own life force (I am) which naturally heals, inspires, coordinates, and sustains us. It is that trust and respect, that faith in ourselves, which gives us a sense of authority over our own lives. The reconstruction process helps the Star to become the authority on his or her life.
4. To achieve a greater sense of congruence. Congruence is a state of harmony and wholeness. One's behavior, feelings and perceptions are in harmony with one's inner Self. People in a process toward congruence experience a sense of peace. The energy that becomes available to the Star helps to generate options, solves problems, and create new choices. In its fullest sense, congruence is an expression of the personhood of the Star. It is this personhood that the family reconstruction seeks to make contact with in the Star and family members. Family reconstruction can help the Star discover hidden resources and learn how to make fuller uses of all his or her resources. In the reconstruction process the Star discovers that when he or she is congruent, emotional triggers lose their power and he or she ceases being a victim of his or her past. Family reconstruction can help the Star to acknowledge and accept experiences, past and present, and to realize that he or she is no longer on automatic

pilot, living by rules and assuming dysfunctional stances that stem from other times in his or her life (Satir et al., 1991).

5. To deal with unfinished business from the past. When we find ourselves unable to feel or accept our feelings, reluctant to take risks, stuck in our fear, hesitant to share our thoughts and feelings, and denying what is going on around us, we are probably maintaining inappropriate beliefs from our childhood. When we become aware of our beliefs, we can decide which ones are keeping us from living more fully. We can reassure ourselves that we are no longer children needing to follow a particular rule in order to survive.
6. To achieve freedom from the impact of past events. We cannot change the event, but we can change the impact. We may continue to be controlling because we have an undefined fear of not being in control. We do not know what would happen and that is terrifying. When we can understand our natural pull, we can acknowledge it and then, if we choose, we can gather our courage and let go of the impact.

In the shorter version, transformation becomes the major goal of the family reconstruction. The Star's energy is transformed from a dysfunctional pattern to a more open, free, and healthy pattern. The transformation in the reconstruction changes negative energy into positive energy at the level of feelings, perceptions, and expectations. Rather than straining to suppress or defend against past pains, the Star lets go of unmet wishes and frees up immense energy to spend in meeting current needs and desires. By this major transformation, the Star recognises his or her freedom, choices, inner resources, and possibilities for greater intimacy. The Star thus moves toward a more inner-directed focus and is free from the contamination of his or her past.

Transformation has occurred when a person goes from saying. "I want to be loved" to "I am loved by me." The Satir model sees the Star as having shifted to a place of high self-worth when he or she looks to themselves rather than others for validation and love. Once this change has taken place, the Star is free to choose loving relationships, take a stand for what he /she believes to be right, and focus the energy on productive and creative activities. In the reconstruction the Guide focuses on helping the Star's internal process instead of focusing on the story about a problem. This allows the Star to tap his or her universal yearnings and to transform the perception, the meaning, the feelings, the feelings about the feelings, the expectation, the motivation and action which stems from the yearnings into a new set of meanings, rules, ways of coping and communicating (Satir et al., 1991). The Guide`s emphasis is on teaching and learning, coping with life`s experiences more effectively and less destructively.

The Personal Iceberg Metaphor

The personal iceberg metaphor has evolved into a creative and excellent method to help and to better understand and teach the family reconstruction process. The personal iceberg metaphor acts as a guide to inner process in response to the various experiential sculpts and sharing that occur in the family reconstruction process. It gives a structure that helps the Guide to address the whole person and yet helps the Star to separate past experiences from the present. "Like icebergs, we show only parts of ourselves. Much of our experience lies below the surface. We also show only parts of what we know" (Satir et al., 1991, p. 34). The family reconstruction helps the Star to experience the impact of the past in the present "here and now"" moment.

The personal iceberg metaphor (Satir et al., 1991) is a road map on the "process" highway to life. It serves as a reference for the Guide to enter the world of inner process and to be able to actively engage the client so that the client can make significant transformational shifts within himself or herself The Satir model sees relationships like icebergs in that one-eighth is evident and overt while the other seven-eighths are submerged. The Satir model maintains that the way we develop an understanding of that submerged seven-eighths of individuals with whom we are involved is through our perceptions of the process in our relationships.

The personal iceberg metaphor is now being used extensively as a major transformatonal part of the family reconstruction process. It helps to identfy the structure of our human complexity. When the Guide is able to access this inner system, therapeutic work has the potential to be extremely deep and possibly transformational for the Star at the level of the Self (I am).

The personal iceberg metaphor has a framework of seven components of experience which gives the Guide a way to relate to the participants' inner world: Self (I am), yearnings, expectations, perceptions, feelings, copings stances, and behavior (Satir et al., 1991). It is a conceptual diagram which provides a structure for awareness and understanding of the inner experience of a person. It is a psychological metaphor that represents the human lived experience of the Star, and his or her sense of Self, of others and the world.

The personal iceberg is a powerful metaphor in which the Guide can gain access to increased insight into the hidden inner world of a person. It is an abstract psychological map which conveys the intrapsychic process world of humans (Lum, 2000). It is also a visual concept which can allow the Guide to know how a person makes meaning and interacts within his or her world. With this knowledge, the Guide can facilitate change within the human inner experience: the Self (I am), yearnings, expectations, perceptions, feelings about feelings, feelings, coping, and behavior (Satir et.al., 1991).

The shorter version of the family reconstruction remains a complex process not easy to teach, integrate, and implement. One can teaches pieces of the Satir model in the reconstruction. You can teach how to use the process but you cannot teach creativity or how to translate the therapist's own creativity into process. One must be innovative and creatively incorporate many different therapeutic ideas that fit our own style of therapeutic practice.

The family reconstruction helps clients become their own decision-makers. This occurs when the client takes charge of his own life, stands on his own feet. Satir would say that taking charge to this process of developing our uniqueness and becoming a responsible human, among other human beings is a vital stage of growth. The family reconstruction can bring the outside push that helps this to happen (Suarez, 1989).

A family reconstruction works best when conducted by someone who believes in and reflects the sacredness of life, who recognizes our "universal journey," who leads with heart and soul as well as logic. When we go with heart in addition to head, instead of rigid rules, and when we have a view of exploring instead of presupposing the territory, we will be following the laws of the universe and will discover what our humaness really is (Nerin, 1986).

Satir wrote(Satir et al.,1991):

The premises that underlie family reconstruction are what I believe to be basic human realities:

1. Human beings have the inherent capacities of living productive joyful lives. The challenge is to access what makes it possible.
2. How human beings cope with the events in their lives is the major factor in determining the outcome of any event.
3. Coping is a process learned during the time when the person was most vulnerable (age birth to five), being at the age when there was the least information to judge the validity and usefulness of what was learned. since it was an initial learning and came at a time of great vulnerability, it is almost written in blood.

4. Human beings have the capability to divert, suppress, repress, project, deny, or distort their natural inherent capabilities to conform to what they perceive to be the demands of survival.
5. At any age, most people can learn new ways of fully thinking and behaving.
6. We are walking manifestations of what we have learned.

Summary

Instead of being preoccupied with pathology, illness, or pain, the family reconstruction process focuses on promoting wellness. The reconstruction process helps the body and mind move beyond stress, survival, and coping to a more positive way of expressing and experiencing life. New eyes see old situations in a new framework, especially in relation to the Self. It is a way to regain and own our wholeness.

The family reconstruction gives people a chance to see themselves and family members in a way that exposes their beliefs, ignorance, unawareness, and misunderstandings. The process also lets people experience each other's real intents of acceptance and caring. Perceiving the human frailties of these patterns in relation to their own parents, most people are able to grow toward higher self-worth. And that is the level of self-esteem at which transformation occurs at the second level of change, thus moving beyond the content of the problem and the behavior of the Star. This usually includes changing the expectations, perceptions, and feelings. To make the transformation possible, it may also mean going back to the basic yearnings. The second-level change has a strong transformational effect on the Star (Satir et al., 1991).

The reconstruction model is both structural and continually changing, forever evolving and integrating new ideas and styles to grow with the ideas and styles of individuals who act as guides. It carries on the tradition of Satir to incorporate whatever works as a practical vision of therapy, and allows for an infinite amount of diversity. Family reconstruction was never a static vehicle. Fortunately the model invites each guide to continue to learn and to change. The professional assumes an awesome responsibility when he or she becomes willing to guide a person through an experience markedly enhanced for the Star through his or her total immersion in the process.

The Satir model of human communication and growth continues to be a major alternative for the present stage of history. It is a model that is ever changing and continues to teach us more and more about what Satir did. It is my belief that as time goes on, the model will continue to change with the new insights and awareness that each artist will bring to it. We will always be gratetul to Virginia Satir for her gifts of courage, clarity, compassion, and confidence. She offered people a choice, a challenge and a path. Satir Centers and Institutes are now operating all over the world to do just that.

REFERENCES

Corey, G. (2001). *Theory and practice of counseling and psychotherapy.* Mount Vernon, NY : Wadsworth.

Horne, A. M. & Ohlsen, M. M. (1982). *Family counseling and therapy.* Itasca, IL: Peacock Publishers.

Lum, W. (2000). *The lived experience of the personal iceberg metaphor of therapists in Satir's brief therapy training.* Unpublished masters thesis. University of British Columbia, Vancouver, British Columbia, Canada.

Nerin, W. F. (1989). Satir is very learnable: Trainees lead changes in family reconstruction. *Family Therapy News* (March/April): 3.

Nerin, W. F. (1986). *Family reconstruction: Long day's journey into light.* New York: Norton.

Satir, V., Banmen, J., Gerber, J. & Gomori, M. (1991). *The Satir model: Family therapy and beyond.* Palo Alto, CA: Science and Behavior Books.

Suarez, M. (1999). *A biography of Virginia Satir.* Burien, WA: Avanta, the Virginia Satir Network.

Wegscheider-Cruse, S. (1994). *Family reconstructon: The living theater model.* Palo Alto, CA: Science and Behavior Books.

6

Transformational Change—

Based on the Model of Virginia Satir

Carl Sayles

We as individuals carry many assumptions about change. One of the constants experienced in life is that change happens. Heraclitus, in about 500 BC stated, "Nothing endures but change." Many believe they can control the context of their surroundings to the point that change happens by their directing. So, if change is happening all around us, what part do we have control of?

Change is an issue talked and written about frequently, with a set of assumptions that are often deeply buried in cultural, social, ideological, and personal histories (Mahoney & McCray-Patterson, 1992). In looking at change, it is important to expand our beliefs or perceptions about change and appreciate its role in daily life. There are basic assumptions in the practice of psychotherapy about human nature and how people change. These assumptions are rarely verbalized, but have a profound impact on how and why people change, because assumptions, if not recognized and acknowledged, can keep us frozen or stuck, making decisions that limit our choices. Virginia Satir's process of change is a way to assist people in making choices that raise self-esteem, provide self-accountability or responsibility, and move a person toward being more congruent with self and others. The intent in this article is to give the reader a better understanding of the process of change, the assumptions that limit change, and the transformation that comes as we discover our congruent self and give "self" voice. Furthermore this article carries the aspiration to describe how the transformational process of change can strengthen and deepen the therapeutic process.

Transformation within the change process, using the Satir model, is based on connecting people at the level of their yearnings, expectations, perceptions, and feelings (Satir et al., 1991). The result of that connection is seen in a person's ability to share, value, and accept themselves in making conscious, congruent choices. As we become more consciously congruent, we grow more whole, we are open to new discoveries, and we want to understand more. We seek out new opportunities to test what we do know, versus the judgment or misdirected advice of others. The search for the resources that people possess within themselves, as opposed to focusing on what "should or could have been" brings us to the place of "transformation." The goal is not to eliminate what no longer works, but to add to what already exists to "transform" the meaning and understanding of the entire event (Satir et al., 1991).

The transformational change process is about having more, not because someone gave it to you, but because you uncovered the resource within you that is already sufficient. The goal is to change and transform the behavior, not to eliminate it. When we attempt to eradicate something in our lives, the physical and emotional cost is often very high, frequently resulting in people returning to a prior level of coping. Looking at change through this transformational lens, we can help people in the process of discovery, awareness building, and understanding, transforming their survival stances into more congruent ways of speaking their truth at that moment in time (Satir et al., 1991).

Virginia Satir closely watched the people she worked with, and in watching them, she discovered that there were stages in the change process. The Satir model identifies six stages in the change process, but to emphasize the change that takes place, transformation was added to the model by Banmen (1998). He identified seven stages in the change process: (1) Status Quo, (2) Foreign Element, (3) Chaos, (4) Transformation, (5) Integration (6) Practice (7) New Status Quo. Change, as we are using the word, is an internal shift in our belief that results in an external change (Satir et al., 1991). This shift in belief happens as the person becomes more trusting of the process, acknowledges his or her own resources, and feels like change is possible. To better understand the stages in Satir's change process, an overview of some of the basic beliefs regarding psychological change is advantageous.

Exploring Change

The theories of change in psychology have a profound impact on how change is viewed and practiced, based on an assumption about human nature and the possibility of change. Four basic historical theories involving psychological change are rooted in psychoanalytic, behavioral, humanistic, and cognitive processes, each having subsets or versions within them, but their basic premise regarding change remains the same. Looking at the change process through the lens of psychological development in history, we can see the benefits in using a model that keeps a person moving to a deeper, more connected place within himself or herself. Within the context of the Satir model, that deeper and more connected place is where transformation happens. Satir, although unique in her understanding about change, was humanistic in her approach (Loeschen, 1998). She believed that people can change and grow, and that they can do it by learning new ways of thinking, doing, and being. In addition, she understood that change is an internal shift that brings about an external change in the way a person interacts with the world (Satir et al., 1991). These two assumptions lie at the heart of this therapeutic approach. Within these two assumptions we discover that making a different choice can bring a sense of worth to a person.

The Satir model offers people the possibility of transforming their old way of interacting by making different choices and being more congruent. This possibility can change a person's belief about herself or himself, raising self-esteem, and giving them hope. Using this process provides the therapist with the opportunity to be present with a person in the midst of his or her deepest pain and despair, empathically connected in a way that moves beyond simply feeling to a deeper level of feeling the feelings as the person moves inside. Moving toward the person's own felt sense of what is going on, at that moment in time, facilitates new perceptions and internal acceptance of past events (Satir & Baldwin, 1983).

Satir made a choice early in her work to move away from the more linear cause-and-effect approach toward a system-oriented or systemic way of perceiving the person and the world he or she lives in (Satir et al., 1991). The Satir Process Model uses these systemic patterns in working with families, couples, adult individuals, and children to help those living within the system to understand their relationship to it and make a conscious choice. In looking at other theoretical approaches from a psychoanalytical perspective, the therapist was seen as a blank screen upon which a person could project her or his thoughts, beliefs, or feelings–associated with significant others, waiting for that crucial moment of transference to occur and bring about change (Corsini & Wedding, 1989). The behavioral therapist was seen more as a technician with little emphasis given to the relationship between therapist and client. There was a sense of neutrality in the relationship that kept the relationship focused on a physical change, rather than the emotional aspect of change that Satir believed in. Within the Satir model change happens at a deep level and within a context that is understood, felt, experienced and integrated by both the person in the process and the therapist.

The humanistic approach, although rooted in the psychoanalytical tradition, took on a more positive view of human nature and change, because people possess the ability to change through social and symbolic teaching (Mahoney & McCray-Patterson, 1992). The social aspect was an interactional exchange between therapist and client, while the symbolic encompassed the use of metaphors as a way of deepening the experience. Both social and symbolic aspects are valued pieces of the interaction within the Satir model. Through the use of metaphors, people are able to connect with a part of themselves that otherwise may go undiscovered. From a client-centered approach, the connection is the place where change can begin to happen and the opportunity for growth is seen as possible. The connection between the therapist and client in the Satir model is important, but the most valuable connection is the one the client feels with himself or herself when the transformational change takes place.

There has been a long history among psychoanalytic, behavioral, and humanistic forces with each one claiming to have the answer to psychological change. There was little communication between these forces, which left open an opportunity for yet another force using a more cognitive approach (Corsini & Wedding, 1989). The cognitive theories began to dominate research on learning, memory, motivation, and social psychology (Mahoney & McCray-Patterson, 1992). Cognitive theory places emphasis on a more interactive, rather than a linear and directed approach to change. This more cognitive aspect of change is present within the Satir model also, looking at the interaction between a person's thoughts and feelings. A person's cognitive understanding or perception is a valuable way of accessing a deeper sense of what they might be experiencing at that moment in time and the possibility of change. Cognitive understanding can play an important role in the transformational change process, because without a clear understanding of what one believes or perceives it would be difficult to move to a deeper place where "self" can have voice. Ultimately, in giving "self" voice, the Satir model uses numerous different aspects of each model to bring about change.

Context for Change

Change happens all around us. Satir spoke of change as another way of talking about life. Transformational change requires an understanding of how perceptions of the world enhance or diminish our ability to change. Having already established that change happens, Satir indicates that change that is transforming is made in a safe, trusting and accepting environment (Satir et al., 1991). Satir was a master at creating a safe and accepting environment where the transformational process, which brings about change, could take place. The Satir model brings that transformational opportunity to both the client and therapist. This is not "Satir magic," but a fluid energy movement that carries people toward a positively directional goal (Lum, 2000). To move positively directional, the focus in therapy needs to shift beyond the story, experience, or history a person carries with them and explore its impact on the person's internal process. Internal change is then experienced, resulting in an external shift in belief (Satir et al., 1991). This internal shift or change is more inclusive of the whole person, integrating approaches that change only the exterior or behavior of a person. This internal change happens in that positive movement that Satir called life.

In exploring life experiences and their impacts, an opening to new perceptions and internal acceptance of past events brings an experiential process that is felt at both an internal and an external level. When that internal process is felt and experienced transformational change occurs. The basic assumption regarding the way change happens within a system is rooted in the belief and conviction that every person is unique and worthy of love. This unique worthiness is an important truth and core concept in understanding the person and his or her potential for change and wholeness (Loeschen, 1998). This potential holds in it the hope that this felt experience has value.

Growth and change happen in an open and functional system, where people are heard, valued, validated, and acknowledged. Moving toward understanding transformational change requires an awareness of what Satir called a way of perceiving the world. The way in which a person perceives or views the world is a valuable key in assessing a person's willingness to look at changing. How people define relationships, the person, an event, or their attitude toward change are four universal truths that characterize all people and their relationships with others (Satir, 1991). These universal truths are rooted in two dichotomous concepts. The hierarchical view and the growth view represent the fundamentally different assumptions or truths that are carried by people and have an impact on the process of transformational change (Satir & Baldwin, 1983). When looking at the model through the hierarchical lens, humanity is viewed as inherently "bad" or "flawed." Rules and standards that are established determine identity within the system, and differentness is not tolerated or valued. The emotional costs of living in a hierarchical system are feelings of inadequacy, despair, depression, hopelessness, and rebellion (Satir, 1988). A closed system, such as this one, is a place where people conform in order to survive. It produces a person or persons that are insecure in relationships and have little or no voice in the relationship. The belief, within a hierarchical system, is that the only options available are the choices already made or "no" choice at all. It is not an environment that promotes risk taking or choice making. Rather, it is a place where self-worth grows more doubtful, with a deepening dependence on other people (Satir, 1988). For self-worth to flourish and grow, people need to be heard, validated, and acknowledged.

The growth, or organic, view provides an opportunity for people to be heard and acknowledged by seeing the potential goodness of all people. By building on that potential, the uniqueness of an individual is encouraged and accepted as an important self-identifier, with differentness being valued. The impact of living in an environment were a person is valued brings with it a feeling of hope, openness, acceptance, worth, and uniqueness. In this environment, relationships are based on mutual appreciation of each person's uniqueness. Making choices, when each person is valued and appreciated, makes the inevitability of change part of each person's internal system or schemata and thereby raises the feeling of worth within the system. Increasing the feeling of worth within the system creates the opportunity for hopefulness, acceptance, growth, and change. As self-worth grows to a more reliable level, where self-confidence can be experienced and drawn more from the self, the potential for growth is built.

As people begin to experience self-confidence, hope, and acceptance, relationships grow. Relationships in the growth or organic view are more equal with each person's uniqueness being valued and appreciated. Looking at a person in terms of her or his uniqueness—versus roles, rules, and need for control—puts an emphasis on the process of relating, moving it away from the possession of power and dominance in the relationship. There is an appreciation for the relation of all things, regardless of position. Events are understood as coming from many different variables, are encouraged, and are seen as an opportunity for change. Viewing change as a natural part of the ongoing process moves people in relationship toward a place of being able to realize their potential and connect with others (Satir, 1988).

Process of Change

To facilitate the exploration of change in the Satir model a case example will be used as a point of reference.

> Jack and Jill have been married 14 years and recently moved 3,000 miles. They come to therapy because they cannot communicate with each other any longer. Jack, 46, works in the computer industry and appears quiet and unemotional. Jill, 52, works in the medical field and is outspoken and animated in her interactions. Jill struggles with a lack of trust in the relationship because of Jack's two-year emotional relationship with another woman prior to their relocation. Jack struggles with not being able to provide for Jill's emotional needs because of her fear of being alone. They would both like the relationship to work out.

For change to take place within a family or system, four prerequisites need to be in place. These important basics are a loving atmosphere, trust, a believable image, and a willingness to be in limbo. A loving atmosphere is essential so that as Jack and Jill begin to explore and experience new ways of believing and seeing the world harsh or judgmental tones that tend to push people into hopeless darkness can be averted. A loving atmosphere is a place where truth can be spoken without fear. When trust is present, sharing a new truth or vision is not scary or fear producing. A believable image is based on the notion that change can actually lead to a deeper place of understanding and not simply back into confusion and chaos. The prerequisite to change that is often most difficult to achieve is a willingness to be in a state of unknowing. This involves a decision that once chaos is reached Jack and Jill are willing to stay there and work the process through. Each of these fundamental truths has its own life cycle. It comes into being as people become more aware of the need to change. This awareness does not always come easily. It can be a moment of intense pain or overwhelming joy. But when the opportunity comes, a choice can be made. The opportunity, or yearning, of Jack and Jill is to experience these fundamentals within their relationship.

The seven stages in the change process are what make the internal shift in belief to an external change possible. This internal shift cannot happen without an accepting environment first being established. This environment is necessary in building trust as the person experiences, explores, and acknowledges his or her feelings. As the feelings are felt and articulated the old belief is transformed into a new understanding, leading to a new belief. This new belief affects a person at the level of self, which brings about a new awareness of what is externally possible. This process happens as a person moves through the seven stages in the change process. These stages include the status quo, foreign element, chaos, transformation, integration, practice, and a new status quo. As the model has developed, a deeper understanding of the change process has evolved. In the movement from Chaos to the place of Integration a transformational shift takes place. This is where the client enters the process and begins to work on what brought her or him to therapy. For Jack and Jill this was a frightening place, because it meant developing a level of trust and intimacy that they said they wanted, but now had to act on. They needed to trust that they would be heard, honored and valued as they moved to a new level of risk within the relationship, opening them to the possibility of transformational change. The goal in this work is to change the internal process, which will have an impact on the external behavior of a person, family or system.

Status Quo

Status Quo is a place of balance within a system. This balance can come at a very high cost to one or many within the system. It can also be present by virtue of living in a system where expectations are clearly identified and people are encouraged to take risks. Status Quo is usually the place where the need for change becomes known, because what worked at one time no longer works (Satir et al., 1991). The pull to remain with what is familiar plays a big role in maintaining the Status Quo within a system. When a system is in Status Quo it becomes more predictable and there is an increased level of reliability in how it operates. The Status Quo of a family or system is rooted in the felt experience of each person living within that system. The result feels right, true and familiar (Satir et al., 1991). For Jack and Jill what worked and felt acceptable was different, but they established a familiar pattern around how they maintained their relationship. But was the balance healthy and could it go on?

When a family or system is in healthy balance every person contributes and his or her contribution is considered. No one gives more than they receive. Open dialogue between members is encouraged and valued and is not dependent upon age, gender, or status within the family or system. Negative behaviors are talked about in a way that does not lower a person's self-esteem or belief in themselves (Satir et al., 1991). They continue to see and understand each other as valuable even when experiencing conflict within the system. Conflict, in a healthy system, is an opportunity to explore and move to a deeper level. It can be a symbol of what is going on in the system without blame or judgment of the person. Jack and Jill do not live in a healthy status quo. They live in a system that is unbalanced and emotionally charged, but not always articulated.

In an unhealthy system there is a level of stability, yet the cost to keep the system stable is very high and requires a great amount of energy on the part of each person. Resentments build, fear and anger are not acknowledged, unmet expectations and yearnings are pushed down, all at a high cost to those in the system. There is limited intimacy and a lack of closeness. Within this closed unhealthy system Jack and Jill struggle with reestablishing intimacy, with little hope of moving forward. Expectations are high with rules to reinforce the expectations. Coping to survive is going on at every level of the system. People are placating, blaming, being super-reasonable, or irrelevant simply as a way to avoid feeling the pain of living or being in a system where individual value is not respected. In a system in which people are paying more than they receive back, esteem and value are low while worth as a person is close to nonexistent (Satir et al., 1991). Change is viewed as unnecessary, silly, or wrong. The risk in challenging these beliefs could result in emotional or physical harm to those living within the system. The risk for Jack and Jill couple could be the end of their relationship.

A basic belief within the model is that people do the best they can with what they know, understand, and perceive at that moment in time. This reframing of behavior is not a way of excusing the person from what they might have done, but it is a way of acknowledging that we cannot know what we were never taught, saw, or experienced (Satir et al., 1991).

Known patterns are usually continued until something relatively drastic happens and someone in the system seeks help or is put in a position where help is given without choice. The intensity of these patterns may increase to the point that the behavior brought on by the crisis becomes unacceptable or unbearable for those in the system. For Jack and Jill the pain of continuing to cope grew to a place of intolerance. In acknowledging the pain the process of change has begun. The unbalanced nature of the relationship was acknowledged and the opportunity for change was explored as a foreign element was invited into the system.

Foreign Element

The Foreign Element is an aspect of the change process that comes from outside the system. It could be an event such as the birth of a child that is joyous and full of wonder and amazement. It could also be an arrest for driving under the influence of a controlled substance, such as alcohol or cocaine. Both of these events disrupt the status quo and come from outside the system. A birth is usually thought of as having a positive influence. But when it is the fifth child in a family that financially is struggling to support four, the unbalancing that occurs could have a negative impact on the entire family system. Old ways of coping could once again be activated and in that moment in time the system is thrown into chaos with little hope and few options. The return to old coping patterns is often the only way people can get through an event, employing blame and denial as the key coping functions to survive.

Another form of foreign element could be a person outside the system. In the case of Jack and Jill the foreign element would be the psychotherapist. For the therapeutic process to work, this outside person needs to be accepted by members of the system in a safe environment. Establishing a safe context for change to take place is an important fundamental building block in working therapeutically with a person or family (Satir et al., 1991). Without safety the opportunity for change is not created. The context for change is established in the connection with people, validating them and facilitating their growth (Loeschen, 1998). Along with establishing a safe context for change to take place the model provides a congruent way of communicating that is powerful and effective in working with families, couples, and individuals. It takes great courage to move away from the safety of the Status Quo within a family system and risk sharing what is real in that moment.

Some of the barriers that prevent the therapist from establishing a context for change are the expectations, beliefs, feelings, and yearnings that people carry. Many of them are rooted in rules and based on beliefs that come from years of reinforcement. Starting where the person is then and adding from that place to make it possible for change to happen creates an element of safety (Satir, 1988). Another common barrier to change includes the fear of not being "enough" or maybe being too much to handle. Many people carry rules that negate feelings. Rules that negate feelings are more deeply rooted than any other feelings. Often these rules are family based and result in not feeling integrated, being uninterested, feeling empty, never feeling quite good enough, and being driven in one closed direction (Satir et al., 1991). To get our life energy flowing we need to identify and change the rules that keep us stuck. Jack and Jill had a difficult time expressing the rules that existed within their family system because they were not aware of them. Exploring the blocks to what they want and need gives both the therapist and the couple an opportunity to move forward. Building that basic trust relationship with Jack and Jill establishes a bridge to what can be in their relationship.

Once a context of safety is established the system begins to soften and becomes more receptive. As those living within the system acknowledge the patterns taking place and open themselves to the process of exploration of expectations and beliefs, the process becomes more conscious. This unfolding moves the family system away from the familiar Status Quo toward the inevitable Chaos.

Chaos

A healthy form of Chaos is characterized by a willingness on the part of one or more people in the system to risk moving into territory that is unknown or unfamiliar (Satir & Baldwin, 1983). For Jack and Jill this is a place they can easily become stuck, feeling hopeless and not able to move. Getting a commitment from them to work on the issues now being explored is vital in moving them to a new level in the relationship. In effect this Chaos means the system is no longer operating in the same predicable patterns that it has in the past (Satir et al., 1991). It can be a risky place for people, because being able to calculate the expectations of the family ensured safety, survival, and, most important, stability. This chaotic place can paralyze people with fear and anxiety and a feeling that every support that ever worked has now been taken away. Acknowledging the fear and anxiety by normalizing the chaos in the family system provides something for people to hold onto while they experience new felt emotions (Satir et al, 1991).

New possibilities do not appear obvious to those living in this now unbalanced family system which is feeling the loss of control, the overwhelming feeling of fear and the unknown. The notion of new possibilities and the opportunities that can accompany this new way of thinking and feeling can free those in the family to speak and feel. It can also move a person or family toward a positively directional choice that they might not have been aware of before. This is where transformation begins to happen. Clients can often feel something new and exciting, even in the midst of the chaos.

Jack and Jill find themselves struggling with the new felt feelings as they begin to express to each other the feelings that have been deeply buried and created block to their relationship. Jack, who struggles with intimacy, begins to talk about his wanting to reach out and touch Jill, but Jill's emotional neediness scares him. Jill expresses her longing to be touched and fear of being alone and not really knowing if she now wants intimacy in the relationship.

The coping styles of each person in the system are specific to that person. But the motivating force behind the behavior is universal. Coping patterns insulate the person from feeling what is really happening in the moment. For a therapist, challenging that coping comes in the form of acknowledging its place, value, and strength. Since coping patterns do not allow an individual's self-worth to be expressed the symptoms of the person or family can take over the expression in terms of nonverbal, intellectual or semantic issues (Satir et al., 1991). The Chaos stage of the change process is one way of exploring and transforming these old copings into new ways of being.

Systems whether they are functional or dysfunctional generally have a predictable set of expectations and behavior patterns (Satir et al., 1991). Recognizing the value of Chaos in the change process can help people to acknowledge the fear of the unknown. It can allow the therapist to speak the unspeakable things in the family system, lowering anxiety and replacing uncertainty with congruence and presence. Being in this place of Chaos can also be a positive motivator, moving people toward more conscious awareness of the issue and create a place or opportunity for choice. Without the Chaos no transformation of the old survival coping patterns can occur (Satir et al., 1991). For people to move to a healthier, more functional way of being Chaos is an essential part of the journey. Without the Chaos the work of experiencing the feelings, perceptions, expectations, and yearnings is difficult, if not impossible, to accomplish. In considering Jack and Jill, we find them in this place of

Chaos struggling to be heard and acknowledged. It is a place where they feel vulnerable and uncomfortable with each other. They are challenged to not use old ways of coping, blaming, or placating, but to be open and honest with each other. This is a time when emotions that have not been expressed can be named and shared. For Jack and Jill it is a time when the relationship feels and looks different.

In moving through the Chaos phase of the model, a place of transformation emerges. It is a place where the depth of exploration can happen. The client therapist relationship at this point must be strong to offer a sense of stability to the client. Trust grows and sharing deepens moving a person to a point of exploring "what is." The past can be brought to the present in a safe way to be transformed and healed. The impact of the past can be felt and acknowledged with the opportunity to change being clearly felt in the present.

Transformation

This phase of the Satir model is where emotions are acknowledged and felt at a deeper level than many have felt or experienced before. Transformation is deeply connected to the self of the person doing the work. The emotions that are felt and experienced are stored in the cells of the body and brain as memories. Changes in the cell are picked up by nerve impulses traveling across the cell membrane to produce a corresponding change in behavior, physical activity, and mood (Pert, 1997). The transformational shifts that are felt by clients are biological changes that take place at the cellular level corresponding to a change or shift in mood and or behavior. What is experienced and felt is real to this person in that moment in time. This shift brings a person closer to the core self, which can be a very scary place for many people, but it also can be a place filled with many valuable resources and a sense of hope. Transformation is a place where the universal yearnings to be loved, acknowledged, and accepted can be met by the individual "self."

Transformation lies at the core of the changes within the Satir model that have happened. Today the Satir model looks at this transformation process through the metaphor of the iceberg. The Personal Iceberg Metaphor first conceptualized by John Banmen and collaboratively developed by Satir, Banmen, Gerber, and Gomori (1991), uses the human internal experience as a guide to the person's inner process. What gets transformed or shifted is the person's relationship to an event that previously may have been unknown, unacknowledged, and unfelt. The memories that were formed and stored in the body are no longer needed as a way cope with life. Life shifts from a way of coping to survive to a way of being in relationship with the self that is grounded and connected to the person.

The impact of this transformation is felt as different parts of the person are transformed. Feelings that previously controlled a person are felt and acknowledged, putting the person in charge of these feelings that once controlled them. Perceptions that were the basis for believing an event that happened in the past are now based on an individual's truth living in the present. Expectations, based on the past, that keep a person stuck, blaming external events for what is currently happening are transformed as a person takes charge of events in her or his life, acknowledging the feelings, beliefs, and deeper yearning. Transformation happens as people take charge of their feeling, perceptions, expectations and yearnings.

In the context of the Satir model the opportunity to resolve unmet expectations and unmet yearnings is where transformation takes place. The self or core of the person gets to be in charge –not an event from the past. This is where in the process of change, change is experienced and felt. The life force or essence can radiate through the whole person as one experiences transformation. Some therapists such as some at the Mental Research Institute call this second order change. Moving persons through this transformational stage brings them face-to-face with a question of worth. Are they worthy of this choice and ready to move forward to a new way of being and doing? It means the exploring of expectations, perceptions and unmet needs and coming to a place where the congruent choice is "yes, I am worth it" (Satir et al., 1991).

Within the Satir model it is not a matter of choosing one issue over another; it is a matter of exploring the difference and making a choice. Out of this new awareness, which brings about an internal transformational shift, an external behavior change can be the result. Choice is knowing that you could go back to the old Status Quo or the Chaotic craziness, but also knowing the cost of going back and being able to weigh the value of going forward to that new place of possibilities. One of the ways the model brings people to this place of choice and transformational change is by giving them hope. It is through hope that people can rebuild and move to a deeper level of self-understanding and self-acceptance (Loeschen, 1998).

Jack and Jill used this transformational place well to do their individual work, but they also worked on the couple relationship. This was difficult for them, because they were not sure if they were going to have a long-term relationship. This brought chaos to the couple which was talked about and processed, bringing them to a positively directional goal where feelings were shared along with perceptions about the level of intimacy in the relationship. Sharing regarding their individual struggles with intimacy surfaced family of origin issues that were then explored and beliefs shifted. Moving to a deeper place the yearning they both carry to be loved, accepted, and heard began to float up. This becomes an exciting place for the couple to work, because the transformation of thoughts, feelings and experiences becomes real and tangible. By their own choice they are now ready to move to a place of Integration, Practice and New Status Quo.

Integration and Practice

With transformation being experienced and felt, integration and practice will anchor the person or system in these changes. Integrating these newly experienced parts can help reduce the conflict that people might feel in experiencing and building a new connection with self that has self-esteem. An important role the therapist has, in this place of integration, is to anchor the significant changes in perceptions, feelings, beliefs, and behaviors. As people become more comfortable with this new way of feeling and experiencing themselves, what once felt strange and awkward becomes more familiar and provides a level of comfort (Satir et al., 1991). One way this is done, using this model, is to help people make decisions about their lives without making the decision for them (Satir & Baldwin, 1983). Supporting the person and the choice they made keeps them in charge of their lives and acknowledges the trust and willingness of the person to take risks, bringing us back once again to anchor the transformation that happened.

Practice takes place as people take away what has happened in the change process and work with it. This is the homework part of integrating a new behavior and is an important aspect of the change process. For Jack and Jill couple practice could involve them looking together at the impact the change they experienced during the session could have on the new possibilities that have been explored. This practice increases self-esteem and value as they take away and use this new way of relating to themselves and to each other.

New Status Quo

Movement forward brings us to a New Status Quo, a healthier balance where people can be heard and acknowledged more fully. A new sense of control has taken the place of the old more familiar way. A new way of perceiving self develops where people begin to trust the new more functional way of interacting. An increase sensed of hope emerges along with a new self-image (Satir et al., 1991). Living in this new Status Quo feels more natural. The environment becomes a place where creativity is released and people feel valued for what they have to offer. There is a new awareness of freedom at the internal as well as the external level of being.

The couple has now begun to practice new ways of talking to each other. Feelings are being shared, heard and acknowledged by both of them. Intimacy has begun to slowly move back into their lives, giving them a renewed sense of hope and excitement for their relationship. They are beginning to ask each other how they feel in the relationship and are stopping to listen and integrate what the other person is sharing. They are seeking out a common interest to keep the positively directional momentum moving and intimacy growing.

Conclusion

So what part of change do we have control over? The Satir model of 2001 and beyond looks at transformation and change through the metaphor of an iceberg. Transformational change happens as people look at the impact of an event on their lives and make a choice to be in charge of how the event affects their life. Very early in life people receive important information about themselves and learn not to pay attention to the internal messages and feelings which perpetuate a belief. This belief then gets translated into ways of coping to survive with little thought given to the impact of the event. The Satir model allows people to take risks in an environment that is less risky and can engender hope.

Transformation is a situation in which a person experiences, at the core of herself or himself, the possibility of being in charge of what is felt, believed, and experienced. The old body memories that brought this person back to re-experience the pain can be felt, changed, and integrated. What emerges in this transformational process is a person who believes, not only in himself or herself—which raises self-esteem—but also that change is possible, because it has been experienced. Transformational change happens as people embrace the pain of the past in the present and feel the difference in the core of their being. The process of transformation begins with a person, full of possibility, taking the risk "to be more fully human."

References

Banmen, J. (1998). *Stages of change.* Presented at the Advanced Intensive Residential Training Program. Federal Way, WA.

Corsini, R., & Wedding, D. (1989). *Current psychotherapies* (4th ed.). Itasca, IL: F.E. Peacock.

Loeschen, S. (1998). *Systemic training in the skills of Virginia Satir.* Pacific Grove, CA: Brooks/Cole.

Lum, W. (2000). *The lived experience of the personal iceberg metaphor of therapists in Satir's systemic brief therapy training.* Unpublished master's thesis, University of British Columbia, Vancouver, British Columbia, Canada.

Mahoney, M. & McCray-Patterson, K. (1992). Changing theories of change: Recent developments in counseling. In S. Brown & R. Lent (Eds.), *Handbook of counseling psychology*, pp. 665–87. New York: John Wiley & Sons.

Pert, C., (1997). *Molecules of emotions.* New York: Touchstone.

Satir, V. (1988). *The new peoplemaking.* Palo Alto, CA: Science and Behavior Books.

Satir, V., & Baldwin, M (1983). *Satir step by step: A guide to creating change in families.* Palo Alto, CA: Science and Behavior Books.

Satir, V., Banmen, J., Gerber, J., & Gamori, M. (1991). *The Satir model: Family therapy and beyond.* Palo Alto, CA: Science and Behavior Books.

7

Transformations in Therapeutic Practice

Stephen Smith

Virginia Satir believed that how she interpreted her perceptions of the world was the basis for everything she did, including how she behaved as a therapist. This was true for all therapists regardless of the theory that the therapist used (Banmen & Satir, 1981). "As I perceive my picture of what the world is all about and how I am in it, it's going to be the basis for how I proceed in the world .. . So that whatever I am doing represents the way I'm seeing . . ." (Satir & Banmen, 1982, p. 24). In her training of therapists, Satir sought to teach her students new ways of perceiving the world and therefore new ways of perceiving the therapeutic.

In this chapter, we are going to explore some of the important and unique perspectives that Satir used to develop her transformational therapy, including the way she looked at people, open and closed systems, the therapeutic relationship, and the process of change. We will then look at the implications of these perspectives in Satir's training of therapists. Lastly, we will describe contemporary training in the Satir model that is currently being given internationally by John Banmen and Kathlyne Maki-Banmen. We will include some research into how this training changed the way a group of trainees looked at their roles as therapists, their relationships with clients, their relationships with themselves, and their understanding of the therapeutic process. Inclusion of the research is provided in order to answer the question of whether or not training in the Satir model is transformational for students as it was when taught by Virginia Satir. This research is based on the work done by Wendy Lum (Lum, 2000).

Satir's View of People

Satir saw people as having three births. (Satir & Banmen, 1983, p. 115). The first was the union of sperm and egg, which activated the life force, and created a new manifestation of the life force. Satir held that people were the co-creators of their lives in conjunction with this life force. The inclusion of this concept of a force that unites all human beings is the spiritual foundation of the Satir model. All people are created from the same process and are connected to the same source. Therefore, everyone has the same value.

The second birth was the physical birth from the womb, when people are born into a pre-existing family system totally dependent on their caregivers for survival. In order to survive babies need to conform to (or please) that system in some way. It is literally a matter of life and death, as babies are totally incapable of meeting their own needs. Satir said:

> We're all born into a survival relationship with our parents. We can do nothing for ourselves. If no one hears our cries and acts on them, we die. Or if they act on them in delayed fashion, that becomes the basis on which we formed our lives (Satir & Banmen, 1982, p. 67).

Hence, a person's notions of reality, and their place within it, are constructed through their interaction with the family system. This concept of constructed reality implies that this is an unconscious process and takes place below people's level of awareness. Therefore, how they cope with life is directly related to the kind of family system in which they were raised, and the kind of perceptions of reality and assumptions about reality that that family had.

The third birth was "when we become our own decision makers" (Satir & Banmen, 1982, p. 45). People have no conscious choice over the first two, but the third birth occurs as a result of a successful search for wholeness and a new consciousness of self. This new consciousness of self is an awareness and appreciation of "how we shep(h)erd, and understand, and nurture, and discover the miracle that is a human being" (Satir & Banmen, 1982, p. 165). Satir believed that until people became aware of the survival messages of the past, they would continue to behave in reference to those messages whether or not those messages had any relevance to their present situation. Intrinsic in her notion of the third birth, then, is conscious choice based on what a person believes fits for them in terms of their own concept of reality. This means that the completion of the third birth requires that a person let go of those survival messages of the past that no longer fit and retain only those which have value in the present.

As there is no longer any requirement to depend on an external system to meet one's needs, there is no requirement to continue to conform to that external system. The new consciousness and appreciation of self to which Satir referred is a result of the internal system becoming independent of the external system. Wholeness is achieved through access to internal resources only.

Satir saw people as being intrinsically good and that each human being was a unique manifestation of what she called the "Life Force." People were "made as perfect beings to have what we (need) in abundance, and to have ourselves be happy, productive, respected human beings" (Satir & Banmen, 1982, p. 24). Despite this innate capacity for growth, however, Satir said that 95% of the people she met did not have the ability to access the internal resources that they needed. She said "they will represent a varying degree of self-worth and it will be telling me about the survival message" (Satir & Banmen, 1982, p. 69). Those people who lack a sense of self worth will adopt various survival strategies. Satir called such survival strategies coping stances, which include blaming, placating, super-reasonable and irrelevant. She never considered these stances as definitions or labels for people. The stances describe how a person behaves, not who they are.

Satir held that people were not single entities but were, in fact, composed of a multiplicity of parts. These parts could be conceptualized in many ways but are generally based on role. Some examples could be a son or daughter part, a parent part, a warrior part, a sensual part, a professional part, and so on. Parts have different opinions, feelings, yearnings, expectations, and behaviors. Each person can be understood as being composed of a community of parts that have a relationship with each other and a person's internal health can, in part, be determined by the nature of that relationship.

Satir believed that all people were capable of growth and could learn how to access these resources regardless of previous life experiences. This belief fosters an attitude that no one ought to be considered hopeless or incapable of change. Even if the client feels hopeless, the belief of the therapist that positive change is possible brings hope into the interaction.

Satir's Systemic Perspective

Satir looked at systems in terms of where they were on a continuum that considered how open or closed that system was (Satir & Banmen, 1982, 1983), that is, how rigid or flexible the system was in terms of order and sequence. She asked four questions to determine where the system could be placed on the continuum: what was a person's definition of a relationship, definition of a person, explanation of events, and attitude toward change (Satir & Banmen, 1982, p. 26).

A closed system, according to Satir, is hierarchical in nature and based on a threat and reward model. That is, the powerful could reward what they perceived as positive behavior and threaten to punish what they perceived as negative behavior; "a closed system always has rules that have some kind of punishment underneath" (Satir & Banmen, 1983, p. 660). System rules contain exemplars or paradigms about what one should or ought to think, feel, see, expect, want, be, and behave, and system energy is used to maintain structure. Therefore, relationships are defined by who is up and who is down in the hierarchy: people are defined in terms of their role (which gives ascribed status). Events are explained in a linear cause and effect fashion to determine who is at fault, and the closed system resists any change that does not maintain the hierarchical structure.

Choice is limited by rigid system structure defined and maintained by rigid system rules. Therefore, a child born into a closed family system will be obliged to find its place within the structure and fit itself in, rather that have the structure make an accommodation for it. The child quickly learns that choice is based on what fits for the system rather than what fits for itself.

Satir referred to the open system as a "seed or organic model" (Satir & Banmen, 1983, p. 219). System energy is used for growth and, because it is not bond up in maintaining structure, can flow freely to where it is needed. Relationships are defined in terms of equivalency of value, people are defined as a combination of sameness and differences, events are explained in a systemic, reflexive manner, and change is accepted and welcomed. Satir said that in the open system "(t)o be open or closed (is) under your conscious choice" (Satir & Banmen, 1982, p. 48).

A child born into such an open system will find that the family structure alters to accommodate its needs in a reflexive manner. Therefore, choice will not be limited to what meets system needs as the child's own needs are accounted for as well.

Systemic Perspective of People

Satir perceived that the internal parts of a person constituted a system (Satir & Banmen, 1983) and that these internal parts interact with each other. Because Satir made direct connections between the intrapsychic and the interpersonal, her notions of open and closed systems not only described the external world but the internal one as well. Whereas an external system may be seen in the relationship between constituent parts of a family, community, or country, an internal system may be seen in the relationship between the constituent parts of a person. Whether the internal system is open or closed can be discerned through the four questions about definition of relationships, definition of people, explanation of events, and attitude toward change.

A closed intrapsychic system is organized around a hierarchy of parts whose status is determined through role. For example, a man who bases his sense of self worth on acquisition of monetary wealth may value aggressive parts of himself that promote success in the business world and devalue parts that do not contribute to such success. It is not likely that these devalued parts will be paid much attention and therefore they will have little influence in this intrapsychic system. In this way less valued, and therefore less powerful, parts can be blamed for system problems and any change which threatens this hierarchical structure is problematic.

An open intrapsychic system is based on equivalency of value for all parts and role determines when a part is most active according to what is needed at that time. This requires that a person accepts all the parts of themselves and all parts are attended to. As parts do not have to struggle between themselves for power, blame is no longer needed to maintain structure.

As internal system needs are met on the inside, there is no longer a requirement to respond to the external system in a particular way. This independence from the external system means that a person may live in an external system that, by Satir's definition, is closed and yet have an internal system that is open. Therefore, although external choice may be limited by circumstance, internal choice is always present. This internal choice is defined by options in how one copes with external impact. Satir considered that although people could not always control the external impacts, they could make choices in how they coped with them.

It is possible, therefore, to be congruent even in the most oppressive surroundings. As an example of this, Satir cited the experience of Victor Frankl, who saw himself as a choicemaker even though he was an inmate at a Nazi death camp. That is, even though he had no choices in terms of his external environment, he had some choices in how he reacted to it. Therefore, as inner and outer systems interact, the internal system can remain independent and efficacious. Self worth, then, becomes an internal, and not an external, construct.

Reality itself is a system construct. Satir believed that her way of looking determined what she would perceive. She said: "We see only what we expect to see. And I wonder how many of you have already discovered that your eyes have the ability to see,… isn't your eyes, it's what you expect to see which controls what you see" (Satir & Banmen, 1983. p 245). Therefore, objective reality cannot be perceived as it is. All people filter what they see through their interpretations and construct the meaning of what they see from them.

Implications for Therapy

The relationship between therapist and client also constitutes a system. If we apply Satir's four questions to therapeutic systems, we can locate those systems on an open and closed continuum. In the closed system, the relationship between therapist and client is determined by their respective roles. The therapist is engendered with power through the possession of expert knowledge and the ability to label the pathology of the client. Satir said, "When I entered the field of psychotherapy, people were looked upon as flat entities to be manipulated by some sort of authority who knew what was good for them" (Satir & Banmen, 1982, p. 84).

The relationship between client and therapist is informed by the power, or lack thereof, inherent in each role. The therapist has the right, even the obligation, to define the client on the basis of whatever symptom of pathology that the client demonstrates. Such definitions of clients are located in an expert knowledge to which only the therapist has access and therefore is external to the client's intrapsychic system. It is assumed that this expert knowledge provides the therapist with an objective perspective. The focus of therapy, therefore, is on the symptom because that is what is perceived to be wrong with the client. The main role of the therapist, then, is to evaluate various elements of the interpersonal or intrapychic system to determine which part he or she believes is at fault and needs correcting. This normative function of the therapist extracts the client's problem from its own context and places it within the contextual map of the therapist.

Whatever problems the client may be experiencing can be blamed on the symptom and ultimately on the client, as the client is the carrier of the symptom. If the client cooperates and participates in the removal of the symptom, the problems should disappear. The uncooperative client is frequently labeled as resistant, and therefore as still to blame for the continued existence of the symptom. When examined in this way, the relationship between therapist and client can be seen as a struggle for power. Whichever one "wins" can impose their way of perceiving the world on to the "loser." Given the structural inequity of power between therapist and client, it is unlikely that the client will succeed in maintaining his or her view of reality.

If the definition of a client is constructed in reference to an external measuring stick, then so is the direction for change. The direction for change is prescribed by notions of how the client should behave, believe, think, feel, expect, or yearn. Compliance with these norms, therefore, is a valid treatment outcome as the therapist (perhaps unwittingly) acts as an agent of social control. The corrective function of the therapeutic intervention is to ensure the client's alignment with external structure and promotes the maintenance of the status quo. Satir considers this, in the closed system, as the "tyranny of the one right way, and of course, the one in power has it" (Banmen & Satir, 1981, p. 49).

When the client was considered the carrier of the pathology, he or she could not be trusted to determine treatment outcomes and interventions could be applied to the client "for their own good." Indeed, the client was required to stand in opposition to the part of him or her that carried the symptom as the client internalizes the values of the therapist. Both client and therapist remain embedded in a closed system as Satir refers to the closed therapeutic system as a "judge and compel" (Banmen & Satir, 1981, p. 78) model of therapy. For example, a judge may compel a person who has been convicted of drunk driving to attend a centre for the treatment of alcoholism or else be incarcerated. The treatment centre may use an abstinence model of intervention and have the requirement that the client admit to being an alcoholic and agree to cease all drinking forever for the treatment to be deemed successful.

The client may not believe that he or she is an alcoholic, but in order to placate the judge the client may make such an admission. The client, therefore, has no power to decide on what the official treatment outcome should be. The attitude toward change on the part of the client in such circumstances is likely to be fearful and resistant. Even if the client needs to make come changes in when, where, and how much alcohol he or she consumes this is unlikely to take place.

In the open system, the relationship between therapist and client is based on equivalency of value and acceptance of one another's spiritual base. Satir says "So people equal people in terms of value and everyone is a manifestation of the life-force" (Banmen & Satir, 1983, p. 226). This implies that power is shared and not held more by one or the other. The therapist defines the client in terms of his or her own uniqueness, not as compared to an external paradigm of pathology. During therapy, the context of the client is the primary focus. This requires the therapist to enter the client's system to seek to understand it in terms of its own context. There is no such thing as an objective point of view; every way of looking is equally subjective in that every perspective is considered to be unique to whoever holds it.

As the therapist comes to understand the client's meanings instead of imposing his or her own, the meaning of resistance also changes. Satir considered that resistance came from the client's need to preserve what they had in terms of safety rather than moving blindly into the unknown (Satir & Banmen, 1983). Therefore, as the therapist creates safety and trust within the therapeutic relationship, resistance will disappear. Satir says that resistance is a way of "having something that is really OK before you leave what you've got" (Satir & Banmen, 1983, p. 216).

Events, and therefore problems, are explained as resulting from the interaction of elements. Therefore, symptoms are located in the relationship between components rather than being vested with any particular component. This moves the focus of any interventions from specific system elements to the process between those elements. Hence, the concept of blame is not longer useful or even valid. Rather than removing the problem from the context, the problem is understood within the context in which it occurs. As the problem is understood within its own context, so then is the solution which is considered to exist within the client and able to be accessed through an appropriate intervention.

Freed from the normative function, the therapist can engage the client in a collaborative rather than a coercive relationship. As the client is naturally seeking wholeness (Satir & Banmen, 1983), the task of the therapist is to locate ways that this goal can be accomplished. The goals of therapy, therefore, are internally constructed and based on the context of the client rather than imposed from an external paradigm of right and wrong. This implies that the client can be trusted to establish his or her own goals instead of being required to accept the goals determined by the therapist. During therapy, the attitude of the client towards change is likely to be open and welcoming when this approach is used.

Satir's View of Therapy

Satir considered that therapy was additive rather than subtractive because the goal of therapy was to add health not to subtract symptoms (Banmen & Satir, 1981). Symptoms were to be cherished and appreciated as indicators that all was not right within the system. Therefore, the symptom was not the problem and should not be the focus of an intervention. Satir assumed that once the underlying dynamic was resolved, the symptom would no longer be needed and would disappear. She said "it's how to develop health, rather than to get rid of ill-health. Now if I do this, develop health, there is no need for ill health" (Banmen & Satir, 1981, pp. 82–83). In general terms, Satir defined the underlying dynamic as low self-worth. Low self worth meant that a person would undervalue his or her own thoughts, feelings, wants, and the like, and overvalue those of others. The resources inherent in these parts of a person would therefore be lost and symptoms would arise. For example, a person who believed that they needed the approval of others in order to have value could spend much time and energy seeking such approval at a tremendous cost to themselves, and therefore develop various symptoms. Developing health, in this instance, is not the removal of approval seeking; that is a universal human need not a symptom. Rather, developing health would involve a person learning how to meet his or her need for approval internally instead of externally.

As Satir believed that each human being had what they needed in terms of resources, the goal of therapy therefore is to assist the client to access what is already there. She said (Satir & Banmen, 1983, p.72):

> Please, never delude yourself that you're putting anything in anybody. You're not even putting anything into yourself. What you are doing is accessing the miracle that you are. And the whole thrust of therapy is making that accessing possible.

We do not put any resources into anybody but assist in changing the internal relationship between parts so that what is there can be used. "What can I add to what is to make it possible for people to come over here? The process of transformation." (Satir & Banmen, 1983, p. 233) This process of transformation is intended to change the relationship between the parts from one of judge and compel, to discovery and choice. The outcome of discovery and choice is conceived to be acceptance and honoring of all the parts so that the energy contained in them can be accessed.

Satir's four requisites for change are a loving atmosphere in which to engage, trust between therapist and client, a believable image of how things could be different, and a willingness to be in chaos during the change process. The loving atmosphere creates a setting where the self can be explored in a curious rather than a judgmental way. Trust in the therapeutic relationship means that the client can let go some of his or her survival strategies. A believable image fosters hope and opens possibilities. Satir considered the lack of a believable image to be the root of resistance. Clients are simply not able to see how they could be different within a given situation and therefore do not believe that choice is actually present. For example, a person standing on a rock in the middle of a river is unlikely to be very willing to move unless reasonably convinced that he or she can take the next step and land in a safe place.

A willingness to be in chaos means that a client can let go of what he or she is familiar with and try something new. The chaos comes from moving from what he or she knows to an unfamiliar place that he or she will not know. Safety while in chaos is derived from confidence in one's process for dealing with the unexpected not in preventing the unexpected from occurring. Therefore, safety is derived from predictable process not predictable structure.

All parts, Satir believed, have resources that the system can use. However, when a system is closed, the resources are bound up in maintaining the status quo. When a system is opened, there can then be a free flow of resources to where they are needed and can be used to facilitate growth. As the presence of the problem is conceptualized in terms of lack of access to the resources that the system has, the place of intervention is the relationship between the parts to free those resources. The goal of therapy, therefore, is transformation in the way the system relates to itself, in essence a change in its way of being. Because of the connection mentioned above between the intrapsychic and interactional system, this transformation then changes the way the system interacts with the external world.

Use of Self in Therapy

The therapist's use of self is a concept that has been recognized as a significant aspect of therapy (Satir & Baldwin, 1983). Satir really stressed the huge significance of the use of self and she believed that, "using oneself as a therapist is an awesome task....I focus in depth on the personhood of the therapist. We are people dealing with people" (Satir & Baldwin, 1983, p. 227). By becoming aware of his or her self in various contexts, the therapist will have access to more creative and flexible ways in which to genuinely connect with clients (Haber, 1994; Satir, Banmen, Gerber, & Gomori, 1991). How the person sees himself or herself will strongly effect his or her presence as a therapist. If the therapist has become aware of certain aspects of how he or she operates in his or her own life, this awareness will empower the therapist to become more effective (Andolfi, Ellenwood, & Wendt, 1993; Satir & Baldwin, 1983). "While therapists facilitate and enhance patients' ability and need to grow, they should at the same time be aware that they have the same ability and need" (Satir & Baldwin, 1983, p. 21).

Therefore, the therapist needs to be aware that he or she is in a reflexive relationship with a client. Therapy is not a one-way street in which the impact only moves from therapist to client; the client has an impact on the therapist as well. The therapist requires sufficient self-awareness to be conscious of the impact that the client is having on them, and the skill to deal with that impact. Transference and countertransference are not considered to be expected parts of the therapeutic relationship. It is the obligation of the therapist to do the personal work necessary to ameliorate the impact of his or her own life history both on the client and themselves.

This is identical to Satir's concept of the third birth. The therapist, having completed a search for wholeness and new consciousness of self, does not require the client to be a particular way. The therapist has worked successfully through his or her own issues and therefore has no expectation that the client is in any way there to meet the needs of the therapist.

Therefore, what is required of the therapist is the conscious use of self. This requires a deep self-knowledge and confidence that the therapist accesses during the process of working with clients as a matter of course. Satir described this as being fully present in the moment, as the personhood of the therapist is not shed at the office door but brought into each and every interaction. In this way, the self of the therapist can be considered as an important instrument for change.

Congruence

One of Satir's (1972) key concepts was the idea that a healthy person would be interacting with the world from a position of congruence. She identified congruence as a healthy way of being when a person is able to honestly connect with the self, other and context and is the foundation for living in harmony within oneself and with others. Congruence, therefore, is located in a healthy relationship between a person's constituent parts. Satir believed that congruence was never static but had to do with the process of being oneself.

Satir believed that if a person were congruent, then he or she would be able to freely express himself or herself verbally and nonverbally from a place of truth. As Satir and Baldwin (1983) suggested:

> A congruent person is in touch with his feelings, regardless of what they are. He does not judge them, does not criticize himself for having them, just views them as a thermometer of his inner condition at the moment. By acknowledging what is there, the therapist is in a position to use himself freely; he is better able to see, hear, and make decisions without being encumbered by an inner dialogue.

Congruency, therefore, is a necessary quality for a therapist to have as he or she is able to manage the impact from the client in healthy ways.

Congruence cannot be understood as a static state. It is, instead, located in the process of relationship between one's constituent parts. A person may have many different thoughts or feelings about what is happening. Congruence is present in how these differences are integrated. Therefore, congruence does not require that a person expresses every feeling or thought as they happen, but that one makes a conscious choice about what to express based on the needs of the self, of others, and of the context. It is congruent to decide to placate a traffic officer in an attempt to avoid a ticket when one feels angry over a perceived injustice of enforcement. It is not congruent to believe that there is no choice in how one behaves in moments of stress.

Training

The training is entitled Systemic Brief Therapy in the Satir Model and is currently provided by John Banmen and Kathlyne Maki-Banmen. Programs have been given in Canada, the United States, Hong Kong, Taiwan, Korea, Singapore, and many countries in Europe. Locally, in British Columbia, Canada, two level one and one level-two training is given every year plus a one-week intensive session each summer. The level one and two programs are five weekends, one per month, in duration. The foundation for the training is the book *The Satir Model: Family Therapy and Beyond* (Satir, et al, 1991).

Participants learn various elements and techniques of the model including family mapping, the personal iceberg metaphor, the personal mandala, family sculpting, parts parties, meditation, and coping stances. They observe demonstrations on how to use these elements and techniques with clients and engage in practice sessions with each other. In practice sessions, trainees take one of three roles alternately; they can be therapist, client, or observer. This affords every trainee with the occasion to experience the transformation inherent in the application of the Satir Model. For example, participants complete their own family map as a course requirement. This means that the trainees look at the impact of their upbringing on whom they are today. This also provides those with unresolved family issues the opportunity to explore such issues and, with the assistance of the trainers or other trainees, achieve a measure of resolution.

Trainees are encouraged to attempt to track three separate channels simultaneously in every therapeutic demonstration or practice session: first, what is happening for the client, second, the process of therapy, and third, his or her own reaction to what is happening. In short, participants are asked to be aware of themselves, of the other (client or clients), and of the context in which the interaction is occurring. The expected outcome of learning to be aware of the three channels is an increase in the congruence of the trainee.

As the training progresses, participants not only learn new ways of looking at clients and the therapeutic endeavour but learn about themselves as well. Therefore, the focus of the training is not just on the doing of therapy but on the being of the therapist as well. For example, as trainees practice using the techniques with other trainees for resolving family of origin issues, he or she in turn is also practised upon by others. This is an intentional, not accidental, result of the training as these experiences provide the trainee with opportunities to work through his or her own unfinished business and move towards a more congruent and less reactive state of being. This intended outcome of the training can be connected to what Satir referred to as working on the personhood of the therapist.

Research

The Lum (2000) study used a phenomenological approach to the integration of one aspect of the Satir model, the personal iceberg metaphor, into the therapists' personal and professional development. The purpose of the study was to find out what impact this integration had on the trainees surveyed. The small sample of nine participants means that the results are not generalizable to all people who take the training but such was not the intent.

The Personal Iceberg Metaphor

The personal iceberg metaphor is a conceptual diagram that provides a structure for understanding the inner experience of a person. Satir said "like icebergs, we show only parts of ourselves. Much of us lies below the surface" (Satir, et al., 1991, p. 34). The metaphor includes seven components of the inner self: Self/I am, yearnings, expectations, perception, feelings, coping stance, and behavior. These components are universal for people regardless of culture, ethnicity, or heritage. However, it is important to remember that though the structure is universal, the manifestation will be unique with each person.

Results and Discussion

Two interviews were conducted with each participant and themes were extracted from the transcripts. While the experience of each of the trainees was unique to that individual, there were themes that were common to them all. We are not going to report on all the results of the study as that is beyond the scope of this chapter. Instead we will include three of the main themes for the purposes of discussion.

The first theme that arose from the data was a reported increase in awareness. The trainees recounted that not only did their awareness of their clients increase but their awareness of themselves as well. This new awareness of self involved what they carried into therapeutic sessions; their thoughts, feelings, assumptions, and attitudes, their culture, their upbringing, and how this all related to their process of choosing therapeutic interventions. As they became more cognizant of their reactions, they were better able to manage their internal state and therefore be more in charge of how they behaved. They therefore became conscious of themselves as existing within a relationship with their clients, interacting as part of the same system and having very human reactions to what was happening. This indicates the development of a more conscious use of self and ability to be more fully present in each moment during therapeutic encounters with clients.

The second theme extracted out of the data was a feeling of respect and reverence for the client and for themselves. The use of the iceberg metaphor introduced the trainees to the incredible complexity of people and required the therapists to inquire at the deepest levels of their clients. Therefore, clients are no longer the two-dimensional objects of Satir's early training but full three-dimensional beings, each with the potential for growth. Some respondents related this to personal spiritual growth with an accompanying respect and reverence for self. This was connected to an increase in the existence of acceptance rather than judgment of self and of others and a lowering of reactivity. One participant in the study stated "because I'm not judging them, I'm not judging me."

The third major theme was a move from looking at events and behavior to looking at the internal impact. As the therapists learned how to inquire into the impact, they were required to look at the meaning for the client of what had occurred. This inquiry into meaning meant that the trainees were required to enter the client's system, and understand what was there in terms of its own context. As meanings are unique to each individual, this indicates that the trainees have begun to understand the subjective nature of reality and the importance of entering the client's system on its own terms. They have begun to forego the notion that, as the therapist, they have a view of reality this is somehow more objective and therefore more true than the perceptions that the client may have.

Transformation for Therapists

In her own training of therapists, Satir sought to change the way her trainees looked at the world and therefore the way they looked at their clients. Her hope was that her trainees would accept the value of working with clients in an open rather than in a closed system. She said that her model "asks us to look at human life in quite a different way, with both a reverence and a sacredness and a reality that we haven't been able to do before" (Banmen & Satir, 1981, p. 70). Given Satir's connection between the intrapsychic and the interpersonal, those trainees who were successful in learning a new way of looking at human life also learned a new way of looking at themselves, with reverence and a sacredness.

What is clear in the results of this study is that what the participants in the Banmen and Maki-Banmen training describe as their transformation in the training corresponds to what Satir wished for her trainees; they have changed the way they look at both their clients and themselves. Specifically, what is evident is movement toward more open intrapsychic and interpersonal systems.

The transformation that occurred for participants in the study is then, by Satir's definition, a change to a more open system. The relationship between therapist and client is now defined as one of equals rather than a relationship determined by inequalities of power. Therefore the myth of objectivity on the part of the therapist is eschewed, as the trainees appreciate that they have no more right to define reality than the client does. Power is coupled with obligation as the therapist is more obliged to answer for his or her behavior than is the client. A person is defined in all of his or her complexity, rather than by role, behavior, or symptomology. Roles define sequencing and behavior, not status. There is a recognition of the other as a "spiritual entity, sacred, effective, physical, emotional being, capable of growth" (Satir & Banmen, 1982, p. 43). Events are explained within the context of the system, not in reference to an external paradigm. The process by which the system attempts to cope with symptoms, not the symptom, becomes the focus of the intervention. Change is not directed by the obligation to conform to external needs and wants, but by the expressed internal needs and wants of the client.

The transformation to a more open system is particularly evident in the way trainees learned how to relate to themselves. While learning to be more accepting, more trusting, more connected with clients, they were learning how to be more accepting, more trusting, more connected with themselves. They can now experience themselves in the full range of their humanity, in contact with all parts of themselves, not locked into the narrow focus demanded in a hierarchical model of therapy. This acceptance of self leads the trainees to an appreciation and understanding of their own need to grow.

Conclusions

During her lifetime, Virginia Satir brought a unique, dynamic, and transformational vision to the practice of psychotherapy and family therapy. She developed a way of seeing the world that had a great impact on the lives of her clients. As her therapy was transformational for clients, so was her training transformational for therapists. Her hope was that others would come to share her vision.

The results of the study show that her vision, as expressed in the training of Systemic Brief Therapy in the Satir Model given by John Banmen and Kathlyne Maki-Banmen, continues to transform therapists. As the trainees learned the Satir Model, they changed the way they related to clients and the way they related to themselves. They did not perceive clients as flat, two-dimensional objects to be manipulated but as sacred beings of amazing complexity and possibility. Though participants in the training likely entered the program looking for a new way to do therapy, what they found was a new way of experiencing themselves, a new way of being.

References

Andolfi, M., Ellenwood, A. E. & Wendt, R. N. (1993). The creation of the fourth planet: Beginning therapist and supervisors inducing change in families. *The American Journal of Family Therapy, 21* (4), 301–12.

Banmen, J. & Satir, V. (1981). *Virginia Satir and the University of Utah.* Delta Psychological Associates, Inc., North Delta, British Columbia, Canada.

Haber, R. (1994). Response-ability: therapist's 'I' and role. *Journal of Family Therapy, 16,* 269–84.

Lum, Wendy (2000). *The lived experience of using the personal iceberg metaphor: From Satir's systemic brief therapy training.* Unpublished master's thesis, University of British Columbia, Vancouver, Canada.

Satir, V. & Baldwin, M. (1983). *Satir step by step.* Palo Alto, CA: Science and Behavior Books.

Satir, V. & Banmen, J. (1982). *Avanta's process community II, Virginia Satir's summer institute.* Delta Psychological Associates, Inc., North Delta, British Columbia, Canada.

Satir, V. & Banmen, J. (1983). *Virginia Satir verbatim 1984.* Delta Psychological Associates, Inc. Delta Psychological Associates, Inc., North Delta, British Columbia, Canada.

Satir, V., Banmen, J., Gerber, J., & Gomori, M. (1991). *The Satir model: Family therapy and beyond.* Palo Alto, CA: Science & Behavior Books.

8

Family Reconstruction

Gloria Taylor

Family reconstruction is described as follows in *The Satir Model* (Satir et al., 1991), the definitive account of the work of Virginia Satir:

> Family reconstruction is an intervention developed by Virginia Satir of reintegrating people into the historical and psychological matrix of their own family of origin. One the major Satir vehicles for change, family reconstruction provides a way of seeing ourselves and our parents with new eyes and thus seeing the present and the future in a new perspective. This new perspective provides us with access to greater possibilities, more freedom, and an enhanced sense of responsibility (Satir, et al., 1991, p. 205).

In this chapter, I shall share my perspective as an active therapist and educator.

At work in this intervention are all the concpts and philosophies which are Satir's hallmark. Using techniques of Gestalt, psychodrama, reenactments, and presence, the potential to see and hear old events in new ways manifests as transformation. Satir was intent on facilitating complex and natural changes on many different levels of being. As she said in her foreword to Nerin's (1986) *Family Reconstruction: Long Day's Journey into Light:*

> The past contains the history of events that have already occurred. It is the learnings from the past that form the approach to the present. To change the perception and the experience of the present so that it can become a stepping stone to a

healthier future, I needed to somehow introduce ways to stimulate new learnings to take place. I knew that new learnings were possible. This process had to be powerful enough to allow the surfacing of vulnerability and the development of new relevant ways to cope (Satir, 1986).

As she would say, "We can always change shit to compost!" Compost has been defined as: "a highly complex set of biological, regulated capacities, change of beneficial characteristics at many levels" (Partridge, 1983). It is clear to me after the many reconstructions that I have witnessed or facilitated that "beneficial characteristics at many levels" are indeed the frequent outcome of a family reconstruction. Satir often had the luxury of three days or longer in which to develop several aspects of a multigenerational reconstruction. As well as having enactments with the person having the reconstruction and his or her immediate family of origin, she was afforded the time to assemble the parents of the parents, their siblings, and often their parents. She thereby could reveal many historical possibilities heretofore unimagined by the "star" in the family.

Today, there occasionally will be a workshop presented by Avanta, the Virginia Satir Network, and others who are still able to take the time required for a reconstruction of several generations. It is more often the case that a weekend is devoted to some basic Satir learnings with a reconstruction, which last no more than three hours, is part of the weekend. I have had the privilege of guiding many reconstructions in North America and abroad. Students at Waterloo Lutheran Seminary in Waterloo, Canada, may take my family of origin class at the masters level as part of the course requirements for clinical membership in the American Association for Marriage and Family Therapy. We meet for 14 weeks during which the students create their genograms and prepare for a possible opportunity to the "star" in a family reconstruction. In my private practice I offer groups for the community which may lost as long as 12 weeks, focus on the Satir model, and which sometimes include family reconstructions of two to three hours duration.

The Satir Learning Centres of Ontario is one of many affiliates of Avanta whose mandate it is to offer Satir tools to the community of Kitchener Waterloo. From time to time, the members of the SLCO gather for an intensive training to learn how to facilitate reconstructions. The participants work in pairs and with my supervision are able to be each other's "star." The worldwide affiliates of the Satir network all offer the opportunity to study the work of Satir.

My Intent

Since family reconstruction seems to be an underutilized tool, it is my intent to make it available to more practitioners and to distill the process to fit into three hours. I promote workshops with descriptions and objectives of family reconstructions. There are some suggestions for collection family of origin information prior to the workshop. /a reconstruction requires 10 or more persons, including both sexes, if possible. Selection of the "star" is a process involving personal interview with interested people who show willingness to change. The stars may emerge in the early stages of the workshop during the initial exercises and when people begin to more clearly understand the process and experience the openness of the group.

As I listen to the Star and ask questions, together we are able to establish which parts of the person's history hold the most promise for growth. Sitting together, the Star and I establish a connection, beginning to trust one another. We are gently envisioning how life might look I this were a successful reconstruction. I encourage the Star to articulate concrete examples of desirable outcomes. For example, "I will remember to give my sister more opportunities to help me instead of always acting like the firstborn who has all the answers." Eliciting goals in this gentle fashion helps the Star become clear about desirable and accomplishable change. Also, the facilitator knows where to hold the action and which events or key members to attend to.

Transformation occurs in many forms including a move from coping strategies to congruence, from blaming others to understanding their behavior, from triangulation to one-on-one contact, from self-judgment to affirmation and possibly acceptance, from resentment to compassion, from criticism to curiosity, from hostility to honesty, from analysis of others to self-discovery, and from diagnosis to ownership. In Virginia Satir's words, the movement is from "shit to compost."

Whether a group has assembled for a weekend, series of meetings, or a class of several months, the process and principles remain the same. Group member learn the importance of remaining in context and refraining from any temptation to judge, evaluate, or offer advice regarding the work at hand. As I guide and encourage participants' process, I take every opportunity to ensure that the trust among us is solid. Part of that trust is the confidence that every story is safely kept within the confines of the group.

While all of our stories differ in content, that which we have in common is our internal response to external events (below the waterline on the iceberg metaphor. Satir et al., 1991). As with an iceberg, most of which is out of sight, only our behaviors are visible or audible to others. Exploration of everything below the water line is revealing therapeutically. It would be true to say that we all know the experience of sadness, loss, frustration, and peace. When participants in a reconstruction respond from their internal truth-in-context they are offering useful information to the Star. Below the water line there is much that is universal and all that makes us human.

Change after a reconstruction is immediate in the way that new perspectives are. For example, a star may suddenly understand that her parents' behavior had everything to do with their own grief and coping strategies and was not about her as an inadequate child. The lasting and ongoing effects are subtle and internally shape-lifting. People close to us respond to the changes as well, sometimes in surprising ways. A student recently reported, for example, that one week after his reconstruction his estranged father sent him a cheque for a considerable amount of money in a letter full of remorse for his lack of parenting skills many years earlier. The long-term changes alter physical , emotional, and relational aspects of the self in healing ways.

While each reconstruction seems to follow a path of its own design, there are some important principles and ordered steps to follow. The setting is important. Participants are most involved when the space that is created affords a sense of trust, confidentiality, peace, and quiet, as well as camaraderie. The participants in the group can gain an appreciation of the process and the basics of Satir's approach through the provision of handouts and readings (i.e., Satir et al., 1991) or through the leadership of a Satir practitioner from whom they can learn by doing.

The following description of a facilitated reconstruction group demonstrates the possibilities for change for each participant, whether or not they choose to be a star in a construction of their own. Assume that this is an ongoing group that meets on eight occasions in which six actual reconstructions occur. The first meeting is spent creating an atmosphere of trust, setting the guidelines, clarifying peoples' expectations, and answering questions regarding the process. The final meeting is celebratory, allowing everyone to expand on his or her experiences, shifts in awareness, and gratitude toward one another. We close the group with a ritual of our own design and restate our affirmations regarding the chances we will continue to expand.

Steps and Principles

1. The group is led in an appropriate meditation or guided fantasy. We begin in this way in order to bring all participants into the present with an attitude of openness, curiosity, and support. Meditations, as Satir used them, connect the intellect to the intuitive and affective parts of us. They highlight our capacity to relate within and without the "I–Thou"-ness in each of us. (Satir et al., 1991, p. 300).
2. The facilitator debriefs the previous week's reconstruction. This step allows the star to share new insights and awareness one week following his or her reconstruction. Role players also may add new perspectives gained during the week. Such perspectives are useful to the star and often resonate with certain similarities to the role player's life.
3. The new star shares with the facilitator some of the details of the historical event in question and some of the goals for desirable change as a result of this work. Beginning to set the atmosphere for all the participants at this stage creates a kind of working trance. As the new context begins to unfold, all the people in the room are gathering pertinent information that will be required for role playing.
4. As the star mentions key family members, the facilitator's assistant (who can be a group member) creates a family map on a board in large clear print, including three or four descriptive adjectives as well as primary coping mechanisms for each member. This process provides the role players with easy access to relevant surface details about the family throughout the reconstruction. It also helps create a working sense of the star's rich experiential responses to the family events being enacted. I think of this experiential reality as the space/time context in which the reconstruction takes place.
5. The facilitator invites the star to choose role players as family members, as well as to select an alter ego to play the part of the star when needed. The alter ego shadows the star in order to be as close to the experience as possible. The role players place sticky name tags on their chests as aids for everyone in the "family." The time spent during this name tagging process allows the role players as well as the star to sink into the new "reality" of this family in the present time and space.
6. The star uses various parts of the room to create relevant space in this new context. For example, the front left corner of the room is

now the dining room, and "Mom" sits at the end of the table. Or perhaps the room is divided into parts of town, the province, or the globe in which the story will unfold. This mapping of the new context is another means of creating the new space/time context and deepening the trance for all the participants.

7. The star places the role players in postures and sculptures and allows the scene to unfold with possible dialogue and movement. Role players have some freedom to express themselves, but not enough to take over the process. At some point the facilitator may choose to have the star exchange places with his or her alter ego or to have them engage in a dialogue. This is an intuitive option that needs to be well timed for its transformative potential, for example, tapping into yearnings. Yearnings are those universal longings to be loved, accepted, validated. How yearnings were satisfied or not satisfied in childhood has a major effect on how we develop, mature, and deal with our feelings. The events-in-historical-context provide role players with internal responses to external events, providing authentic conversations, expressions, and feelings.
8. The initiator must stay aware of time in order to be able to get into and out of the reconstruction in the time allowed. This keeps the momentum building, peaking, and winding down with time left to debrief and de-role.
9. Role players are debriefed at the conclusion of the reconstruction. They are to share their observations, feelings, insights, and feelings from the point of view of their role. Then they are invited to apply any of this that pertain to their own life and family. This helps to make the distinction between "my" life and the role of family member, although there is often an uncanny similarity.
11. The last role player to speak is the alter ego "self." This role is special insofar as the alter ego has been a shadow/participant for the star and is likely to have validating feedback an/or new information for the star. Feedback from the alter ego may underline the star's own thoughts and feelings, provide additional depth to the story, and, often, offer a wider range of choice for the star.
12. Finally, the star is offered the opportunity to speak, although he or she may choose to process the work internally, knowing that the next meeting will provide another occasion to speak. This anchors the entire experience for the Star, allowing her or him to explore the new depth and intricacies of herself or himself (below the water line of his or her iceberg).

13.After each role player has spoken, any observers who had no role may speak. They comment on what they saw and heard and how to apply it to their own circumstances. Then all are invited to close their eyes, to hold on to all parts of the experience that are relevant to themselves, leaving the remainder to the star. They recall their own names and identities, open their eyes, give their name tag to the star, while saying in a clear voice, "My name is . . .." This step assures that roles are divested of their power and that no confusion of identities will remain outside the context of this particular reconstruction.

With each passing week, the group members appear demonstrably more clearly and close. Over the years I have been deeply moved when group members have commented, as they frequently do, "I feel as though I know all these people and they know me better than my own family, but I don't know any of their last names."

Unexpected changes take place after reconstruction. It is as though family members and close friends of the participants are altered in some ways by the work, although they have any conscious awareness that any work has taken place.

What follows is a description of a reconstruction that demonstrates the above steps and principles. The context is the family of origin class at the Waterloo Lutheran Seminary, which was mentioned earlier.

"Deb's" Reconstruction

The group is encouraged to close their eyes, to allow their breath to release any tension, and to take themselves into their centers. They are lead in a Satir meditation and then invited to gently reenter the present space and time. After some comments about the previous week, a star joins me to sit and reflect on aspects of her early childhood. She is able, finally, to articulate some goals for her work.

I will call the star "Deb." Her parents fled from a small country to another in Europe during World War II. As she understand the story, her father insisted on leaving the uncertainty and chaos of a war zone in spite of her mother's protects. He chose to move himself and his pregnant wife to a safer home in Canada. Deb's mother, six months pregnant at the time, was frightened at leaving familiar supports behind, but was overruled by her husband's decision. The passage by ship was nearly intolerable for her.

Shortly after arriving in Canada, the mother miscarried the pregnancy—a son—and the heightened stress seemed to be more than this young couple could withstand. Deb's father began to leave his wife, returning from time to time. When he finally disappeared for good, he left his wife with a three-year-old daughter, who barely remembers having a father.

As Deb begins her story, she comments, as an aside, "I have such a small family and have had such a good life, I am afraid their will be nothing to work on here." She is able to say, after some reflection, that there seems to be a hollowness in her chest that never goes away. She places both hands over her heart as she says this.

Deb chooses role players to represent hr mother, father, and miscarried brother. The remainder of the group is moved to a corner of the room, which Deb designates as her country of origin, and are given the role of representing all of the relatives who were left behind when the young couple immigrated to Canada.

As the "parents" begin discussing the decision to leave their country, "Mom" is very frightened and reluctant, and "Dad" is heavy with the responsibility of a pregnant wife. The "realness" of their predicament emerges in palpable ways. The unfolding scene brings them to their new home in Canada, where they are without friends or family and facing the impending birth of their first child. Role players, at this point, are very expressive and "living" the experience. At the loss of this first child, a son, the "family" in Europe seems to be holding a collective breath. Mom n Dad are at a complete loss for words and comfort.

At this point in the reconstruction, Deb is invited to speak to her "dead brother." Seeming to be very open to this loss for the first time, she has much to say to and about him. Through her tears, she shows sorrow for losing him, telling him what a difference his life would have made to her life. It seems as though Deb is pouring out the yearnings and unmet expectations of her early life for the first time ever. She voices her anger and disappointment to her "father" and hr admiration and empathy for her "mother;." When she is finished speaking to her "family," she looks up. Her face is shiny and open.

Now we hear from all the role players as they express the effects the roles have had on them as well as the ways in which they have been reminded of similar feelings in their own lives. The "family" members who had to watch from "the old country" express feelings of futility and helplessness at their inability to be of any use to the stranded couple and demonstrate unabashed awe at their courage. Deb's alter ego confirms many of Deb's feelings and perceptions, adding more description to the "whole of it." We move on.

Deb's Reflections on the Family Reconstruction

Deb offered journal entries following her reconstruction. The following excerpts are those that I have chosen from her entries:

> A feeling of release, of a burden lifted, of freedom. A sense of insight into a puzzling aspect of my father's behavior, not his character. A recurring, gnawing headache. This environment, only incidentally a classroom, feels safe—people trust not only you but also each other. The non-invasive, supportive bonding achieved in that environment among a group of people who still don't even know all the names of their fellow students is remarkable and wonderful.
>
> Some comments on my reactions: Because my father's absence made it impossible to express my love or fulfill my desire to receive it, these tender feelings and my desire to express them either dried up or hid. My tears on Friday were prompted, I think, by being able to express my yearnings, not my love. While I had not repressed these feelings, I was building up defenses which I have maintained all my life. These defenses were breached on Friday. Hence my sense of a burden lifted.
>
> That my father decided to leave our home country at least partly for the safety of my mother and her unborn child is a new possibility for me to consider. I had simply accepted at face value that he did not want to fight in another war. I have to let this work in me for a while.
>
> The role player's portrayal of my father was what I yearned for—reflecting, echoing hauntingly what my husband was like: tender, loving, giving, honest, a straight arrow. It is four years since he died and I have been puzzling about my feelings of denial and resentment. Do I feel vulnerable? Unprotected? Time will tell.
>
> From childhood until menopause I have had severe headaches. Consistent with the placating stance, I have tended to be obedient and approval-seeking. Perhaps I have switched stances to super-reasonable. School and learning have become safe, comfortable, and successful for me. Friday's experience has been an important growth in perspective for me. For the people who come to me for counseling, I shall do my best to provide a safe, supportive environment and growth opportunities.

These journal entries came one week after Deb's reconstruction. They are a fine example of the sort of reflection that I hear in the debriefing sessions the week following a reconstruction, and even later.

Change through Reconstruction

As one who sees therapists as agents of change, I know of no comparable vehicle to family reconstruction for transformation at all levels of congruence. At the first level of congruence, we accept our feelings as they are. At level two, we are in harmony with our Self. This third level of congruence involves being in harmony with our Self and our life energy, spirituality, or God (Satir et al., 1991).

Change at any of these levels produces several other by-products: self-confidence, awareness of choice, and access to more inner resources. These in turn help change the person's dealings with the outer world, including making his or her relationships more intimate and communication more effective. People around this person change also. Satir's metaphor of the family members as parts of a mobile aptly presents the family as a system. As one aspect of the mobile moves, so do all the others, not however in ways that are predictable. Using Satir's methods, the have the privilege to assist the transformation process. From my perspective, there is no greater honor.

References

Nerin, W. F. (1986). *Family reconstruction: Long day's journey into light.* New York: Norton.

Satir, V. (1986). Foreword. In W. F. Nerin, *Family reconstruction: Long day's journey into light* (pp. v—xii). New York: Norton.

Satir, V., Banmen, J., Gerber, J., & Gomori, M. (1991). *The Satir model.* Palo Alto, CA: Science and Behavior Books.

9

Youth Suicide Intervention Using the Satir Model*

Wendy Lum, Jim Smith, and Judy Ferris

This article is intended to share how the Satir model (Satir et al., 1991) can be used to understand and treat youth who are suicidal. Youth suicide is a major concern in Western society, and measures need to be explored to reduce suicide among the adolescent population. In the United States the suicide rate among adolescents and young adults tripled between 1950 and 1980. The rate for people 15–34 years old during that time and throughout the 1990s remained at approximately 15 per 100,000 population. By 1996, suicide was the third leading cause of death for adolescents and young adults (Maris et al., 2000). The suicide rate for 15–24 year olds is 12 per 100,000. The rate for 5–14 year olds is 0.8 per 100,000. Approximately 10,200 people ages 15–34 years old kill themselves each year and 4,700 from ages 15–24. These numbers show the tragedy of despair amongst young people.

Everall (2000) highlighted the fact that in Canada, suicide is the second leading cause of death for young people aged 15–24 years. Banmen (2000) suggested that youth suicide is a significant concern for mental

* Portions of this paper were presented at the Canadian Association for Suicide Prevention (CASP) Conference, Vancouver, B.C., October 2000.

health professionals. Youth struggle with internal coping in relationship to their external factors (eg. family violence, disruption during key transitional periods at school, teasing/bullying, loss of significant family member) and this factor may contribute to increased suicide rates. Clearly youth suicide is a societal issue that needs more effective education and intervention for prevention of suicide among adolescents.

Common Therapies for Suicidal Adolescents

The Satir model (Satir et al., 1991) is a unique therapeutic system that offers hope for therapists who wish to connect with and to positively affect suicidal youth in making a choice to live. Satir's model will be discussed in relationship to an actual case study. There are other therapeutic frameworks that are used to deal with youth suicide prevention and intervention. The methods, which are currently used to understand and intervene with suicidal youth, will now be reviewed.

The preferred treatment for working with the suicidal adolescent is individual therapy on an outpatient basis. Richman and Eyman (1990), examine the three major types of therapy used with suicidal patients–individual, group, and family. Issues such as fragile identity, conflicted self-expectations, and difficulty expressing emotions are discussed. Hoover (1987) looks at the self in regard to suicidal behavior, stating that the distinguishing factor in suicide is the invalidation of the sense of self. Hoover and Paulson (1999) describe the journey away from self as a disconnection from self and others. The return to self occurs through reconnection through feeling, self-awareness, and honouring the self.

Initially, crisis intervention is the treatment used to deal with the suicidal crisis. The immediate therapeutic task is to prevent self-harm. The work of therapy can focus on broadening the adolescent's linkages to a wider network of resources and on the predisposing conditions that make the adolescent vulnerable. Suggested interventions are social skills training, treatment of loneliness, cognitive-behavioral therapy and other behavioral approaches, problem-solving skills, training in anger, and aggression management. Solution-focused brief therapy uses the client's strengths, competencies, resources, and successes (ability to be resilient) to bring about change (Fiske, 1998). This approach emphasizes cooperation between client and therapist and offers tools in the form of questions when working with suicidal children and adolescents to help divert their attention from problems to possible solutions.

Ellis and Newman (1996) link cognition and suicidality. They state that hopelessness, problem-solving deficits, and perfectionism as well as dysfunctional attitudes and irrational beliefs are characteristic of individuals contemplating suicide. Cognitive-behavioral therapy is used with both adults and adolescents. This is a collaborative model in which client, therapist, and the family identify the client's problems, strengths, and previous attempts at problem-solving. Problem-solving skills are further developed, and the client learns to develop alternative interpretations and beliefs so that suicide no longer seems the only viable option. Freeman and Reinecke (1993) refer to the techniques of activity scheduling, mastery and pleasure ratings, graded task assignments, behavioral rehearsal, social skills and assertiveness training, bibliotherapy, in vivo exposure, and relaxation, meditation, and breathing exercises. Cognitive techniques useful in developing adaptive responses to dysfunctional thinking are described. These include understanding of idiosyncratic meaning; decatastrophizing, guided association discovery, cognitive rehearsal, and development of cognitive dissonance.

Dialectical Behavior Therapy (Linehan, 1993; Linehan, MacLeod, & Williams, 1992) also uses a problem-solving strategy. However, it differs from cognitive behavioral therapy in that it tries to make the techniques more compatible with psychodynamic models. Fiske (1998) suggests DBT be modified for use with children and adolescents. Constructive goals and reasons for living are the basis for this model.

The goal of psychoanalytic/psychodynamic approaches is to gain insight into the unconscious conflict of the client. In summarizing these approaches, Maris, Berman, and Silverman (2000) refer to object relations theory, which states that suicidality represents a failure in the task of separation-individuation. Research on attachment styles among suicidal youth supports this aloneness.

Goals of family therapy are modifying communication patterns, increasing support for the adolescent's attempts at self-care, and improving the family's problem-solving behavior. A central goal is to develop an understanding within the family of the meaning of the adolescent's suicidal behavior and to improve family functioning (Berman & Jobes, 1997; Maris et al., 2000). Group therapy provides a social support network for suicidal clients and provides a milieu where social skill development can take place. (Maris et al., 2000) Themes emerging from group psychotherapy are family relationships, peer relationships, and the control of potentially overwhelming feelings and impulses (Richman & Eyman, 1990).

Satir Model Therapy

Virginia Satir initially developed a model of intervention that focused on personal growth and accessing life energy for healing. Since then it has been developed further for use with suicidal clients to choose life. The Satir model (Satir et al., 1991) has many applications for therapists to learn in strengthening connection with suicidal youth. This model recognizes that all human beings strive to survive and to grow. Satir had great faith in people's ability to grow, as long as there is breath (Satir & Banmen, 1983). Satir believed in the life force that all humans have access to, and her therapeutic work was aimed at releasing this life force from within the person (Banmen & Banmen, 1991). When youth are suicidal, there is less energy for living, although they may summon up the energy to commit their final act. This model encompasses many aspects of theory and enables therapists to gain insight into the inner world of youth and their ways of coping. The Satir model recognizes the impact of family of origin disappointments, rules, expectations, and relationships. By working through and healing past unresolved hurts and resentments, youth may be better able to move in a positive direction toward future growth.

Within the Satir model, the Personal Iceberg Metaphor (Banmen, 1997; Satir et al., 1991) is a conceptual framework of the inner experience, which can be used to assess, understand, reflect, interact, change, and transform youth. This concept is an intrapsychic psychological map of the inner world. There are seven components within the Personal Iceberg Metaphor (Self: I am/Spiritual Core, Yearnings, Expectations, Perceptions, Feelings about Feelings/Feelings, Coping Stances, and Behavior). The metaphor concept allows therapists to understand their own as well as another's intrapsychic experience. The Personal Iceberg Metaphor enables therapists to process youths' internal world, while at the same time acknowledging their external world.

Inner Experience

Behavior of the Suicidal Youth

The acting out behavior and verbal communication of suicidal youth is an expression of his or her internal experience. The Satir model looks at behavior and verbal communication as the result of the inner world of youth. Through using the Satir model and by focusing on changing adolescents' internal world, destructive external behavior has the stronger possibility of being positively changed. Satir's Personal Iceberg Metaphor (Satir et al., 1991) acknowledges behavior as only being a one-eighth part of the whole person, and that 7/8ths is hidden from external view, thus the iceberg metaphor.

In dealing with suicidal youth, therapy has often been focused more on identified behaviors. Some of these behaviors are displayed such as running away, disruptive behavior, challenging comments and actions, resistance to others, chronic nonattendance at school, noticeable mood changes, body movements, nonverbal responses, substance abuse (drugs and/or alcohol), sexual acting out, giving away possessions, and verbal comments (Banmen, 2000). Suicidal teenagers have a higher possibility of experiencing disruption and unpredictability within their family environment (Everall, 2000). Suicidal actions or intentions can be seen as a sign that within youth's internal worlds, there may be a sense of hopelessness, helplessness, despair, and disconnection.

Coping Stances of the Suicidal Youth

Satir (1972) suggested that in order to survive, people cope in different ways under stress. The four coping stances are referred to as the placating stance, the blaming stance, the super reasonable stance, and the irrelevant stance (Satir, 1972; Satir et. al., 1991). Satir also viewed relationships as involving three crucial components: self, other, and context. This is how a person acts and feels in relationship to oneself, in relationship to another, and depending on the situation or environment in which the relationship is taking place.

Suicidal youth who use the placating stance under stress may not highly value themselves, but will value the other person and be aware of the context. These teenagers live in their feelings about themselves, others, and the world. The placating suicidal youth may experience a deep sense of worthlessness, unworthiness, hopelessness, and helplessness. There may be behaviors that indicate depression, and a deep unhappiness about themselves and their life. Suicidal adolescents may reject themselves, while expecting that others have given up on them. The rejection could manifest as a giving up on themselves, which will inhibit their own life energy, hence possible depression. Suicidal youth may be very unhappy and disappointed that their needs are not being met by others (Banmen, 2000).

Suicidal youth who use the blaming stance under stress value themselves and are aware of the context, but will not value the other person with whom they are in a relationship. These adolescents have high expectations of others and the world. When their expectations are not met, a blaming stance will occur. The blaming suicidal youth may feel a deep sense of inner isolation and loneliness. Outwardly they may display verbal and/or nonverbal anger towards others through acting out, bullying others, drug abuse, and delinquent behavior. These teenagers may also feel aggressive, revengeful, and indignant.

Suicidal youth who use the super reasonable stance under stress will be focused on the context, information, and details of situations. The super reasonable suicidal youth may feel very fragile, and have a deep sense of isolation from others and within themselves. These youth may create distance from others by isolating themselves with books, games, and computers. Their behaviors may manifest outwardly through perfectionistic, obsessive, and/or compulsive behaviors.

Suicidal youth who use the irrelevant stance under stress, have no sense of belonging or sense of connection. Disconnection from self can be a constant state of being. The irrelevant suicidal youth may feel extreme pain and sensitivity. They may experience turmoil and chaos externally and internally. They can be very impulsive, spontaneous, and make poor choices due to their impulsive actions. These adolescents may not be focused on tasks or not be present within their own selves. These youth may appear to be funny, joking, and class clowns, but internally the disconnection is extremely and deeply painful. These teenagers may struggle with creating a sense of self or have an inability to create a sense of self.

Adolescents are less able to access their strengths and resources while under stressful circumstances. Suicidal youth could use any of these coping stances, however one stance may be more prominent. Suicide results from a decision that comes from young peoples' inability to transpose stresses in their daily life.

Feelings of the Suicidal Youth

Feelings are our emotional response to ourselves, others, and the context (situations and events). Satir and associates (1991) believed that we have a right to feel our feelings, however we may have family rules that deny the display of these feelings or emotions. Often placating youth may be very aware of this feeling component in their lived experience. Suicidal youth may be flooded with feelings of their emotions, or they can be numbed from feeling their emotions. Teenagers who are suicidal may feel hurt, sadness, depression, loss, abandonment, fear, anxiety, remorse, guilt, self punishment, disillusionment, confusion, and a sensitivity to being criticized by others (Banmen, 2000). The experience of loss can be accumulated over a period of time in childhood (Everall, 2000). Suicidal youth can also feel anger, rage, revenge, and retaliation and be critical of others. There may be a deep sense of rejection and betrayal that can create a helpless feeling. In summary, how suicidal youth cope will influence the kind of feelings that will be internally experienced.

Feelings about the Feelings for the Suicidal Youth

Satir and colleagues (1991) acknowledged the impact that feelings have on oneself, and attributed this to our feelings about having feelings. This is a component that deepens and displays the intricacy of the feeling experience. The feelings about the feelings component have an impact on suicidal teenagers with their sense of self-esteem, self-worth, and adequacy. Suicidal youth may experience feelings of shame, guilt, and worthlessness in relation to their initial feelings. Adolescents who are suicidal may also experience a sense of vulnerability, hopelessness, helplessness, and deep despair.

Beliefs of the Suicidal Youth

Suicidal youth will have perceptions and beliefs that influence their suicidal intentions and behaviors. Adolescents who use the super reasonable stance are likely to be highly aware of and focused on their intellectual perceptions in order to make sense of their world. How suicidal youth view themselves, others, and the world, will affect their decisions about life and death. Chandler and Lalonde (1998) found that four out of five youth (84%) who were actively suicidal did not believe that they had any connection to their past, present, or future. There may be a sense that they have lost control, or have never had any control over their world, and they may feel unable to change their circumstances. Suicidal youth may believe that they have no choice, or that committing suicide is the only choice that is left for them to make. Some suicidal youth may believe that they are emotionally invisible to others and that no one will listen to them. Adolescents who are suicidal may have had numerous losses and believe that such losses will continue in their lives. A sense of being abandoned by others or the world can be predominant. Suicidal youth see rejection as an acknowledgment of their sense of being contaminated or flawed (Everall, 2000). These teenagers may believe that they are losers, and they could be on a downward spiral in relationship to their self-esteem. Some suicidal adolescents may believe that they are unlovable, unacceptable, or incompetent. If these teenagers or their family members have high expectations of them, there can be a sense of failure for not living up to being perfect or successful.

Expectations of the Suicidal Youth

Unmet yearnings will manifest in expectations of others to meet their yearnings, and this can interfere with teenagers' taking responsibility for their lives. Suicidal youth who use the placating coping stance may be self-punishing, and self-victimizing and expect that they cannot affect their world. There can be expectations which are negatively focused. Suicidal youth who use the blaming coping stance can be blaming, accusatory and controlling, especially if they expect others to meet their needs. Their expectations can be unrealistic, imagined, and contribute to disappointments. Often expectations are formed from family rules that involve "shoulds, musts, and oughts." Suicidal adolescents may judge themselves for having failed their own expectations. High expectations that are realistic can help as a protective factor in preventing suicide.

Yearnings of the Suicidal Youth

Satir and colleagues (1991) believed that all humans have universal yearnings for love, validation, belonging, connection, acceptance, acknowledgment, meaning, growth, and freedom. So no matter what age a person is, these yearnings are common, even for the adolescent population. When youths' yearnings are met, then a sense of fulfillment, wholeness, and harmony will be experienced. When unfulfilled yearnings are not met, there is a negative impact on the internal worlds of these youth, and often these can turn into expectations of self or others, which lead into negative behaviors. If youth yearn to be loved and do not feel loved, then they may conclude that they are unlovable. If there is a yearning to feel a sense of worthiness and these yearnings are not met, they may think that they are worthless. When adolescents yearn for connection and these yearnings are not met, there is a disconnection from self. If youth yearn for attachment and these yearnings are not met, they may become detached and this detachment can be from Self: I am and/or God. If there is yearning for belonging, but these yearnings are not met, they may experience social isolation or an isolation from self. When youth yearn to feel acknowledgment and these yearnings are not met, they may feel rejected. If youth yearn for growth and these yearnings are not met, then they may experience a sense of failure and stagnation. Yearnings are a significant component of the inner world that gives meaning to life.

Self of the Suicidal Youth

The Self: I am is one's connection to their soul, essence, core, or life force. It is through this life force that life's energy is manifest. When youth are fully connected with the life force of the Self: I am, then they will experience peace, inner calm, hope, faith, wisdom, harmony, a desire to live, high self-esteem, and a willingness to take responsibility. This deep connection with Self: I am can be a spiritual source for youth, which can also help to provide a sense of meaning in their lives.

When youth are disconnected from the Self: I am, there will be disruptions or blockages in their life force energy (Satir et al., 1991). This disconnected energy may occur as a result of the impact of their family of origin experiences between family members (Everall, 2000; Satir et al., 1991). As a result of this disconnection, youth will experience low self-esteem and self-worth. This inner experience of self will affect youths' intrapsychic world, which will in turn have an impact on their relationships with others. Suicide may be a rejection of the Self: I am, a punishment of Self: I am, a violence toward the Self: I am, or an abandonment of Self: I am.

What Suicide Investigations Teach Us

Wars come and go; epidemics come and go; but suicide, thus far has stayed. Why is this and what can be done about it?"

—Jamison, 1999, p. 24

The experiences of an individual youth suicide will be analyzed in the context of the Satir model. The information of the inner experience of the deceased individual has been gathered from the testimony of significant others in the youth's life through an extensive investigative process. This collaborative view is derived from the case file taken from one of the authors (Smith) from his work as a Behavioral Investigator for the British Columbia Coroner's Service, Canada, where he performs child, youth, and adult suicide investigations. Between 50 and 75 percent of approximately 500 child and youth suicides examined through the behavioral investigation program were not predicted by the parents, service providers, or gatekeepers. This was a surprising number of unpredicted suicides suggesting that precursors to child and youth suicide needed to be understood differently.

Looking at suicide through the theory of the Satir model brings forth new learning applicable to the living. In his work as director and therapist for a youth and family services agency, Smith has also had the opportunity to apply this new learning with suicidal youth.

Many reasons for suicide and attempted suicide have been put forth. We hear a lot about the external factors that are major contributors to the cause of suicide. These factors, including drugs and alcohol, loss and grief, divorce, peer pressure, reduced job opportunities, economic competition, and world tension have all been used to explain the suicidal scenario. The external, contextual, environmental, interactive factors are probably stronger stressors now than in previous decades. Yet, most teenagers seem to handle these stressors well. All of life is within a context. How we handle the impact of various stressors might be a more important consideration than the stressors themselves. The Satir model (Satir et al., 1991) has some basic premises that might fit in our exploration of suicide. Satir believed that human beings have the internal resources they need to survive and grow. She also believed that internal change is always possible, even if we do not have control of our external world. She taught that the problem is not the problem, but how we cope with the problem is usually the problem. She found that most people choose familiarity over the discomfort of change, especially during times of stress. She also advocated that therapy needs to focus on health and growth possibilities instead of pathology (Banmen, 2000, pp.1–2).

The work of the behavioral investigation program is intended to illuminate the human factor in death investigations. Specifically, the program serves to assist the coroner in determining the classification of death and why certain deaths may have occurred and how they may have been prevented.

A behavioral investigation is a voluntary inquiry into the inner experience of the deceased. The information gathered includes: background history of the parents and a multigenerational family history, information about the pregnancy, pre-, peri-, and postnatal history, developmental milestones, marital and family history, significant events in the family and life of the deceased, and school information. In addition, the behavioral investigator gathers testimonial descriptions of the deceased from significant others in the life of the deceased. This process adds important dimensions to understanding how the deceased experienced life. Those interviewed include parents, siblings, relatives, friends, employers, lovers, fellow students, coaches, leaders, teachers, therapist, psychiatrist, social workers, and medical doctors. The collective view of the possible experience of the deceased is gathered through a careful and sensitive interviewing process frequently lasting between three to four hours per interview. With these interviews the investigator gathers a body of information that when viewed through the Satir model (Satir et al., 1991) provides a means to understand behavior as coping.

Behavior patterns are analyzed and reported to the coroner. In addition, the behavioral investigators are required to speculate how each suicide death may have been prevented. This speculation has become the art of understanding the experience of the deceased. Considering behavior as coping as seen through the Satir model shifts focus from the individual act of self death to the story behind the struggle to live and the meaning the individual may have attached to this struggle. For some, suicide appears not to be so much about wanting to die, but more about believing they can no longer endure the pain of living. This suggests that explanations for suicide might lie within himself or herself in relation to the world in which he or she exists.

Case Study

Satir model theory regards behavior as the external manifestation of the internal experience. Understanding behavior in this way provides opportunity for earlier intervention into suicidal ideation. While investigating the suicide death of Paul, a pseudonym for a 16-year-old male, Smith was initially puzzled by the lack of information to explain the reasons for his suicide.

The information from the coroner's office that Smith reviewed, included:

1. The suicide note left by the deceased
2. Interview narratives with the principal of the high school that Paul last attended
3. Attendance and disciplinary files profiles for grades Kindergarten through to and including grade nine
4. School records 1998 to January 1999
5. Eulogy given by high school principal
6. Interview narrative and psychological summary report of school district psychologist.

7. Interview narratives with Paul's parents
8. Interview narrative with teaching staff of the elementary school
9. Psychological research questionnaire completed and provided by the coroner's agent

In addition to the information provided by the coroner's agent, Smith conducted a telephone interview with Paul's mother to gather birth and family system history. The suicide note contained messages of hopelessness and helplessness. It did not explain why or how Paul arrived at the state he was in at the time of his death. Smith wondered what indications he may have given that might have been seen as a precursor if not to his suicide, at least to his apparent suffering.

Through information taken from his school records (Table 1), Paul appeared to be quiet, compliant, and academically successful. When he reached high school he had become uncooperative, oppositional, and bullying in his behavior with absenteeism and suspensions. He appears to have coped with his feelings by withdrawing into himself. Adopting a compliant coping style, as Smith suspects Paul did, prevented others from understanding his personal internal experience.

Paul was unable to externalize his feelings of pain and/or fear. This inability to externalize feelings, in Smith's experience, is likely the meaning of his statement in his suicide note "There is no way I can explain what I did but it was done. I just couldn't go on living." Smith believes that Paul lacked a deeper understanding of who he already was; that in a sense Paul felt he had yet to become a person. This expression from Paul's suicide note gives a feeling his life was not working out and that he lacked connection with his self. This expression from Paul's suicide note also indicates the state of despair he was in at the time of the writing of the suicide note.

Paul succeeded academically in elementary school and appears to have done so with the external support of his teachers. In middle-school and high school, records show he struggled to succeed academically, indicating he may have continued to require external support and likely expected this support to continue as he progressed through his school years. Without this support, his performance dropped off, as did his compliance.

The attendance and comment profiles for grades Kindergarten through Grade 9 as recorded by the school, are a clear indication Paul could succeed academically when sufficiently motivated.

School records for kindergarten indicate Paul presented at school as lacking self-esteem. These perceptions on the part of the school system resulted in academic support. In retrospect his low self-esteem presentation might more accurately have been seen as the external expression of his coping. Understanding externalized behavior as coping with an internal state, nervous and tense behavior for Paul might have been about a deeper level state of fear. Interpreting Paul's nervous and tense behavior as a deep level fear, could have initiated an earlier referral for therapeutic intervention in elementary school. By Grade 3, Paul is experienced at school as withdrawn. His withdrawn behavior withholds his true feelings from the external world, and in Smith's experience this withdrawn behavior might be the first sign that Paul is experiencing feelings of both helplessness and hopelessness.

Table 9.1

Paul's School Records

GRADE	DAYS ABSENT	COMMENTS
Kindergarten	13	Nervous, high-strung, low self-esteem.
Grade 1	13	
Grade 2	25.5	
Grade 3	27	Hesitates to ask for help in class.
Grade 4	Unknown	With learning assistance support achieved a B average.
Grade 5	05	A/B average
Grade 6	8.5	A/C average
Grade 7 (middle school)	35.5	marks dropped. Achieved one B, other marks were C, P and F. Lack of effort, disciplinary problems, missed assignments, disrupting others.
Grade 8	Unknown	several suspensions, spitting, intimidation, fighting, using drugs at school, extortion.
Grade 9 (3 years in grade 9)		marks continue to fall, indefinite suspension, absenteeism, was repeating grade nine for third time with marks ranging from B to F with an average of C-.

With continued support at school he achieved a reasonably high standard of academic success through Grade 7. In his Grade 7 year Paul moved into middle-school at a different geographical location from his elementary school and with different teachers. His marks and the behavior comments from Grade 7 through to the end of his life reflect lack of effort, missed assignments, suspensions from school, fighting, intimidation of others, and drug use. Paul at this time is experienced as uncooperative, manipulative, and passive-aggressive, inviting reactive disciplinary action on the part of the school district. Smith suspects that he was possibly experiencing the combined painful feelings of fear of failure, disappointment, helplessness, hopelessness, and frustration. Smith believes Paul may have been acting these feelings out through lack of effort, missed assignments, fighting, intimidation, and drug use. Had the school district understood these externalized behaviors as coping, they likely would have referred Paul for psychological therapy, rather than only reacting to his behavior through disciplinary measures.

Smith believes Paul was in a desperate emotional state through the later part of middle-school into high school and that this state is reflected in his angry acting out behavior. This was the last attempt Paul was able to make in order to have his life come out right. Smith believes he was likely in deep emotional pain of despair, and that he likely harbored expectations of himself, family, and teachers that had not been met at the time of his death. Without external support Paul was unable to succeed and eventually gave up trying. Smith believes the noncompliant behavior of Paul may have had the purpose of asking for support. By shutting down, he may have carried the hope he would receive the same support in middle-school and high school that he received in elementary school. Smith believes Paul likely experienced this absence of support as painful feelings of loneliness and abandonment, and that his drug use may have served to ease this pain.

Smith discovered that Paul had at times performed acts of self-mutilation by digging into his hand, and exposed skin on his arms with a pencil or sharp instrument. Smith also discovered Paul drew pictures depicting violence and scenes containing blood. This self-mutilation behavior and graphic sadistic art provided another obvious opportunity for therapeutic intervention.

The ability to understand behavior differently may be the key to early intervention and prevention of suicide. Understanding behavior as the external expression of an internal state sees behavior as a dynamic purposeful activity with attached expectations of self and others, and views expectations as linked to deeper unmet universal yearnings. These universal yearnings are directly linked to the individual's need to evolve and, when these yearnings remain unmet, can be the experience of their life not working out.

Suicide Treatment Using the Satir Model

This section will share how a therapist using the Satir model (Banmen, 1997; Satir et al., 1991) might have engaged in treatment with Paul while he was still alive. From the identified case study, Paul could have been referred to a therapist to deal with his sense of inadequacy at an earlier age; unfortunately his referral for therapy in Grade 9 was not initiated soon enough. Therapy could have been initiated at an earlier time when it was evident that Paul struggled with his school involvement. The behaviors he exhibited in Grades 7 and 8 could have alerted friends, family, teachers, school counselors, or principals that Paul was in need of therapy.

In the Satir model (Banmen, 1997) there are four main goals for therapy; to raise self-esteem, encourage better choice-making, increase responsibility, and facilitate congruence. The Satir model recognizes the universal yearnings of all humans to be connected with themselves and with others. By facilitating a sense of connection, the therapist would be able to better explore Paul's commitment to live. First of all, using the Satir model (Banmen, 1997) the therapist would intentionally connect and attempt to maintain connection with Paul throughout the treatment period. The therapist would share an attitude of acceptance, genuineness, and caring. Initially the therapist would assess Paul's energy and willingness to engage in therapy throughout the first session and within each subsequent session. The therapist would use process questions throughout sessions, such as, "What would you hope would happen from our time together?" By listening closely to how Paul had perceived himself, others, and his situation, the therapist would gain valuable information into how to approach the therapy process. The therapist could ask, "Is there anything you would like to change in your life?"

The therapist would listen for a possible goal and helped Paul to define a goal for therapy. The therapist would check to see if he were committed to working with the therapist on attaining his goal. Once a commitment had been made, the therapist would remain conscious of his specific goal throughout the therapy period. If there were resistance from Paul, then the therapist might have to recheck the goal to see if he was still committed to this goal, otherwise there would be further exploration and a reclarification regarding the goal of therapy. "Are you sure that this is what you really want for yourself?"

With regard to self-esteem, the therapist would wonder about Paul's self-esteem, and ask questions such as, "What do you know about yourself? and "Who do you believe you really are?" As noted, it appeared that Paul had low self-esteem and was not well connected to himself. The therapist would explore his relationship to himself, and foster a stronger inner connection to self. "When do you feel most alive?" and "When do you experience inner calm?" The therapist would find ways to strengthen Paul's self-esteem by increasing self-awareness, fostering self-acceptance, and self-validation. One way to get a sense about how Paul saw himself, would be to ask, "What are your hopes and wishes for yourself?" His answer could enable the therapist to understand which yearnings could motivate him to live. In the case of Paul, his dreams of becoming a rock star suggest a desire for acceptance and recognition. The therapist would find out how he could have found an acceptable way to express himself either through singing, playing an instrument, or possibly creating poetry. The therapist might be able to help him to realize his dream, or change his dream for one that could have been attainable.

The Satir model supports the idea of resilience within all people and the belief that each person has strengths and resources to deal with their lives. The therapist would listen to the problem, and reframe the problem into more positive possibilities. As the therapist listened to and continued to be engaged with Paul, there would be exploration on finding out how Paul experienced himself, others, and his world. The therapist could ask, "How do you handle your loneliness?", "How do others see you?", and "When have you felt supported and seen by others?" The therapist would use process questions throughout the therapy process, in order to find out if there were strengths or resources that had been developed by Paul as a result of his situation(s) and relationship(s). For example, "When do you feel good about yourself?" and "What do you do well?" The therapist would be creative in reframing negative perceptions into more positive resources. "Can you appreciate that you have deep, deep feelings, like the depths of a passionate songwriter?" Once the strengths and resources had been identified, the therapist would help Paul to take ownership for his strengths and resources, in spite of any perceived obstacles. "Right in this moment, can you be aware of your love of music? How does it make you feel inside?" Awareness of his strengths and resources could foster increased self-esteem.

One of the four goals of the Satir model is to help the client to make better choices. The choice to live is a crucial goal for the therapist to explore with suicidal youth. "Are you willing to live for yourself and not for others?", "Do you deserve to live in peace?", "Can you make a decision today to live and not to die inside?" Another important aspect of the Satir model is to create experiential moments for the client in therapy. During these moments when Paul was becoming aware of and experiencing his inner world, the therapist would gently challenge him to make some choices about his life. "Close you eyes and as you become aware of the pain, can you send compassion to that painful place, so it can begin to breathe?"

If the therapist sensed that Paul had suicidal thoughts, it would have been important to explore whether he was willing to live for himself. The therapist would ask Paul to make a decision to live at the level of self while he was immersed in an experiential moment. "In this vulnerable place, can you find the inner strength to live and grow?" If Paul did not feel hopeful, then the therapist would suggest, "Will you accept my hope for you, so that we can work together until you gain your own hope?" The therapist would ask, "Are you willing to make a decision not to hurt yourself, while we are working together to change things?" If Paul felt suicidal when he was away from the therapy session, then the therapist would help him co-create a plan for coping that Paul could agree to.

Increasing responsibility is another one of the four goals of the Satir model. Working with and changing expectations is also a fundamental concept in the Satir model. Helping a client to either accept his or her expectations or to change those expectations can facilitate a client to take on responsibility for his or her life and to make different choices. If the therapist heard any regret(s), then exploration could occur with having Paul accept that these were his expectations. The therapist would suggest that if Paul accepted and owned his expectations, then he could have been more willing to fulfill his expectations and let go of his expectations of others. "Are you willing to make a decision to stop hurting yourself, and to ease your pain?" and "How can you let go of expecting that they should know about your painful hurt, when you hurt yourself?" If Paul would not let go of his expectations, then the therapist would explore the costs for him in keeping these expectations. The therapist would suggest that he meet his own yearnings for acceptance and validation, instead of waiting for others to meet his yearnings. Together they could make a concrete plan on how Paul could meet his yearnings. "How can you extend a caring, helping hand to yourself?", "Are you willing to give yourself the gift of life, instead of waiting for someone else to give your life to you?" "Is it time to let love inside?"

The facilitation of congruence, the last of the goals in the Satir model, involves helping with the ability to be honest and truthful in actions and words coming from one's internal experience. As clients become more aware of interactions with self, other, and the context, there can be the opportunity to develop congruence. Gaining an understanding of the impact of Paul's past experiences in the family and within the school system would be very useful. "What happened for you when no one seemed to pay attention to you anymore?" The therapist could also include Paul's family in family therapy, and involve his parents or siblings in the therapeutic process. The therapist would explore his past family experiences and past social experiences, and then work on reducing any negative impacts in the present. "Are you still waiting for your parents to really see you?" By changing how he experienced his memories of the past, Paul could have been freer to live his present life. "Your parents gave you the gift of life, are you now ready to accept their gift into your heart?" "Are you willing to forgive your parents for not understanding you in the way that you needed?" "Can you now forgive yourself for not taking better care of yourself in the past?" When Paul was not burdened by negative perceptions of himself or others, then he would have been more able to become congruent. "Can you allow yourself to live with your mistakes, without having to punish yourself for having the courage to live?"

Another important aspect of the Satir model would be reflected in the therapist's listening closely to how Paul verbalized his world and any meaningful metaphorical words or concepts. The therapist would closely listen to and respond with specific and intentional conscious responses. "Are you willing to shine a warm, bright light on the part of you that feels isolated and invisible?" The pace and the tone of the therapist would match Paul's energy level and pace in order to have created a close therapeutic relationship and shared language.

The Satir model also encourages therapists to strengthen their own abilities for observation of self, the client, and the context of the session. Throughout the session, the therapist would be observing in these three different ways. The therapist would pay close attention to Paul's language, connection, and responses; pay attention to the responses that he or she shared with him; and would watch his or her own inner responses to Paul's comments and interactions.

The therapist would notice Paul's inner experience through using the framework of the Personal Iceberg Metaphor. The therapist would listen to, watch for and pay attention to Paul's inner experience by using the components of the Iceberg metaphor. The therapist would be using his or her intuition to comprehend what kind of intentional responses might have been most effective with him. The therapist would be watchful of his behaviors, coping, feelings, feelings about having his initial feelings, perceptions, expectations of himself, expectations of others, expectations of his world, yearnings, and Self: I am. The therapist could ask questions that speak to the inner components of Paul's world. For example:

- (behavior)"When you cut yourself, what is the wound saying?"
- (coping) "How do you cope with the rejection?"
- (feeling) "How do you feel right now as we explore this?"
- (feelings about the feelings) "What is the feeling that lies beneath your anger?"
- (perceptions) "What do you think would stop the pain?"
- (expectations) "What do you expect they should have done when they saw your wounds?"
- (yearnings) "If you were to live in that way you had hoped, what would be happening for you instead?"
- (Self: I am) "Can you allow your favorite music to soothe your soul?"

The therapist would look beyond Paul's initially withdrawn behaviors or his later external acting out behaviors. The transformational experience would be more likely to occur after the therapist was able to facilitate Paul's acceptance, acknowledgment, forgiveness, honoring, loving, and commitment to his Self: I am. By helping to change Paul's inner experience of himself, this would create the space for healing and growth. The Satir model would give the therapist a map into understanding Paul's inner experience. It can also help the therapist to support him, to make new decisions to live, to increase his self-esteem, and support Paul to become more responsible for his life and to encourage congruence within.

Conclusion

Current treatment modalities often may address only separate components of youths' inner experience. The Satir model gives a framework that encompasses an integrative and holistic view of their inner experience. This model can be effectively applied to the prevention, intervention, and treatment of suicidal youth. We can now begin to understand suicidal behavior differently by exploring and changing the inner world of youth. Seeing suicide through new lenses allows the focus of treatment to be internally based and transformationally focused. The Satir model offers hope for therapists in facilitation of deep inner transformation in youth. We need to instill hope in youth, so that they can look forward to having a positive impact toward their future. As more of our young people find meaning and reason in living, there will be great hope for this and the next generation of youth.

References

Banmen, A. & Banmen, J. (Eds.). (1991). *Meditations of Virginia Satir: Peace within, peace between, peace among.* Palo Alto, CA: Science and Behavior Books.

Banmen, J. (1997). *Invitational training: Satir's systemic brief therapy.* Bellingham, WA: Unpublished paper.

Banmen, J. (2000). *Suicide prevention: A treatment alternative.* Suicide Intervention & Treatment Task Force: Satir Institute of the Pacific, Vancouver, B.C.: Unpublished paper.

Berman, A. L., & Jobes, D. A. (1991). *Adolescent suicide: Assessment and intervention.* Washington, DC: American Psychological Association.

Berman, A. L., & Jobes, D. A. (1997). *The treatment of the suicidal adolescent.* Washington, DC: American Psychological Association.

Chandler, M. J., & Lalonde, C. (1998). Cultural continuity as a hedge against suicide in Canada's First Nations. *Transcultural Psychiatry Research Review, 35* (2), 191–219.

Ellis, T.E., & Newman, C.F. (1996). *Choosing to live: How to defeat suicidal behavior through cognitive therapy.* Oakland, CA: New Harbinger.

Everall, R. (2000). The meaning of suicide attempts by young adults. *Canadian Journal of Counselling. 34* (2), 111–25.

Fiske, H. (1998). Applications of solution-focused therapy in suicide prevention. In D. Deleo, A. Schmidtke, and R.F.W. Diekstra (Eds.), *Suicide prevention: A holistic approach* (pp.185–97). Dordecht, the Netherlands: Kluwer.

Freeman, A., & Reinecke, M. A. (1993). *Cognitive therapy of suicidal behavior: a manual for treatment.* New York: Springer Publishing Co.

Hoover, M., (1987). *Suicide and the self as process: Self validation– invalidation.* Unpublished masters thesis, University of Alberta, Alberta, Canada.

Hoover, M. A., & Paulson, B. L., (1999). Suicidal no longer. *Canadian Journal of Counselling, 33* (3), 227–44.

Jamison, K.R. (1999). Night falls fast. New York: Vintage Books.

Linehan, M.M. (1993). *Cognitive-behavioral therapy of borderline personality disorder.* New York: Guilford Press.

Linehan, M. M., MacLeod, A. K., & Williams, J. M. G. (1992). New developments in the understanding and treatment of suicidal behavior. *Behavioral Psychotherapy, 20* (3), 193–218.

Maris, R. W., Berman, A. L., & Silverman, M. M. (2000). *Comprehensive textbook of suicidology.* New York: Guilford Press.

Richman, J., & Eyman, Jr. (1990). Psychotherapy of suicide: Individual, group, and family approaches in current concepts of suicide. In D. Lester (Ed.), *Current concepts of suicide* (pp 139–58). Philadelphia, PA: The Charles Press.

Satir, V. (1972). *Peoplemaking.* Mountain View, CA: Science and Behavior Books.

Satir, V., & Banmen, J. (1983). *Virginia Satir verbatim 1984.* North Delta, BC: Delta Psychological Associates, Inc.

Satir, V., Banmen, J., Gerber, J., & Gomori, M. (1991). *The Satir model: Family therapy and beyond.* Palo Alto, CA: Science and Behavior Books.

10

The Satir Model With Female Adult Survivors of Childhood Sexual Abuse

Anne Morrison and Judy Ferris

There are various therapeutic approaches to working with female adult survivors of childhood sexual abuse. This article will explore the range of approaches and specifically examine the benefits of the Satir model (Satir et al., 1991) which stresses the impact, not the "story," of the abuse. A case example will demonstrate the therapeutic efficacy of the Satir model.

Child sexual abuse is sexual contact between a child and an individual in a position of power and authority. It is a sexual act imposed on a child who lacks emotional, maturational, and cognitive development and ranges from fondling to intercourse between a child in mid-adolescence or younger and a person at least five years older (Sgroi, 1982; Courtois, 1988; Dolan, 1991; Briere, 1992).

Estimates of the prevalence of childhood sexual abuse in the United States range from 15 to 33 percent for females (Freeman-Longo & Blanchard, 1997; Finklehor, Hotaling, Lewis, & Smith, 1990; Briere & Runtz, 1989), and 13 to 16 percent for males (Finklehor et al., 1990). Studies show the majority of child victims are female and that one in five children may be sexually abused prior to age 18. In Canada, the report by the Badgely Commission (Badgely, 1984) estimated that 1 in 4 girls and 1 in 10 boys would be sexually abused before they reached the age of

18. In 1996, children under 18 were the victims of 22 percent of assaults reported to the police (Canadian Center for Justice Statistics, 1996).

Treatment of Sexual Abuse

Female survivors of childhood sexual abuse usually present themselves for therapy as they are experiencing difficulty in one or more of the following areas: cognitive, emotional, physical/somatic, and interpersonal (Kirschner, 1993). Webb and Leehan (1996) further define these areas as a lack of basic trust in self and others; deeply ingrained feelings of low self-esteem; a sense of powerlessness and lack of control; difficulty in identifying, acknowledging, and disclosing feelings; and a lack of interpersonal skills which hinders the ability to form relationships. Therapy attempts to address these areas either individually or in group therapy.

Individual Therapy

There are many approaches used in individual therapy for female survivors of childhood sexual abuse: psychoanalytic and object relations, psychodynamic, existential and humanistic, solution-focused, cognitive-behavioral, social learning theory, family systems, and feminist therapy. A comparison of these approaches can be found in Brown and Ballou (1992), Cantor (1990), and Dutton-Douglas and Walker (1988).

Courtois (1988) summarizes four philosophical principles inherent in therapy for female adult survivors of sexual abuse: to treat the sexual abuse directly as well as its effects; to use traumatic stress, feminist, and family systems theories to understand the effects and to plan treatment; to individualize the treatment; and to foster the development of a therapeutic alliance and a safe environment. Walker (1995) suggests outlining the client's areas of strengths in order to build on these and to set the climate for re-empowerment. Dolan (1991) uses solution-focused strategies. Solution-focused strategies effective for the initial phase of treatment have been developed by Berg (1990); de Shazer (1982, 1984, 1985); de Shazer, Berg, Lipchik, Nunnally, Molnar, Gingerich, and Weiner-Davis (1986); Lipchik (1988); Lipchik and de Shazer (1986); O'Hanlon and Weiner-Davis (1989); and Dolan (1989).

Group Therapy

Group therapy is used alone or in conjunction with individual therapy. The nature of the group process breaks down the sense of isolation survivors often feel. Usually a professional therapist leads therapy groups, but there are also self-help groups led by adult survivors. Safety of the group is paramount to therapeutic effectiveness, and this is not always found in self-help groups where the facilitators may not be trained in group process.

The general goals for therapy groups are breaking down the sense of isolation, providing a supportive environment, providing a consistency to promote trust, providing opportunities for problem solving, learning to express and deal with feelings, and learning interpersonal skills (Webb & Leehan, 1996).

Courtois (1988) recommends group therapy to alleviate secrecy, isolation, and stigmatization. Briere (1989) believes self-esteem is enhanced and members feel less deviant in a group. The opportunity to interact with peers and to build meaningful relationships and share common concerns is beneficial to adult survivors (Courtois & Leehan, 1982; Drews & Bradley, 1989; Fowler, Burns, & Roehl, 1983). These approaches attempt to address the effects of abuse on the cognitive, emotional, physical/somatic, and interpersonal areas.

Satir's Concept of Treatment

The Satir model is based on the premise that everyone has basic needs, or yearnings, that strive to be fulfilled in order to accomplish inner peace (Satir, et. al, 1991). These yearnings—to be loved, to be validated, to feel heard, to be respected—are often what drives human behavior, as people search for ways to meet these yearnings. At the core of everyone's being is the essence, life energy, or soul—that area of "being" rather than "doing." This inner core can be the center of inner peace and harmony and is accomplished when one's yearnings are met. People often describe this state as being fully human or fully alive.

According to Virginia Satir, if people's yearnings are fulfilled, they are freed to be positive choice makers. People also become responsible for their internal and external worlds, so that they feel in control of their lives and no longer trapped as victims. They realize that they have the ability to experience wholeness and harmony; they are able to experience their various inner parts and enable them to work together in harmony. Negative energy from various inner parts, such as condemnation, hatred, and guilt can be neutralized, or transformed, to a positive place that becomes a resource for the person. For instance, a person might transform her inner judge to a reflective part that allows a fuller access to perceptions, without negative judgment. The internal judge then can be transformed to wisdom to examine possibilities and decide on one's course of action. The result is that one's inner reflective part does not have to take on extra negative energy which works against the feeling of congruence; the result is that the person then has a reservoir of positive energy to fuel her life essence.

John Banmen helped to conceptualize Satir's depiction of the rich inner world of perceptions, feelings, expectations, yearnings, and core life energy into a model of an iceberg that has eight layers (Satir et al, 1991). At the tip of the iceberg is the behavior that one sees and hears. Often people look for solutions at the behavior level, and sometimes they are successful. However, it appears that more lasting change can be effected when they examine their inner world, or the seven other internal layers of their iceberg, in order to become aware of their inner parts and move them into internal harmony. The other parts identified in the iceberg, then, include:

- Coping Pattern: (Placating; Blaming; Super-Reasonable; Irrelevant)
- Feelings (joy, fear, excitement, sadness, anger)
- Feelings about feelings (shame, guilt, confusion)
- Perceptions (beliefs, values, mind-sets, thinking or cognition)
- Expectations (of oneself; of others; from others)
- Yearnings (to be loved, feel respect, validated, understood, heard)
- Self — inner core (one's soul, life essence, life energy)

One's sense of self is fueled by an inner harmony that is achieved by having one's outside behaviors congruent with one's inner state. This is particularly important in the understanding of sexual abuse.

Satir's Approach to Sexual Abuse

Virginia Satir believed that every person is a growing human being, capable of making responsible choices, of achieving self worth, and accomplishing inner and outer congruence. In applying her principles to the treatment of those who are sexually abused, the Satir model emphasizes the positive growth potential of the individuals who are seeking help. Clients are experienced and treated as growing human beings, with resources to be tapped, and potential to become revitalized human beings. The clients are seen as people with strengths and untapped resources that can unlock their inner worlds of pain, self-doubt, fear, and/or other internal struggles that are preventing them from feeling fully alive and worthwhile.

People who are experiencing sexual abuse, therefore, are seen as having a growing life force, fully capable of achieving internal harmony and congruence, rather than as victims of external pain that controls their lives. Many other forms of treatment emphasize the belief that the therapist needs to enable the client to re-experience the pain, face the trauma, or complete any unfinished business by directly confronting the abuser. The Satir model, on the other hand, has a less prescriptive approach. It is based on the belief in the clients' internal strengths and capacities to know just how their treatment needs to unfold and what are their best choices for how to process the impact of the abuse. In fact, a therapist who assumes that he or she needs to enable the client to re-experience the earlier pain from the abuse will be creating a situation that actually can traumatize the client. One has to question the purpose of why a therapist would guide the client into self-revelation which leads to re-experiencing abuse. Such an approach works against the main tenet of the Satir model: to create a safe, welcoming setting for clients to do their work, based on the therapist's belief and conviction that clients have life energy to be tapped and internal resources to rediscover that which will enable them to achieve a full life.

Once clients enter into their internal experience, they intuitively know what boundaries they need to maintain as they do their internal work. Clients do not need to recreate any external replica of the original abuse, or follow a certain pattern of how to resolve its impact. Occasionally, it may be helpful to examine the context of the experience, that is, the clients' perceptions of their family relationships, without going into the story of it. Rather, the focus of the treatment is on the present impact of the abuse on the clients' present behavior, and how the past has shaped their internal world as reflected in the iceberg metaphor. For instance, clients may have a very small sense of self, which affects their yearnings, so that they do not feel worthy, lovable, or deserving of respect. This can leave them focused on placating others or ensuring that others' needs are looked after before their own. Clients who have a belief that they are less worthy than others, or perhaps feel contaminated by their past, will often feel shame around their internal feelings of sadness, fear, and internal anger at the abuse.

The work that would need to be done for such persons, then, would be to enable these clients to experience their potential, to discover that they are worthwhile and worthy of a quality life, to learn to reframe their previous beliefs into guidelines that support their inner sense of self and are not based on needing to placate others. They could process the inner sadness and anger and reintegrate these feelings into a vulnerability and sensitivity that can work for them, without having to stay expressed as crippling depression or anger. Clients can learn how to establish positive boundaries and self-regard without having to re-experience the earlier trauma. The end result of this treatment, therefore, would be to enable clients to create a new inner sense of self, by defusing the pain from the inner turmoil of fear, anger, or depression, or by transforming negative feelings into positive resources that work toward a positive inner sense of self. Energy that was previously channeled into negative, self-defeating feelings and experiences can be recaptured through the accomplishment of positive inner energy working toward a new internal harmony. We will now discuss the dimensions of the Satir model in practice in more detail.

The Treatment Approach for Female Adult Survivors

Initial Contact

The Satir model stresses the importance of making contact and building trust with every client. In the first interview, therefore, it is important to offer a welcoming, safe, confidential setting for the client. What distinguishes the approach would be the therapist's interest in discovering how the client wishes to proceed. The therapist helps the client to explore goals. The first phase of treatment, therefore, would enable the client to begin to have some hope for herself, that she is worthy, that she has resources, and actually has strengths she can tap into to discover a new level of being. Together, the therapist and the client set some positive directional goals, such as to strengthen her emerging positive self-esteem and to transform the impact of past hurts and anger into positive energy that fuels her new confidence and enables a clearer sense of self.

Treatment

The treatment approach includes using the Iceberg metaphor to explore the impact of the abuse on each of the client's eight internal levels of being: feelings; feelings about feelings; perceptions; expectations; yearnings; sense of self, and how this is expressed through one's behaviour and coping stances. The therapist can also access the client's world by exploring how the client has internalized the expectations of others. The therapist helps the client to reframe the rules she sets for herself about ways she believed she had to behave in order to fit into the family's expectations, into new guidelines which support a more positive self concept. For example, a client may have learned in her family of origin that angry feelings were to be avoided in order to "keep everyone happy." As an adult, the client discovers that anger can be her own gateway to positive self-expression and the client learns how to assert herself so that she feels heard and understood. The therapist can help that person realize that she can be responsible for her own feelings and that she can establish her own boundaries and sense of personal safety.

The therapist must also work with the client's unmet expectations, as a typical impact from sexual abuse is that the client's expectations for a certain childhood experience or adult state have been compromised. As a child, the client felt helpless and may carry inner sadness and anger about the ongoing loneliness and emptiness that she lives with as an adult. Also, a client who has been sexually abused often isolates parts of herself as the only way she has to deal with the abuse so that she does not have to experience it in her consciousness. This can lead to dissociation and out of body experiences so that the client has a distorted body image and does not comfortably connect with her body through physical intimacy. Careful exploration of how the client needed to separate out parts of herself as a child, but how she no longer needs to live that way as an adult, can help the client begin to integrate some of her individual parts.

Maki-Banmen's work on client's parts is an excellent resource for this exploration (Maki-Banmen, 1999). Maki-Banmen has changed the focus and format of Virginia Satir's Parts' Party so that the client can be guided to actually experience each of her inner parts, discover which parts are taking the most energy, find out what these parts are yearning for, and discover new resources which can transform some of the negative internal energy and enable the client to integrate what was previously painful into their awareness in a transformed state of energy. This is especially helpful when working with a client's inner child (parts) so that the client learns how her childhood loneliness can become nurtured by other inner parts as an adult so that the child grows up and forms a new inner security which takes its place within the client's new adult positive identity.

As the therapist enables the client to explore her internal world, especially the meaning she has made of the impact of the sexual abuse, the client's internal iceberg will shift. For example, feelings of anger, shame, hurt, will become less powerful and not define the whole person; the client will be able to accept the feelings and use the energy in a positive direction. She will realize that the impact of the abuse does not comprise her whole being. She will realize that she has an inner energy that stands apart from her experience which she can gain access to and which will help her to reframe the meaning of her experience. She will discover that she is more than her feelings. The client will see that her self-perceptions were carved by earlier conclusions of how she saw herself, or what rules she had to live by. She will see that she can redesign the rules to fit her new internal beliefs that she is worthy and has resources to guide her through life. She will discover that her internal parts no longer have to be in conflict with one another, but can be understood as separate entities, each yearning to be accepted, understood, and validated, and each then can be transformed into a positive role for her internal well being.

Clients will emerge with a new internal freedom that enables them to live from an inner source of harmony and positive life energy. They will have transformed their inner sense of self by exploring the impact of the abuse without having to work very much with the story which traditionally so often has guided the client's revelations in traditional modes of therapy. It appears that working with the impact of one's life experience results in much more lasting internal changes than reworking the sharing of the story of the earlier incidents. The Satir model, based on self worth, capability, and inner resources, is a powerful tool for therapists to practice. One of the authors (A. M.) will now share a case example of working with the Satir model to enable a female client who was sexually abused to discover new inner freedom and a fulfilling life.

Case Study

Carol was a 29-year-old woman, married for 11 years, and mother of a 19-month-old baby girl. Carol requested individual therapy after she had completed two different levels of a support group for women who had suffered sexual abuse as children, which the authors co-facilitated. The group co-facilitators used many Satir techniques to help the women build more self- awareness and begin to process the impact of their abuse. The therapists taught the women the Iceberg Metaphor as a tool to understand their internal experiences and how the different levels worked together to define their sense of self. The women began to realize that their internal chaos could be understood, and therefore made less frightening, when they processed their internal experiences through the Iceberg. The therapists also worked with the women around their perceptions of themselves and the world around them that had been shaped by their experience of the abuse. The women began to shift their view of the world as a dangerous place to one that could be safe and they began to learn new ways to set boundaries for themselves and others. The group created a safe setting to view themselves differently—as individuals who were worthy—not permanent victims in life. Women emerged from the group with a stronger sense of self apart from their experience of abuse; they realized they had positive life energy; and they began to build much more positive self-concepts. They realized that they no longer had to live their lives to fulfill others' expectations. They began the process of integrating their childhood vulnerabilities into positive resources.

Through the group experience, Carol began to accept herself as a person of worth, became much less driven by her anger at the abuser, and became more able to connect directly with group members. Carol was very appreciative of the supportive, resource-based group therapy approach, as she previously had endured two different sets of individual counseling (as a child and again as a teenager), which had focused on identifying the abuser and re-experiencing the emotional pain of the abuse. Her counseling had also set up the expectation that Carol would need to file charges against her abuser (her father) and confront him again if she were to attain inner freedom. Carol found our group focus of exploring the iceberg and transforming the impact of the abuse much more helpful. At the end of the two groups, Carol felt she had made a good beginning, but that she needed some individual sessions in order to complete her inner healing.

I (A. M.) saw Carol about 10 times, usually spaced every three weeks, over a nine-month period. When Carol shifted her work to focus on her relationship with her husband, she invited him to join her for marriage therapy. We had approximately 10 conjoint marital appointments between August 1999 and June 2000, at which point the couple had achieved a positive, rewarding marital relationship. Carol concluded her work with one final individual appointment to take stock of her individual healing and celebrate her inner freedom.

For the purposes of this case study, I will focus on the individual work that I did with Carol, and her individual therapy sessions. I will discuss how I made contact with Carol, look at her presenting problems and the development of her therapeutic goals, study her family of origin, determine interventions, and outline the results achieved.

How Contact Was Made

The group sessions had helped Carol to realize that she was entitled to work through the impact of her childhood sexual abuse in her own way. She still felt damaged from the abuse. Throughout the group experience, Carol rarely made eye contact and hid from the world behind long blond hair that covered most of her face.

When Carol came for her first individual appointment, she was nervous, her voice shook, and she could hardly make eye contact. I could feel her "scared rabbit" kind of demeanor and could also see a lovely gentleness that seemed to be just below her surface. Carol trusted me from experiencing me as a group co-facilitator. Therefore, I built on that trust and helped her to feel safe and welcome to be who she was with me without fear of judgment. My office is very relaxed and private and easy to settle into, so I built on that comfortable setting and helped her to relax and take more risks to share her inside processes.

It seemed to me that Carol had really been damaged by some of the previous therapeutic techniques that she had described in the group, such as making each person in the circle share all the details of the abuse out loud to the whole group, one at a time, around the circle, as well as the belief that healing would only come if one filed charges and confronted the abuser. I could feel the pain that Carol carried from the abuse, and I was not about to wade into her world and make her restate or re-experience it. Similarly, I was not about to dictate what she needed to do face-to-face with her abuser. I did not believe that such confrontation was the only route for Carol to let go of her crippling inner anger, but would rather would deal with what was underneath the anger.

Carol said that she wanted help to feel better about herself, to better understand the impact of her abuse beyond the raging anger that she carried inside of herself, and to find ways to be less afraid around people. I will recreate some of the dialogue that took place to illustrate some of the process and focus.

Client: " I am angry so much of the time and I hate feeling that way. I can be a real bitch. I know that others say I need to tell my father off but I do not want to face him, let alone talk about it with him. I can't remember the last time I really felt happy. I think I am a mess."

Therapist: " You know Carol, I admire how you came to the group and attended all the sessions when you were feeling so angry with everyone. And I saw you share your truth with others and really examine what the anger was about. And now you are making a decision to go further and resolve the grip of it all. That takes courage—what a strong spirit you have!"

And so I made contact by emphasizing her courage to commit to individual work, believing that she was worth it, and built on her inner strengths that I had seen in our groups. I commented on how much she had changed from a lot of initial anger and lack of trust in the group to allowing herself to make contact with the other women and the facilitators and how her sensitivity to others and respect for their paths had really given women courage and new hope.

T: "Carol, I know you are saying that you feel helpless and lost and not very good about yourself. But I wonder if you also can remember the wonderful things you offered the women in our group? Can you name what the women said they appreciated about you in our last session?"

C: "No, I cannot remember anything they said."

T: "What about what Marie said?"

C: "Yes, I do remember what she said—because I was so surprised. She said that I was a good listener and that she thought I had courage."

T: "What is it like to now be in touch with what she said? Can you appreciate that you have courage that helped someone else in the group."

C: "Yes, I feel a little less jittery inside when I think of that."

T: "So let's build on that inner strength together Carol, as you begin today. Do you believe that you have resources you can call on as you do your own work—both here in my office and outside, in your own life?

C: "Well, I am beginning to see that could be true, but I am not sure; it is a new feeling for me."

Carol was beginning to see that she actually had resources she could call on for her own work. We immediately cemented our contact on her positive potential as a full human being, not around viewing her as a victim. I emphasized that I saw her as someone with a lot of resources and inner strength, fully capable of discovering more about her positive life energy, and that I was confident she could become the woman she wanted to be. Carol would later say how instrumental that was in her healing, because it was the first time she was given a message that she had potential, rather than the assumption she was permanently crippled by her past.

Our initial goals were to help Carol accept her feelings at this point in time, to find ways to nurture herself so she could feel some comfort and self-care (such as "journaling," hot baths, delight in her new baby) and to begin to value herself more and appreciate her courage and positive life spirit. We explored Carol's family-of-origin experience to understand the family dynamics and relationships and how they had helped to shape Carol's early ways of making meaning of life.

Carol's Family-of-Origin

Carol's family had a mask of niceness and happy relationships but inside it represented a group of isolates, all floating on their own, and not getting their yearnings met. The father was a blamer, absent, unpredictable, and a super-controller. He was an alcoholic, emotionally abusive to his wife, and sexually abusive to his daughters. The mother, a placater-blamer, tried to be everything for everyone and pretended that everything was fine. She lived in a cocoon and turned to Carol for support and protection, so that they were enmeshed. She either placated her husband or was passive-aggressive, so that her anger leaked out in spurts to the children. Carol was the middle of three children with a brother who was two years older, adopted at age three months, and a six-year-younger sister. Carol felt all alone with her pain, with no one to turn to; her siblings appeared to be allied and her mother was unable to hear the truth about Carol's feelings or yearnings. Carol experienced her brother as rejecting, angry, and absent; he dealt with his pain by being irrelevant and to this day does not feel he belongs. Although Carol was somewhat close to her sister, neither could express their real feelings; her sister tended to act out her hurt and rebel against her parents; Carol internalized pain and was the "good girl."

Carol grew up believing that she needed to please others at all costs. She was energetic, compliant, and mischievous, but also fearful, shy, and insecure. She tried to make everyone happy within a chaotic family ruled by a controlling father—alcoholic, outwardly successful and hardworking—and a placating mother who tried to keep everyone believing everything was fine and that they had a "nice" family. Carol experienced sexual abuse from her father beginning at the age of nine; her father also sexually mistreated her sister also. Carol felt the outsider in the family, fearful of her parents' fighting, afraid they would divorce, and uncomfortable with how much her mother turned to her for support. Carol believed that her siblings had a close bond which excluded her; she sensed secrets between them which they did not want to discuss with her.

Carol was the "good girl" who easily internalized blame from her father through his sexual abuse episodes with her and her sister. In fact, Carol assumed blame for all of the family tensions; she was sensitive to the undercurrents between family members, and believed they were all attributable to her failures. Carol was enmeshed with her mother and aware of her mother's sadness with her father. Carol carried the mother's sadness as well as her own. She had enormously high self-expectations to make everyone else happy, and very little sense of self. She felt a lot of shame and assumed she was damaged because of her father's sexual abuse. Carol maintained good grades in school but felt like an outsider and did not have many friends.

As we explored Carol's perceptual past, that is, how she perceived her family from the viewpoint of her childhood, Carol began to be able to see herself more clearly:

T: "What were your parents' expectations of you, Carol?"

C: "My father expected that I would do as I was told and that I should never say anything about how he was with me. My mother wanted to keep peace in our family, so she avoided anything confrontational and wanted me to keep quiet. She liked things to look calm."

T: "So, in your family, was it that 'daddy knows best'?"

C: "Yes, that is it! I never realized that before, but we all knew not to cross Dad and we saw that Mom wanted us to keep him happy."

T: "What goes on for you inside as you say this now?"

C: "I realize that maybe I did not have much choice; I had to keep quiet, because otherwise Dad would be angry and Mom would be sad. She wanted us to be polite with each other . . .."

T: "What else are you discovering?"

C: "That maybe it was not my fault—the abuse and all—I really did not have a lot of choice."

T: "So maybe as a child you did not have a choice, but now as an adult you have lots of choices?"

C: "Yes, now I can't change what happened then, but I no longer want to have this anger, because it is as if he still wins."

T: "What do you mean?"

C: "By keeping all this anger toward my Dad, and now I am beginning to feel it toward my Mom too, he still wins! He has a hold on me!"

The therapist took Carol through each level of her internal experience as a child—through her Iceberg. Carol was able to process the impact of her abuse through her experience of individual relationships with each family member. This allowed her to understand how she was carrying the impact from her past into her present life. It helped her free up more energy to use to let go of the impact of the earlier abuse and experience more inner freedom. As we moved along in our work, our therapeutic goals emerged; they detailed more specifically how Carol wanted to do the work "to become a happier (less depressed) person."

Therapeutic Goals

In terms of the Satir model, we worked on the following therapeutic goals:

1. To shift Carol's self perceptions from someone who is a helpless victim to someone with inner worth and internal resources;
2. To help Carol rewrite family rules that she internalized which kept her relating like a "good girl" and transform them into guidelines for consideration, along with other information and perceptions she formed into her adult belief system;
3. To discover and build a whole new sense of self, moving from defining herself through shame and other feelings, to discovering her many parts, and developing a solid inner core and identity that represented new wisdom (or intuition) to guide all of her parts;
4. To integrate her neglected abandoned child into her adult identity so that she could self nurture herself and fully live in the present;
5. To learn how to set boundaries so that she is in charge of how she experiences relationships;
6. To separate more from her mother, (become de-enmeshed), and no longer take on the responsibility to keep her happy; and
7. To achieve a new sense of self, as a person of worth and dignity.

Therapeutic Interventions

To help Carol see that she was an emerging being, not permanently crazy and set in one way, I taught her the iceberg right away. She was shocked to realize that she had many levels of experience and that her yearnings to feel loved for herself and not for the actions she performed were not weird and that there could be a sense of self or soul at her very core. We focused our work to help Carol discover, build, and experience, her own special positive sense of self. This became a new underpinning to her experience.

One of our first tasks was to focus on the rules by which Carol was living. Some examples:

C: "To do everything in my power to make others happy."

T: "How did that work?"

C: "When I could tell that Dad was angry or upset, I immediately assumed it was because of me and I tried to find ways to make him happy. So I would clean up the house, agree with everything he said , etc."

T: "So this was the 'Father Knows Best' rule?"

C: "Yes."

T: "What were some others?"

C: "To take care of Mom."

T: "How did that work?"

C: "I could tell if she was sad, so I tried to be funny, because I knew she needed a lift and I felt it was my job to make her happy."

T: "Do you still live by those rules?"

C: "I never thought about it that way, but yes—I guess I do! I think it is my fault if my husband is upset and try to do more housework if he seems uneasy, because I generally think it is something I did that causes him to be frustrated."

T: "What is going on for you inside right now?"

C: "I have a pit in my stomach; I feel nauseous."

T: "What is going on?"

C: " I think that is silly for me to blame myself for his every feeling and I am revolted."

T: "Can you see that as an adult, you have choices of how you want to live? That you can actually take another look at these rules and decide for yourself how you want to live now?"

C: "I never thought of it that way—amazing!"

T: "What is it like to realize that you have that choice now?"

C: " I would love to do more of this; this really lifts pressure off of my shoulders. I feel lighter—to think I have that choice!"

We continued to examine the rules Carol had internalized from her family of origin and which still dictated her every move. We spent time going through all of the rules she seemed to live by, traced their origins, how she needed to live that way in order to survive in her first family system, but that many of these rules no longer fit Carol in her adult life. Carol "journalled," reflected, and learned to neutralize the power of the rules so that she could establish her own purposes to live by.

We then did a small version of the Parts Party which helped Carol to identify and de-enmesh some of her negative parts, such as feelings of shame, lack of worth, fear, and criticism. She realized each part had a life of its own and how each part could be transformed and reorganized in her internal world. She saw the positive functions for each of these parts and became much less reactive.

We can summarize some of her work in her own words: "I never realized that I had different components within me. I learned that every behavior is based on the interplay of the parts. I used to think that all of me was the 'gross stuff' and I therefore owed it to the world to make sure everyone knew all the ugly parts of me if I deserved their friendship. I now realize that I do not owe people anything; that it was not all that I am and that I can choose if I share any detail of my life with someone, from a positive core, not from blame or shame."

Besides working on Carol's internal experiences, we also examined how she interpreted the world and others. Carol learned to stop assuming that everyone she met judged her and that a difference meant she had failed; she stopped taking on others' pain (as she had learned so well from her mother) and stood up to her mother about her options and her differences from her mother. Carol and her mother gained some space between them, as well as new honesty in their communications.

Similarly, Carol learned to objectify and analyze origins of conflict that she experiences in life and groups instead of trying to remove it or take the blame. She has become clearer and more assertive at work, with her husband, with family members, and in new ventures she now takes on. For instance, she was recently the only member of her apartment complex management council who challenged a man who was making hurtful remarks to one of the nursing mothers. She was able to stand up to this overbearing man from an inner strength and conviction which helped him to set boundaries and the group thanked her for it.

Carol has become very clear about her own boundaries, and ability to set them, as she establishes her own inner strength.

C: "No one can decide for me how it needs to be with my father"

T: "What difference does that belief make, then, for how you are with him?"

C: "It gives me a freedom to make my own decisions about the kinds of contact I want our daughter to have with him."

T: "How is it for you to make those decisions for yourself? Is this familiar?"

C: (laughingly) "No, it certainly is not familiar! It feels brand new."

T: "What is it like to have this new experience?"

C: "It feels scary."

T: "What else?"

C: " It feels exciting."

T: "So which is bigger for you, Carol, the fear or the excitement?"

C: (smiling) "The excitement, because I can feel inside of me that I really do have the right to make these decisions for myself. It is just new to actually do it!"

T: "Can you appreciate, then, Carol, the shifts you are able to make within yourself? The new Carol is now telling me that she knows she has the right to make her own life choices!"

We see, therefore, that Carol was moving through the first stages of change; she was processing the integration of her new resources and moving into the phase of practicing her new abilities. As Carol continued to build a stronger sense of self and belief in her own abilities, she also became become less judgmental of others, allowing them to have their viewpoints, and not needing everyone to agree with her. This carried over into new relationships and boundaries that she set with her siblings.

C: "When I visited my brother, and he began to criticize my parenting decisions about how to manage our daughter, I told him that I loved him and respected his right to make his own decisions about his family, and that I also expected him to respect who I was and my decisions…it really shocked him to see me stand up for myself with him!"

T: "What was it like to be different with your brother?"

C: (smiling) "It felt great, because I spoke up without having to be angry to get my point across and he seemed surprised, but ever since then he has also seemed to have a new regard for me. I think I helped him to realize how quickly he could make judgments and my stopping that, actually seemed to help him become more accepting . . . we had a great time for the rest of our visit."

Carol has told me that there were various interventions or ways of working which I used that really enabled her to risk and grow: that I have a calm, kind voice; that I am respectful of her no matter what; that I am always in her corner, and she especially liked my pacing. She said that I did not rush her, but helped her complete one portion of work before moving on and I seemed to sense when she was ready to move deeper. She felt she went right through the stages of change, from very strong resistance (which was how she began our women's group), to utter chaos and feeling very scattered and lost; to discovering some new beginnings which she faithfully practiced, made her own, and has now integrated into a new sense of wholeness.

As stated elsewhere, the fact that I did not force Carol to believe she had to confront her father over the sexual abuse, lay charges, or sever all contact, allowed her to find out what was the best approach according to her own inner wisdom. This belief in Carol's inner wisdom was key to her building new inner strength. Carol became able to see herself as a lovable, worthy person apart from her experiences and she was relieved to no longer define herself through her abuse. Carol became able to experience and release the intense anger toward her father, her mother, and her childhood family experiences. She transformed the anger's negative energy into wishing that she had not had to experience the abuse, but accepting that this was a piece of her past. She tapped new energy to set her own clear boundaries as an adult. As Carol became a more whole person, she was able to think of her parents and what their icebergs may have been like. This allowed her anger, hurt, and fear with them to be transformed into new compassion for both her parents and what might have been their internal experiences underneath their parenting behaviors. Carol was then able to find some inner peace and she was relieved to establish ways to keep contact that honored her desire to feel connected, but within her own comfort zone.

Results

I wish I had a physical picture of the Carol I first met and the Carol I know now; she has come into her own so beautifully! She has shed the long hair which hid her and now keeps it cropped close to her face to accentuate her features, not hide them. She makes direct eye contact, she is relaxed and not wooden; and she has let out this lovely gentleness, wonderful playfulness, and great humor and wit which were previously buried. To Carol, the biggest change is that she sees herself as a well person, not a victim. She recognizes that she is not always congruent, but she can spot her overreactions or questions, reflects, and understands them by using the iceberg, makes sense of them from it, and makes shifts.

The following are some of Carol's observations that she has written to describe where she sees herself now:

- When I learned that I really could be the person of my own choosing I started to feel free.
- I had set up a tangle of rules that no one could have lived by, but I was totally unaware of this.
- I have come to firmly believe that I don't have to remain a victim for the rest of my life.
- I am a survivor, a champion of my own decisions and choices. I rely on my own inner voice and myself.
- There are many external things, people, feelings, situations that

may sway me from time to time, but the bottom line is that I am my own keeper.

- Even though the past is non-negotiable, my interpretation is all my own.
- Through my time with Anne I have learned so many things about myself, about choices I didn't even know I had made.
- I learned that the facts I thought were unchangeable simply were waiting for me to change.
- I learned that my behavior is always a direct result of what is happening under the surface for me.
- Through the use of the iceberg I have been able to see (visually) the path emotions and behaviors and yearnings take in my life.
- I have such a better understanding of me. I learned my old rules did not work, and they could be changed. Who would have guessed? It is so exciting to know that my rules are my choosing alone! If they don't work, I rework them; if they do, I keep them.

Conclusion

The Satir model, as developed and refined by John Banmen and currently illustrated in the work of John Banmen and Kathlyne Maki-Banmen and practiced by many members of the Satir therapeutic community, offers a range of treatment tools and techniques which therapists can access to support their client's growth and self renewal. The Satir model is particularly powerful for female adult clients who have experienced sexual abuse, as it enables the therapist and client to work at the level of self, or the core of their being. The client can therefore be freed from the inner conflict without having to re-experience the trauma of the original abuse through techniques which require that the client emotionally re-process the earlier pain. Through the Satir model, the client accomplishes a renewed sense of self and inner congruence which reflects inner freedom and a new quality of life.

REFERENCES

Badgley, R. (1984). *Sexual offences against children and youth in Canada.* Ottawa: Supply and Services Canada.

Berg, I. (1990). *Solution-focused approach to family based services.* Milwaukee, WI: Brief Family Therapy Center.

Brown, L. S. & Ballou, M. B. (Eds.). (1992). *Personality and psychopathology.* New York: Guilford Press.

Briere, J. (1989). *Therapy for adults molested as children: Beyond survival.* New York: Springer.

Briere, J. (1992). *Child abuse trauma.* Newbury Park, CA: Sage Publications.

Briere, J., & Runtz, M. (1989). Symptomology associated with childhood sexual victimization in a non-clinical adult sample. *Child Abuse and Neglect, 12,* 51–59.

Canadian Center for Justice Statistics (1996). *Juristat, 17* (11). Ottawa: Statistics Canada.

Cantor, D. W. (Ed.). (1990). *Women as therapists: A multitheoretical casebook.* New York: Appleton-Century-Crofts.

Courtois, C. (1988). *Healing the incest wound.* New York: Norton.

Courtois, C. & Leehan, J. (1982). Group treatment for grown up abused children. *Personnel and Guidance Journal, 60,* 275–279.

de Shazer, S. (1982). *Patterns of brief family therapy.* New York: Guilford Press.

de Shazer, S. (1984). The death of resistance. *Family Process, 23* (1), 11–17.

de Shazer, S. (1985). *Keys to solution in brief therapy.* New York: Norton.

de Shazer, S., Berg, I., Lipchik, E., Nunnally, E., Molnar, A., Gingerich, W., & Weiner-Davis, M. (1986). Brief therapy: Focused solution development. *Family Process, 25,* 207–22.

Dolan, Y. (1989). Only once if I really mean it: Brief treatment of a previously dissociated incest case. *Journal of Strategic and Systemic Therapies, 8,* (4), 3–8.

Dolan, Y. (1991). *Resolving sexual abuse.* New York: Norton.

Drews, J., & Bradley, R. (1989). Group treatment for adults abused as children: An educational and therapeutic approach. *Social Work With Groups, 12* (3), 57–75.

Dutton-Douglas, M. A., & Walker, L. E. A. (Eds.) (1988). *Feminist psychotherapies: An integration of therapeutic and family systems.* Norwood, NJ: Ablex.

Finklehor, D., Hotaling, G., Lewis, I. A., & Smith, C. (1990). Sexual abuse and its relationship to later sexual satisfaction, marital status, religion, and attitudes. *Journal of Interpersonal Violence, 4* (4), 379–99.

Fowler, C. Burns, S. R. & Ruehl, J. E. (1983). The role of group therapy in incest counseling. *International Journal of Family Therapy, 5* (2), 127–35.

Freeman-Longo, R. E., & Blanchard, G. (1997). *Sexual abuse in America: Epidemic of the 21st century.* Brandon, VT: Safer Society Press.

Kirschner, S., Kirschner, D., & Rappaport, R. (1993). *Working with adult incest survivors. The healing journey.* New York: Brunner/Mazel.

Lipchik, E. (1988). Purposeful sequences for beginning the solution focused interview. InE. Lipchik (Ed.), *Interviewing* (pp. 105–117). Rockville, MD: Aspen.

Lipchik, E. & de Shazer, S. (1986). The purposeful interview. *Journal of Strategic andSystemic Therapies*, *5* (1–2), 88–89.

Maki-Banmen, K. (1999).

O'Hanlon, W. H., & Weiner-Davis, M. (1989). In search of solutions. New York: Norton.

Satir, V., Banmen, J., Gerber, J., & Gomori, M. (1991). *The Satir model: Family therapy and beyond.* Palo Alto, CA: Science and Behavior Books.

Sgroi, S. M. (Ed.) (1982). *Handbook of clinical intervention in child sexual abuse.* Lexington, MA: Lexington Books.

Walker, L. E. A. (Ed.). (1988). *Handbook on sexual abuse of children.* New York: Springer.

Walker, L. E. A. (1995). *Abused women and survivor therapy.* Washington, DC: American Psychological Association.

Webb, L. P., & Leehan, J. (1996). *Group treatment for adult survivors of abuse.* Thousand Oaks, CA: Sage Publications.

11

The Use Of Self of the Therapist

Wendy Lum

The development of the self of the therapist is a significant aspect of becoming an effective therapist. The use of self has been recognized by various therapists as being the single most important factor in developing a therapeutic relationship (Andolfi, Ellenwood, & Wendt, 1993; Baldwin, 2000). Virginia Satir was a strong advocate for the self of the therapist and spent much time focusing on this aspect during her therapy training programs. It is important that therapists resolve unfinished family of origin issues in order to heal and to prepare themselves to be therapeutically congruent. Just as clients carry negative impacts from the past, therapists also carry their own negative impacts from past events. Therapists who are emotionally healthy are more likely to have worked through their own personal issues. If therapists have not resolved these issues, there is a strong possibility that they will have a variety of reactions to clients' problems, for example; getting stuck, avoiding the issue, skewing the information, or losing focus. The use of self allows therapists to be fully present for their clients.

The Satir Model (Satir, Banmen, Gomori, & Gerber, 1991) was written to integrate Satir's vision, philosophy, therapeutic beliefs, goals for therapy, tools, and techniques into an inclusive therapeutic method. This model has been used to train therapists in powerful therapeutic skills, as well as to explore how to use the self in therapy. To clarify for the purpose of this article, the Satir model does not view self-disclosure as use of self to clients. A therapist's self-disclosure to clients most often takes away from a client's inner exploration.

Satir in some exceptions, would share her self mainly for a teaching purpose. As an example she once stated, "Now when my mother used to tell me I was mouthy, let me tell you what I thought she meant. She meant I was disagreeing with her" (Satir, 1983). In Satir therapy, the sharing of self is encouraged only to capture a teaching moment, and is not used for the creation of connection or to strengthen empathy. The use of self encompasses much more than sharing a common experience of self with clients. A different use of self is enhanced by being in touch with, being aware of, and monitoring self. By heightening their own awareness, therapists will be better able to prepare and center themselves before sessions. This practice enables therapists to be emotionally available to connect deeply with their clients' inner worlds.

The Satir model encourages that therapists and clients become fully human and congruent. It is not possible to be congruent at all times, yet it is important that therapists strive to be congruent at all times within their therapy sessions. Therapists will not become congruent if they neglect to work through their own personal issues because of discomfort, avoidance, resistance, or denial. Satir believed that if therapists were congruent, there would be no need for transference or counter transference, rather that therapists would model the possibility of how to stay more connected with themselves. Therefore she strongly supported the development of congruence in all therapists, so they could relate with clients without using projections. When therapists are congruent, they are fully present, whole, centered, and in a state of peaceful harmony.

The Satir model promotes a heightened awareness for therapists and clients alike. Awareness in this model means being aware of one's inner process, accepting of what is, knowing one's self, and looking at possibilities (Banmen, 1997). Therapists need to be able to observe oneself and to be able to reflect upon oneself in order to develop awareness. The increased awareness of therapists will benefit clients' exploration and the therapeutic processing of issues. The Satir model gives therapists the ability to address both intrapsychic experiences and interactive systems. The use of the self of the therapist facilitates the therapeutic process to be growth oriented, creative and respectful. Clearly the use of self of the therapist is very pertinent to the development of the therapeutic profession.

The Satir Model's Four Goals of Therapy

The Satir model (Banmen, 1997) promotes four goals of therapy: to increase self-esteem, to foster better choice making, to increase responsibility, and to develop congruence. These four goals are not only applicable to clients, but are important for the development of the self of the therapist.

Increase Self-Esteem

Satir recognized self-esteem as the foundation to creating a connection within one's own deepest self. Self-esteem is important in order to have a sense of self-confidence and empowerment. The self-esteem of therapists, also has an impact on how these therapists interact with their clients. "How do I feel about who I am?" "What do I think about my own worthiness?" "What would help me feel better about my own competence?" If therapists feel good about themselves, then they are more likely to trust their own intuition and therapeutic process interventions. When therapists have high self-esteem, there will more ability and flexibility for making better choices. Both clients and therapists have unresolved issues from their family of origin which have an impact on their level of self-esteem. Therapists' professional esteem could suffer if they are not able to be accepting or understanding of their clients' responses and growth. Therapists using the Satir model are encouraged to increase their self-esteem by being gentle and kind to themselves, not judging themselves, accepting who they are, and acknowledging their intuition and abilities. As therapists increase their self esteem, they are more likely to believe in their own therapeutic capabilities.

Self-Care of the Therapist. One of the popular vehicles of the Satir model is the self mandala metaphor which describes the wholeness of a person. The eight areas of the self mandala (see Figure 11.1) include: physical, sensual, nutritional, intellectual, emotional, interactional, contextual and spiritual areas (Satir et al., 1991).

Self-care is necessary in all eight areas in order to promote a sense of wholeness and balance. The Satir model recognizes the eight areas of the self mandala as significant for creating and maintaining harmony within self and with others. Therapists could ask, "How am I maintaining balance in my personal and professional life?" "How can I take better care of myself?" "How have I been ignoring my spiritual life?" "When I only focus on a few areas in my life, what is happening in the other areas that I have overlooked?" Since Satir's death in 1998, the self mandala has continued to be an important tool for self-care and for creating and maintaining inner harmony.

Table 11.1

Self Mandala

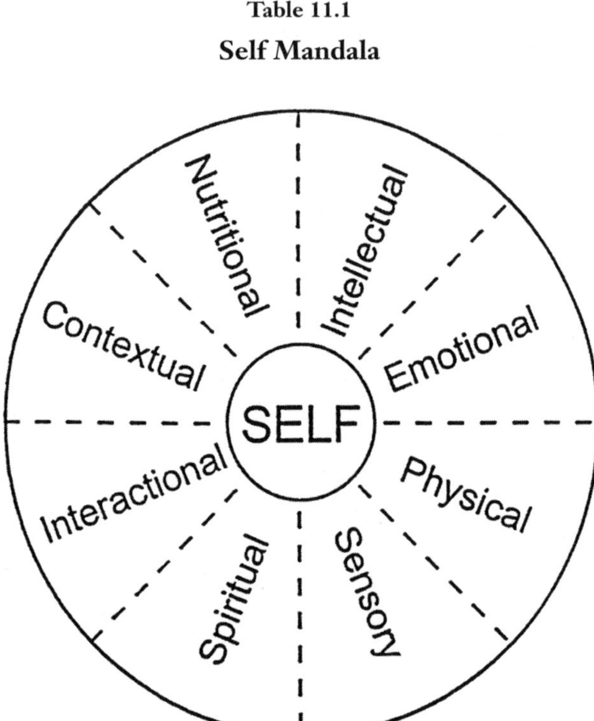

If therapists are to promote the health and wellness of their clients, then they must also be actively pursuing health and wellness within their own lives. "Compassion fatigue" can drain therapists' energy, and foster discouragement, irritability, and depression (Pieper, 1999). Many therapists strive to care for others, and sometimes they may neglect attending to their own personal needs. Therapists cope with stress and burnout in different ways.

Therapists who become overly responsible and pleasing are most likely to experience burnout (Fish, 2000). Fish notes and supports Satir's view that therapists at risk for burnout are too emotionally involved with their clients. Fish found that in their personal and professional lives, burned out therapists were expending energy, yet neglecting to replenish their own energy. It is important that therapists take the time to center themselves, become aware of themselves, and to set clear boundaries between themselves and their clients. As therapists take better care of themselves, they are more able to remain resilient in spite of professional stressors. "I'm exhausted after seeing so many clients today who were in pain, so I'm going to stroll by the ocean in order to clear my mind." Satir recognized that as therapists accepted and acknowledged their feelings, then life energy would be able to flow more readily, which means they would be more able to connect with self (Satir & Banmen, 1983). Satir model therapists today are encouraged to practice self-care, so that they can be more deeply connected, effective, and present with their clients.

Strengths and Resources of the Therapist. Satir focused on strengthening clients' resources as an important aspect of therapy. Just as clients are not always aware of their strengths and resources, therapists are not always aware of their own strengths and resources. "What strengths and resources have I gained from my own family of origin?" As therapists are better able to gain access to their own strengths and resources, their sense of self-esteem will grow. They will have a greater access to their own innate qualities that can support healthy therapeutic relationships. "How can I focus on my client's strengths and not on their regrets?" Satir model therapists are encouraged to accept, acknowledge, "own", and access their strengths and resources (Lum, 2000).

Foster Better Choice-making. Satir believed in the possibility that there are three choices in any given situation. It is important to move a client away from an either or choice, and toward open exploration of at least three choices. Satir model therapists are challenged to become aware of choice points for intervention that arise throughout their therapy sessions. "What choices do I have in this moment that will move my clients in a more positive direction?" Congruent therapists and clients are freer to make choices from an empowered state. "I trust my intuition and I'm going to point out the discrepancy between what he says he does and what he actually seems to do." Satir model therapists are encouraged to make choices to become more congruent in their personal and professional lives, and to facilitate choices amongst their clients (Lum, 2000).

Awareness of the Therapist. Satir believed that therapists could effectively increase awareness in their clients through using process questions. Initiating and guiding effective therapy is an intentional and consciousness raising process. Therapists share observations in order to heighten their client's awareness of themselves within their situation.

"I noticed that when you smiled, you were shaking your head as if to disagree." When therapists have access to self awareness, they gain information which can contribute to the development of congruence (Lum, 2000). "I wonder what could be happening inside me right now? I noticed that I became very tight in my stomach as he cried." The Satir model promotes the internal monitoring of therapists' inner worlds, which can increase access to crucial therapeutic information and experiences (Lum, 2000).

Therapists who are not able to track clients' process interactions, are more likely to become bored, and confused, and to feel inadequate and detached (Pieper, 1999). "I am uncomfortable, but I have to hide it from my client." It is important that therapists be able to monitor and observe their own internal processes, intuit what might be happening within their client's internal processes, as well as to observe the interactions between family members. To reflect upon our own impact on processes and to engage in ongoing self assessment will facilitate self growth and increased consciousness. The development of awareness and intentionality enables Satir model therapists to both closely follow and guide their clients (Lum, 2000).

Satir encouraged therapists to be able to access these senses and suggested that freedom to feel, see, speak, smell, and taste is vital for the health of all people. Satir model therapists are encouraged to increase their conscious awareness in order to enhance and heighten their clients' experiential auditory, visual, sensory, kinesthetic, and olfactory senses. Satir model therapists are also encouraged to become aware of their inner world in relationship to the therapy process and to individual and family systems. The development of observation skills is a fundamental aspect of training to become an effective therapist. The ability to observe oneself will enable therapists to develop more effective strategies and interventions. Therapists will better refine their processing skills by becoming aware of what is said and how things are stated. Satir believed that people make decisions based on both the conscious and unconscious worlds, and she encouraged therapists to hear with their "inner ear" and to see with their "inner eye" (Reik, 1948; Satir & Banmen, 1983). Satir model therapists are strongly supported to develop their own inner attention and intuition (Lum, 2000).

Satir encouraged connection to the self through promoting deep breathing within meditative experiences (Banmen & Banmen, 1991). The ability for self reflection allows therapists to heighten the awareness of our unconscious world and bring it into consciousness. "What am I responding to?" "How is my breathing right now?" "I wonder why I'm feeling so blocked inside?" Satir model training facilitates the development of experiential moments for therapists to develop inner awareness and reflective moments (Lum, 2000). Awareness is the key to moving people from an incongruent state to the state of congruence (Lum, 2000; Satir & Baldwin, 1983).

The Therapists' Perceptions of the World. Satir explored four areas of perceiving the world: how we define a relationship, a person, an event, and attitudes toward change (Satir et. al., 1991). There are significant differences in perception between a negatively focused hierarchical model and the positively focused directional growth of the Satir model. How therapists view clients will affect how therapeutic relationships will develop. When therapists view clients as victims, this will disempower and discourage clients from accessing their own inner resources to deal with their situation. "How am I responding to my client as I listen to their beliefs?" "What were my family rules that have presently affected me in a negative way?" "Her issues seem so close to my own personal struggles, I wonder if this will get in the way of my effectiveness as her therapist?" The Satir model encourages therapists to become aware of, and to acknowledge, and change any beliefs that are negatively affecting their ability to congruently process their clients.

Increase Responsibility. Responsibility is another goal of the Satir model therapy. Satir encouraged therapists to take responsibility to work through their unresolved issues, and she used family reconstruction to support therapists' personal healing of family of origin blockages. Therapists have a responsibility to respond to their clients compassionately, nonjudgmentally and transparently. To truly hear what is behind the words and interactions of clients will take therapeutic artistry on the part of the therapist. Therapists will be more effective if they have the ability to respond to both the context and the process of therapy. It is the therapist's responsibility to decipher and to maintain clarity on which issues are triggered by the therapeutic process, and which are the client's personal issues (Satir & Baldwin, 1983). Clients can be very sensitive to the therapeutic relationship and may sense if there are any biases, resistance, discomfort, unresponsiveness, or disrespect coming from therapists. Thus it is necessary for therapists to become aware of their own internal processes and not to allow judgment or reaction to affect their ability to be fully present with the client. Satir also believed that in order to help external family systems to become more whole, therapists must first heal and become whole within their own internal systems (Satir & Baldwin, 1983). “If I’m still reacting, I wonder if there is something that I haven’t yet healed?” Satir model therapists are encouraged to resolve hurts from their family of origin which may still be having a negative impact on their present life.

Baldwin (2000) also acknowledged the use of power in the therapeutic relationship, and therapists with limited awareness could misuse their power in non therapeutic ways. As a part of being responsible, therapists and the therapeutic profession must strive to earn and to maintain credibility and accountability within the general public. Therapists can provide a crucial service to help people heal injustices, and deal with vulnerabilities, hurt, and pain. Due to the sensitive nature of clients’ problems, it is necessary that therapists act responsibly. It would be irresponsible for therapists to blame their clients for any negativity that occurs in the therapeutic relationship. “I wonder if there is something that I’ve missed?” Therapists may cause damage if they are unwilling to acknowledge how they conduct their use of self (Satir & Baldwin, 1983).

It is important that therapists behave and interact responsibly to ensure acceptable practice and in order not to be challenged in criminal or civil court. Legal proceedings can be initiated to gain answers to questionable therapeutic practice. Competent therapists must strive to adhere to the policies , regulations, and ethics within their professional association in order to maintain responsible standards of practice. Satir model therapists are encouraged to take full responsibility for themselves and to respond congruently with their clients.

Training the Self of the Therapist. Satir was passionate about training therapists to improve their competencies, as she focused on the use of self of the therapist. Yet many instructors, supervisors, and students still do not have the opportunity to explore their own self as therapists (Kramer, 2000). Many training programs have not focused on development of the self of the therapist, and this is an area that gets neglected (Baldwin, 2000). Kramer (2000) suggested that the secrecy that surrounds the discussion of self of the therapist has contributed to the inadequate preparation of future therapists. It is considered very important in the Satir model that training programs expand and develop the training of the self of the therapist.

When training programs neglect to process the self of the therapist, there becomes an implied message which minimizes and gives subtle permission for therapist trainees to ignore the healing of their own unresolved issues (Shadley, 2000). “I’m not going to risk my vulnerabilities, they might judge me to be in the wrong profession." "I have to look competent, otherwise no one would refer clients to me for therapy." "Keep control, it's safer that way" "I don't need any therapy because I've already done my work." Therapist training that integrates skill development and personal competency is needed (Baldwin, 2000). Satir model therapist trainees are given many opportunities to develop the use of their selves. These trainees also greatly benefit from experiencing the therapy process as an actual client, which gives them an inside understanding to the therapeutic process through the Satir model (Lum, 2000).

Competence of the Therapist. Satir put her energy into increasing the competence of therapists throughout her month long residential training programs. It is important that therapists develop competence in order to initiate communication processes, and to be able to deal with ambiguous messages within the family system (Satir & Baldwin, 1983). The Satir model emphasizes that congruence would be the necessary condition for the competency of therapists to emerge and develop. Competency does not mean being an "expert" on the individual, couple, or family. "How can I ensure my competence as I develop and integrate the Satir model?" Therapists who maintain their congruence are more able to be competent in their therapeutic practices (Fish, 2000; Lum, 2000).

Competence is supported in the therapeutic profession through the expectation that therapists engage in continuing educational and professional development. Various organizations (American Association for Marriage and Family Therapy, Canadian Counselors Association, International Family Therapy Association, and others) encourage ongoing professional development and facilitate conferences to educate their members. Satir encouraged therapists to develop their sense of competency through practice and learning. Many family therapy institutes and associations share concepts and methods in which one can grow as a therapist. Satir had stressed that the person of the therapist is more crucial than mainly focusing on the skill development of a therapeutic technician (Baldwin, 2000; Kramer, 2000). Satir model therapy training effectively facilitates the integration of competence and use of self (Lum, 2000).

Ethics of the Therapist. There are many diverse issues that arise in the therapeutic relationship and many peoples' lives have become complicated, complex, and challenging. There is a crucial need for therapists to conduct themselves with integrity and ethically, especially considering the many aspects of various situations for clients. Fish (2000) suggested that it is important that therapists be congruent in order to be better prepared to deal with ethical issues. If the therapist is clear on what an ethical relationship in therapy is, then he or she will be better equipped to handle intricate situations. There are many dilemmas that have arisen that need an ethical response from therapists such as gender, violence in relationships, custody, sexual abuse, and cultural issues. The complexity of family dynamics now includes separation, divorce and remarriage issues, stepfamilies of varying combinations, grandparents rearing grandchildren, and other issues.

The therapeutic profession must strive to create the foundation and education that will develop, guide, and maintain a standard of ethics. Therapists are in a sensitive relationship that is based on trust. Professional organizations have standards in place in order to protect this trust. Therapists must only provide services that they are trained for and not try to exceed their level of skill. "I'm going to refer you to a therapist who specializes in trauma and ritual abuse." There are many unique situations that call for sensitive therapeutic decision making on the part of therapists. The ethical therapeutic relationship must have clear guidelines formed from a strong therapeutic foundation in order to adapt to these rapidly changing times. Satir model therapists are encouraged to become more reflective, and act responsibly and congruently so that they will be ethical in their therapy practice.

Supervision of the Self of the Therapist. Supervision of the therapist is crucial in maintaining responsibility, ongoing training, competencies, standards and ethics. Supervision using the Satir model has been recognized by the American Association for Marriage and Family Therapy. This model of supervision enables Satir model supervisors to therapeutically and experientially process their therapist supervisees' inner worlds through any personal responses, puzzles, or reactions that they may have with their own clients. "How can I support my supervisees to become more congruent?" The ability to process therapist supervisees calls for therapist supervisors to also have a heightened awareness and ability to self monitor, while at the same time supervising and processing their supervisees. It would be the responsibility of Satir model supervisors to strive for personal congruence, while at the same time effectively processing their supervisees' personal and therapeutic issues.

Develop Congruence. Satir strongly challenged her therapist trainees to attain congruence within their therapy practices. Congruence is one of the goals of the Satir model (Satir et. al., 1991). It is a key element toward supporting therapists to become effective in establishing healthy therapeutic relationships. The Satir model promotes congruence as an important aspect for people to be fully human and suggests that there are three levels of congruence. The first level of congruence is to accept feelings as they are. Feelings belong to us and we need to be in charge of them. Through acceptance, acknowledgment, and honoring, therapists can attain congruence. The second level of congruence is to be in harmony within oneself, with others, and with the world. The third level of congruence is to be in harmony with Self: I am, life energy, spirituality, and God.

Congruence is seen as a state of harmony, clarity, and honesty. Congruence would be the result of the therapist trusting oneself (Baldwin, 2000; Lum, 2000). "How much am I willing to trust my hunches?" When therapists are congruent, then they are more able be more grounded and stable as they help to support their client's change (Satir & Baldwin, 1983). Therapists who are congruent will allow their clients to fully explore their issues, without having to react negatively to their clients' responses. It is important that therapists are responsible, to ensure that they will be congruent and competent. "What am I not seeing in myself right now, because I am feeling so conflicted?" "How can I remain grounded even when my clients seem hostile towards each other?" The family system will be supported to heal and change when therapists are able to be clear and congruent. Satir believed that congruence enables therapists to be flexible in their interventions depending on changing family interactions. Monitoring any subtle changes in external modalities would help therapists to pick up any signs of incongruence in their clients (Satir & Baldwin, 1983). The development of congruence is not an easy process and can produce personal discomfort in therapists, which may need to be safely explored (Shadley, 2000).

The development of competence and congruence enables therapists to remain clear of any biases they might have in order not to negatively affect their clients' process (Satir & Baldwin, 1983). Congruence also helps therapists to maintain a sense of respect for the client regardless of the issues or one's personal biases. Satir model training facilitates the development of congruence for therapists, while in a supportive environment with other therapists (Lum, 2000).

Spiritual Self of the Therapist. Satir was aware of the cellular and cosmic aspects of growth in the process of life (Satir & Baldwin, 1983) and suggested that all humans have a life force that has an aspect of divinity and spirituality. She was effective at creating a connection with peoples' energy at the spiritual level (Satir & Banmen, 1983). Satir spoke of the presence of electricity when she worked with therapists and clients and saw life as energy (Satir & Baldwin, 1983). There is research that now confirms Satir's visionary understanding of life energy as contained within the cells of the body (Myss, 1996).

Satir recognized that combining one's intuition and groundedness would facilitate a sense of connectedness to others (Banmen & Banmen, 1991; Satir & Banmen, 1983). Satir saw therapy as a spiritual experience between herself and her client. Now the therapy world is acknowledging the interconnection of therapy and spirituality (Miller, 1999). "How can I honor the essence of my clients?" "How can I facilitate a sense of inner peace right now in this moment?" "What do I know about the sense of divine within my own life?" The therapist would connect his or her soul level with their client's soul level which would create the spiritual dimension (Baldwin, 2000). Satir model therapists are encouraged to explore their own connection to their spirituality in order to be able to process clients' spiritual exploration (Lum, 2000).

Satir's Systemic Brief Therapy Training Program

Training And Skill Developmen. One way to develop awareness, congruence, and competence in the therapist is Satir's systemic brief therapy training program which is sponsored by the Satir Institute of the Pacific and Avanta: The Virginia Satir Network. Banmen (1986) noticed that there was not enough time given to integrate the numerous concepts and tools which make up the Satir model and developed a systemic brief therapy training program as a result of his observations and experience with Satir's month long residential training programs for therapists. "Satir believed that close friend John Banmen . . . understood her therapeutic system more than she did" (King, 1989, p. 30). From the model, Banmen developed the training program, which is presently being taught to therapists by Banmen and Kathlyne Maki-Banmen throughout the world.

The Satir Institute of the Pacific sponsors Satir's systemic brief therapy training for therapists in Vancouver, British Columbia, Canada. The level one program is taught for five weekends over a five month period. The level two program is also taught for five weekends over a five month period. This format has enabled therapist trainees adequate time to practice and integrate the model (Lum, 2000). Avanta: The Virginia Satir Network sponsors a one week residential intensive program in Satir's systemic brief therapy, in either Canada or the United States of America for professional development. Therapists from Asia, Europe, and North and South America have participated in this program which is taught by Banmen and Maki-Banmen.

The Satir model has supported the development of congruence for therapists, as well as for their clients. Satir's systemic brief therapy training promotes therapists to actively and intentionally engage in developing their own awareness, congruence, and competence. Banmen (1986) had been aware that the development of skill was not sufficient to prepare a therapist to be therapeutically competent. Banmen stressed that therapists should not become technicians and only learn techniques. He recommended that therapists bring their personhood and congruence into the therapeutic experience. The integration of skill and self of the therapist is an outcome of Satir's systemic brief therapy training (Lum, 2000).

Satir created many concepts and tools that enable therapists to work with clients in a humanistic way. Some of her key concepts include: family of origin work, triad work, family reconstruction, self as a mandala, the parts party, and the stages of change. Family of origin work explores three family generations looking at the person and his or her experience of their parents (mother and father), siblings, and their maternal and paternal grandparents. Family reconstruction involves physically sculpting a person's family with stand-in volunteers from within the therapy training classes. This process can enable the person to positively change any negative perceptions or experiences from his or her family of origin. The parts party enables persons to explore, own, and transform different parts of themselves by externalizing positive and negative parts. Satir model training programs prepare the therapist through teaching Satir concepts, shared discussions, observations, dyad and triad practice, small and large group sharing of new awareness, learning, experiential processes, and skill development.

Triad Experience. Satir's systemic brief therapy training helps to support the development of intentional conscious choice making in therapists (Lum, 2000). There are many opportunities for therapists to engage in triad work, which includes having experience as a client, a therapist, and an observer/supervisor. Therapist trainees are asked to be willing to risk and expose their vulnerabilities within each triad position. When trainees are in the client position, they are asked to work on an actual personal issue as a client, and not to engage in role play. Therapist trainees have numerous therapy experiences, first-hand as clients for their own real life issues. This gives the trainees opportunity to heal any unresolved issue(s), which better prepares them to be congruent and competent. In the therapist position, the Satir trainees have the opportunity to explore their therapeutic skills and gain insights from themselves with the help from the observer process. In the observer/supervisor position, the trainees will increase their ability to observe and to encourage the congruence and competence of trainees in the therapist position.

Personal Iceberg Metaphor. The personal iceberg metaphor is a relatively a new development which helps to develop the self of the therapist. This metaphor includes behavior, coping stances, feelings, feelings about feelings, perceptions, expectations, yearnings and Self: I am. Internal awareness manifests itself through external behavior and coping (Satir & Banmen, 1983). Banmen (1997) has used the personal iceberg metaphor as a key concept in teaching the Satir Model to therapists in training. The personal iceberg metaphor represents the lived experience of a person's intrapsychic world. This metaphor is a specific tool that gives a framework for therapists to reflect, gain awareness, and effectively intervene therapeutically with their clients. Therapist trainees are also encouraged to reflect upon their own internal processes and to gain awareness of their own inner world.

The personal iceberg metaphor is helping to resolve therapists' unfinished business and assisting them to become more fully human. This metaphor has enabled therapists to gain access to an understanding of the interactive processes that Satir had engaged in through her interventions. In the past, therapists were in awe of Satir's ability to connect with and effect positively directional change with her clients. Some therapists also seemed to believe that only Satir was able to magically intervene with her clients. The personal iceberg metaphor now enables therapists to intervene in intuitive ways, and Satir's systemic brief therapy training program shows that the Satir model is not person specific. Numerous therapists from around the world are discovering that this metaphor facilitates deep change in effective and important ways. Banmen has taught the model in such a way that it is learnable, teachable, do-able for all therapists who are willing to take risks to explore their therapist self.

Lum (2000) conducted a phenomenological study for her master's thesis to look at nine therapists and their lived experience of the personal iceberg metaphor, after they had completed 150 hours of training in Satir's systemic brief therapy training. The Satir Institute of the Pacific was also interested to find out if those therapists had became more congruent and more fully human after involvement in their sponsored training program. Lum (2000) discovered that those therapists gained increased self awareness through reflection, access to inner knowing, clarity, and increased conscious choice making. These changes contributed to their development of the conscious use of self. As the nine therapists integrated the personal iceberg metaphor they developed their strengths and resources that in turn contributed to a sense of professional competency. As they acknowledged their competencies and increased understanding of the personal iceberg metaphor, the therapists noticed that they became more congruent within their personal and professional lives. Those therapists also became aware that as they made deep internal changes within themselves, their relationships with clients positively changed as well. The nine therapists found that as their own personal changes occurred, they became more able to facilitate deep internal changes within their clients. They also reported facilitating spiritual experiences with their clients, as well as personally experiencing a sense of spirituality and interconnectedness with others (Lum, 2000).

Conclusion

The updated Satir model has made therapy briefer by using the personal iceberg metaphor, and this has given the therapeutic community a valid method by which to develop the use of self for therapists (Lum, 2000). Satir's vision, wisdom, and deep understanding of human nature has fostered the movement toward the development of congruence and competence within the therapeutic profession. Therapists must continually work on maintaining self-care, increasing self-esteem, heightening awareness, and being aware of their perceptions of the world. It is imperative that therapists work on developing their congruence, competence, and responsibility. The current therapeutic trend demands that therapists maintain a sense of ethics within their profession. There is also a need for people to have therapists who will explore spirituality with their clients. The Satir Model provides an important and relevant development in the training of therapists to become more competent, congruent, ethical and spiritual.

References

Andolfi, M., Ellenwood, A. E., & Wendt, R. N. (1993). The creation of the fourth planet: Beginning therapist and supervisors inducing change in families. *The American Journal of Family Therapy, 21* (4), 301–12.

Baldwin, M. (Ed.) (2000). *The use of self in therapy. 2nd ed.* New York: Haworth Press.

Banmen, A. & Banmen, J. (Eds.). (1991). *Meditations of Virginia Satir: Peace within, peace between, peace among.* Palo Alto, CA: Science and Behavior Books.

Banmen, J. (1986). Virginia Satir's family therapy model. *Individual Psychology: Journal of Adlerian Theory, Research & Practice, 42* (2), 480–92.

Banmen, J. (1997). *Invitational training: Satir's systemic brief therapy.* Bellingham,WA: unpublished manuscript.

Fish, D. (2000). *Health care practitioner burnout and the psycho-spiritual Satir model: A phenomenological study of managing personal energy.* Unpublished masters thesis, Manchester Metropolitan University, Manchester, England.

King, L. (1989). *Women of power: 10 visionaries share their extraordinary stories of healing & secrets of success.* Berkeley, CA: Celestial Arts.

Kramer, C. (2000). Revealing our selves. In M. Baldwin (Ed.), *The use of self in therapy. 2nd ed.* (pp. 61–96). New York: Haworth Press.

Lum, W. (2000). *The lived experience of the personal iceberg metaphor of therapists in Satir's systemic brief therapy training.* Unpublished master's thesis, University of British Columbia, Vancouver.

Miller, W. R. (1999). Spirituality and health. In W. R. Miller (Ed.), (1999). *Integrating spirituality into treatment: Resources for practitioners;* Washington, DC: American Psychological Association.

Myss, C. E. (1996). *Anatomy of the spirit.* New York: Crown Publishers.

Pieper, M. H. (1999). The privilege of being a therapist: A fresh perspective from intrapsychic humanism on caregiving intimacy and the development of the professional self. *Families in Society: The Journal of Contemporary Human Services, 80* (5), 479–87.

Reik, T. (1948). *Listening with the third ear: The inner experience of a psychoanalyst.* New York: Farrar, Straus.

Satir, V. (1983). *Blended family with a troubled boy.* Kansas City, MO: Golden Triad Films.

Satir, V. & Banmen, J. (1983). *Virginia Satir verbatim 1984.* North Delta, BC: Delta Psychological Associates.

Satir, V. & Baldwin, M. (1983). *Satir step by step: A guide to creating change in families.* Palo Alto, CA: Science and Behavior Books.

Satir, V., Banmen, J., Gerber, J., & Gomori, M. (1991). *The Satir model: Family therapy and beyond.* Palo Alto, CA: Science & Behavior Books.

Shadley, M. L. (2000). Are all therapists alike? Revisiting research about the use of self in therapy. In M. Baldwin (Ed.), *The use of self in therapy. Second ed.* (pp. 191–211). New York: Haworth Press.

12

The Satir Model and Cultural Sensitivity:

A Hong Kong Reflection

Grace Cheung and Cecilia Chan

Virginia Satir came to Hong Kong in 1983 and conducted a two-day workshop. About 300 participants attended the workshop, most of whom were helping professionals. From 1986 for about 10 years, Jane Gerber, Maria Gomori, and John Banmen followed up on what Satir started. As a teaching trio, they conducted each year in Hong Kong Level I and Level II four-day personal growth workshops. Currently, Banmen and Gomori continue to conduct workshops separately in the Satir model in Hong Kong, with Banmen focusing more on the training of trainers.

Today, we already have a number of trainers and therapists in Hong Kong who were trained to practice in the Satir model, and most of them practice in more or less the same way that they were taught. In our view, we should be grateful to these colleagues for having introduced us to the Satir model and for having shown us how the model is practiced in North America. We also strongly believe that as professionals living and practicing with local people, it is our task to adapt the model and/or develop a practice rooted in our own culture.

Need for Cultural Sensitivity

For the German philosopher, H. G. Gadamer (1997), knowledge is irretrievably tied to tradition, the ontological condition which makes understanding possible. While our socio-historical position shapes our experience, our understanding of that experience, and our understanding of the past and the future is itself a product of tradition.

Following Gadamer, there is no other way to understand our clients except by entering into their tradition. This point is also borne out by multicultural psychologists, including Ivey, Ivey and Simek-Morgan (1997), Sue, Ivey, and Pedersen (1996) and Sue and Sue (1990). In their view, theories of counseling and psychotherapy represent a variety of worldviews, each with its own values, biases, assumptions about human behavior, language, and constructs, which may clash with the worldview of the culturally different client. To facilitate change, the therapist must be culturally sensitive.

Change, to be effective, must survive in the cultural milieu. Good individual adjustments are not possible if they do not accord with cultural expectations. This point is particularly relevant in a highly collectivist environment, such as the one we find in Hong Kong. Duan and Wang (2000) say it very succinctly: "An exclusive focus on improving individual satisfaction without considering the cultural demands will not produce any lasting and effective change for Chinese clients", because pursuit for personal fulfillment can be considered "selfish", and what is perceived as being "selfish" is not likely to get any support (pp. 211).

Although Hong Kong has undergone rapid change over the past 50 years, from a society of refugees to a modern, urban, cosmopolitan, and financial center, and although the people of Hong Kong are known to possess most attributes of modernity, including being pragmatic, efficient, outgoing, global-minded, competitive and adaptive to rapid change, studies have shown that traditional collectivist culture is still very much part of the local scene, especially in family life (Cheung, 1985; Ho, 1974; Lee, 1995).

Here, we wish to make two points, which on the surface might seem to contradict each other. First, from our clinical and training experiences, the Satir model has worked very well with many Hong Kong Chinese clients and participants. The Satir model, which approaches individual issues from a systems perspective, placing the individual within the context of the family, offers a valuable resource for assisting Chinese clients as they struggle with issues of stress relating to a collectivist society. Its emphasis on individuality, self-esteem, congruence, choices, freedom, and responsibility provides what is missing in a Confucian collectivist culture. Satir's basic beliefs, her analysis of change at different levels, her vehicles of change, and her experiential training format have also been found to be effective.

While we are impressed with what the Satir model can offer to therapy in the Chinese cultural setting, we are also doubtful. While interviews (Pau, 2000) of participants after training programs revealed that some of the participants were able to recall the positive changes they achieved in the course of the program, the same interviews also showed that after the program, back in their own families, where another cultural regime was in order, and where another set of rules was in force, change for the same participants became very difficult.

Our training experience also showed that approximately one-third of participants felt uneasy about taking part in experiential activities. About half found it difficult to express appreciation and gratitude, especially to their family members. Many participants found it easy to talk about work and social issues, but very difficult to share private intimate thoughts with other participants. They did not even do this at home with their loved ones. The general rule was: feelings were to be kept inside and not to be expressed.

In the clinical setting, we have problems using the Satir model with clients who come from very traditional Chinese cultural backgrounds. Some clients, young ones in their teens, told us they had been protected by their parents since birth. Making a choice might be exciting for some people, but for them, it was a cause for anxiety. The concept of facing conflicts is also foreign to many of our clients. Some said, "The way to manage conflicts is to avoid them. Make big conflicts small, and small conflicts disappear!"

It is our firm belief that the Satir model, as a model, is basically compatible with traditional Chinese culture. The question is: how can we employ it in a culturally meaningful and culturally sensitive fashion? To answer this question, we must first identify the differences in cultural context before we can have any meaningful discussion regarding ways for adaptation.

Adapting Hofstede's (1980), Kim's (1994) and Triandis' (1995) use of "collectivism" and "individualism", we propose to use the terms "hierarchical collectivism" and "egalitarian individualism" to differentiate the two major cultural-psychological patterns and to highlight the distinctive character of their social relationships.

Simply put, the term 'hierarchical collectivism' is used to describe a cultural context, found in most East Asian societies, that puts collective welfare before that of the individual, where identity is defined more by the role a person occupies than by his or her individual qualities or achievements, where respect for harmony, order, and authority is emphasized, and where self-restraint is a virtue to be cultivated. In contrast, egalitarian individualism refers to a cultural context, found in most Western societies, where pursuit of self interests and self fulfillment is the normal order, where identity is defined by personal qualities and achievement rather than by ascribed roles and statuses, where equality and free expression of individual thoughts and emotions are upheld (see Table 1).

Table 12.1

From Hierarchical to Growth Model within a Culture of Egalitarian Individualism

Hierarchical Collectivism	Egalitarian Individualism
Collective welfare comes first.	Self-fulfillment comes first.
Identity attached to ascribed roles rather than individual self.	Identity defined by personal qualities and individual achievement, rather than by ascribed roles and statuses
Respect for harmony and order: Obedient to authority	Personal Development: Equality
Self-restraint	Free expression

Satir Was Sensitive to the Demands Of Culture

All the books we read on the Satir model indicated that Satir herself was sensitive to the demands of culture. She stressed the importance for parents to teach their children to fit in with the requirements of family living, to balance their needs with those of others, and to fit into the demands of culture. In Satir's view, children need to develop skills for coping with and balancing the requirements of you, me, and context (Satir, 1983). Satir's concept of congruence takes into full consideration the three components of Self, Other, and Context. Context is an important consideration for practice, and context includes culture.

At this point, it deems appropriate to take a look at Satir's comparison of the hierarchical model with her growth model, and discuss this in relation to its egalitarian individualist cultural background.

Table 12.2

From Hierarchical to Growth Model within a Culture of Collectivism

Hierarchical Model	Growth Model
People dominate or submit to each other.	Relationships are between equals in value.
People need to conform to role expectations and obey "shoulds" for physical and emotional survival and acceptance.	Each person is unique and can define self from an inner source of strength and validation.
People are expected to think, feel, and act like each other, and to live up to external norms.	Respecting samenesses and differences, people discover themselves and others.
Only one right way exists to do something, and the dominant person knows what it is.	Many ways usually exist, and we can use our own criteria to choose an approach.
People deny their own experiences so as to accept the voice of authority.	People look beyond the obvious event to understand its context and its many contributing factors.

Table 2 gives a comparison of the basic features of Satir's hierarchical and growth models (for detailed descriptions of the hierarchical and the growth model see Satir, Banmen, Gerber, & Gomori, 1991, pp. 6–15).

One of the major goals of therapy in the Satir model is to help people change their perceptions of the world, from the hierarchical model to the growth model. If one takes a close look and compares Table 1 and Table 2, one finds striking similarity between hierarchical collectivism and the hierarchical model on the one hand, as well as between egalitarian individualism and the growth model on the other.

Satir probably did not have China and Chinese communities in mind when she was formulating her ideas about the hierarchical model, but her description of the model captures very succinctly the basic value assumptions of Confucian hierarchical collectivism. It is also interesting to note that values emphasized by the growth model, including equality, individuality, independence, uniqueness, self-direction, diversity, choice, and respecting sameness and difference are values most lacking in traditional Chinese society. For a moment, it seems that the growth model provides the solution to the problems of Chinese society.

It must be noted, however, that Satir developed her model in the egalitarian individualist culture of North America. She took her cultural context seriously, focusing on individual self-enhancement and building high self-esteem. She did this by strengthening abilities to listen, to see, to check meaning, to recognize and express feelings, to feel free to ask and comment, to take risks, to communicate congruently, to take responsibility, and to change. This fitted in very well in an egalitarian individualist culture, where people treasure individuality and equality, yearn to be free and independent, and search for personal fulfillment.

One must also know that in the United States, where the Satir model first developed, values of democracy, equality, freedom, and independence have been upheld for more than 200 years; social security for old age is provided; and at the individual level, autonomy, creativity, ambition, direct expression of thoughts and feelings, and risk-taking ventures are encouraged.

When Satir advocated that people should accept each other as equals in value, regardless of age, color, gender, or health; that each person is unique in his or her combination of human sameness and differentness; that people should interact with one another in multiple ways rather than follow a one-way dominant/submissive direction; that people have the ability to change, expand, love, and grow, to discover and accept one's individuality, one's feelings, and differences, and to freely express them, to feel whole and connected, and to have high self-esteem (Satir et al., 1991), she was articulating a vision which was embedded in the dream of the American people. She spoke their language, and she was understood.

It is quite evident that transition from the hierarchical to the growth model as effected by Satir did not take place in a cultural vacuum. For those who came to be touched and inspired by Satir, their transition to the growth model, although not easy, took place in a cultural milieu that had a set of features that were in consonance with and supported the value assumptions of the growth model (see Diagram 1). Though there would still be people who were not able to integrate equality and individuality in their lives, these values were assumed in American culture. No arguments were needed. These values might not be present in some people's lives, but the same people would accept that they ought to be.

Figure 12.1

From Hierarchical to Growth Model within a Culture of Egalitarian Individualism

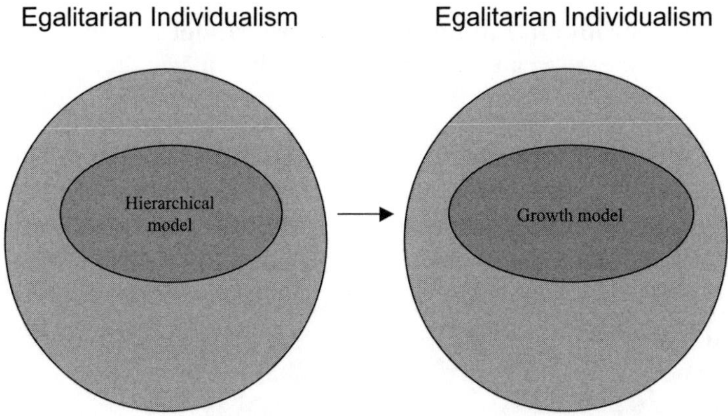

The Question of Cultural Sensitivity

In Hong Kong, the context is totally different. After 150 years of British colonial rule we do have people who share worldviews and values based on individuality, if not also equality. For the majority of people, their family lives are still under the strong influence of hierarchical collectivist tradition. Generally, there is greater concern for collective family welfare than for individual fulfillment, greater emphasis on harmony than on freedom and difference, on filial piety and obedience to authorities than on independence, autonomy, and equality.

Colonial politics add to the weight of tradition. Independence, democracy, and equality have not been generally promoted, not in society, or in schools or families. Although the question of security for the aged has been in public discussion for about 30 years, the implementation of the Mandatory Providend Fund Scheme, which provides very limited old age security, did not become effective until the end of 2000. The idea that adult children should be responsible for the care of aged parents will continue to underlie efforts to maintain the tradition of filial piety and family solidarity for many more years to come.

In this hierarchical collectivist context, any attempt to forcefully make a change from the hierarchical model to the growth model will be sheer imposition (see Diagram 2). The language, beliefs, and sentiments involved will come across as alien to many people. It is very doubtful indeed if transition effected this way will be a smooth one, and this is obviously against the spirit of Satir.

Table 12.2

From Hierarchical to Growth Model within a Culture of Collectivism

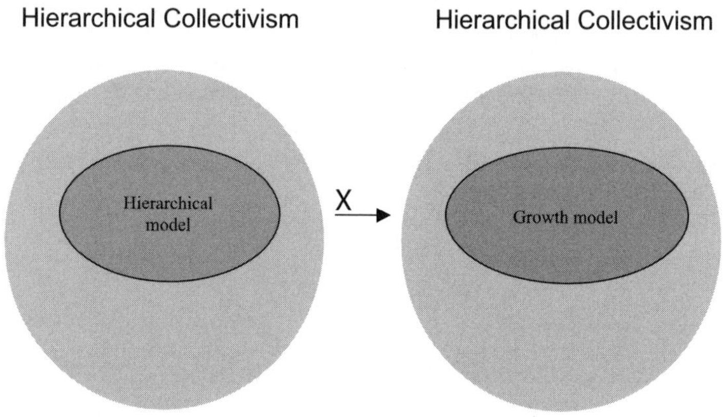

Therefore, working in a hierarchical collectivist culture, the therapist trained in the Satir model cannot go "automatic", but must use the model in a consciously guided and culturally sensitive manner.

Practicing Congruence in a Hierarchical Collectivist Context

Cultural sensitivity involves a number of issues. In this paper, for the sake of brevity, our focus is on congruent communication, which lies at the center of Satir's therapeutic system.

According to our understanding of the Satir model (Satir et al., 1991; Loeschen, 1991; Englander-Golden & Satir, 1990), to communicate congruently means to communicate clearly, directly, specifically, honestly, freely, and respectfully. It means appreciating the uniqueness and equal dignity of self. Taking Other and Context into consideration does not mean conforming to the Other and to the demands of Context. One learns to be respectful of the other. This does not mean taking care of the feelings of the other, but rather trusting that the other has the ability to take care of his or her own feelings.

Simply put, congruent communication is saying things straightforwardly (Englander-Golden & Satir, 1990), rather than in a roundabout way. It is honoring and expressing our deepest wishes. It is a way of reclaiming responsibility and empowering ourselves. It is risky, because while we present our real self, and expose our inner core to the possibility of rejection, we have no guarantee that the other party will respond positively. We are certain only of one thing, that "we give ourselves permission to comment on whatever our deepest truth is at that moment" (Englander-Golden & Satir, 1990, pp.136–137).

In congruent communication, one can say to the other directly, "I care about me, about you, and about our relationship. I can take the risk of discovering that what fits for me at this time does not fit for you" (Englander-Goden & Satir, 1990, p. 138). It acknowledges that there may not a mutual fit, and that it deserves honor and recognition, even if we feel disappointed. It starts with the idea of "I love me. I value me," and out of this feeling for ourselves, "we can love and value others."

The idea, as we understand it, is to love and value ourselves first, and then love and value others. And in our view, this practically corresponds to what Satir considered Level I congruence (Satir et al., 1991). Guided by this understanding, we have been able to help many clients overcome their relationship problems, but not with clients who come from traditional Chinese backgrounds.

Many clients expressed having difficulty to communicate congruently, particularly when they had to deal with people occupying a senior status in the hierarchy, for instance, with parents and elder siblings. They simply could not bring themselves to say what they truly wanted to say.

Many participants of personal growth programs also found it difficult to directly express their thoughts and feelings. It was not something they were used to. That was never permitted. Others said, "Congruence is a very foreign, or Western way of thinking and communicating. We Chinese do not do it this way. We are never as direct in expressing our thoughts and feelings, because it hurts. We do not say everything we want to say. We always keep about 70% to ourselves."

The problem lay in our centering the focus on Level I of Satir's model of congruence. In our training and clinical practice, we were not paying enough attention to congruence at Level II. We thought we had to help the client or the participants go through Level I first before they could come to tackle problems at Level II. At this point, a brief recapitulation of the three levels of congruence is in order.

Satir and associates (1991) differentiated three levels of congruence (see Table 12.2), with high self-esteem as its common objective for all three levels. In our view, change at Level I takes place within the cultural framework of egalitarian individualism. The focus is on the self, specifically on being honest with our feelings, on choice, freedom, and responsibility as described above.

In our understanding, Level II of congruent communication aims at change beyond egalitarian individualism. Although the focus is still on the self, it is a self that reaches out to others and context. It is at a new state of wholeness, inner centeredness, and harmony, defined in terms of people being at peace and harmony with themselves, with others, and with context.

At Level III, people enter the realm of spirituality and universality (see Table 3). In her later years, Satir gave a lot of attention to these aspects of becoming more fully human. She encouraged people to become aware and connected with the universal life force that creates, supports, heals and promotes growth. In therapy, Satir sees all people as being filled with the life force, with some people not so well connected with the energy of the life force. The job of the therapist is to move in and activate the energy that is there, creating a movement which is healing in itself (Satir et al., 1991; Kramer, 1995).

Table 12.3

Congruence at Three Levels

	FOCUS
Level I: Feelings	Awareness Acknowledgement Ownership Management Enjoyment
Level II: The Self ("I am")	Centeredness Wholeness Harmony
Level III: Life-force	Universality Spirituality

(Source: Satir et al., 1991, p. 68)

While Level I indicates what is generally suppressed in Chinese culture, Level II and Level III echo similar values in Chinese culture.

While focusing on feelings at Level I as a way for people to affirm individuality, equality, freedom, uniqueness, choice, and responsibility is a very effective way of beginning therapy in an egalitarian individualist context, as clients pick up such ideas easily and will not find too much resistance to such ideas in their cultural environment, doing the same as a beginning step of therapy in a hierarchical collectivist culture, in the way we have done, demonstrates cultural insensitivity.

Unlike the situation in egalitarian individualist cultures, where individuals are considered to be autonomous, and interpersonal relationships are based on principles of mutual respect, equality, non-interference, and detachability (Kim, 1994), individuals in collectivist cultures conceived of themselves as embedded in a network, interrelated through their ascribed roles, according to which their duties and obligations are prescribed.

In the Confucianist collectivist society, human relationships move out from the center in concentric circles. Each circle represents a specific relationship, carrying a set of obligations and responsibilities. At the center of the circles is the self, and all self-realization is connected to realization of obligations and responsibilities in each circle of relationships (Fei Xiao Tung, 1981).

The first circle, and the circle which constitutes the most fundamental relationship of all, is the relationship between father and son. When it comes to conflict between expectations and obligations, the Chinese make filial piety the primary and highest virtue, taking precedence over all other virtues and responsibilities.

In Western society, the adult child stands on equal ground with the parent, having as much right as the parent in his or her pursuit of self-care. In Chinese culture, the adult child is forever a child in the eyes of parents, and in accordance with dictates of filial piety, the "child" has to value parents more than self, take care of parents before taking care of self.

In traditional Chinese society, concern for others comes before care for self. Confucian morality demands that a person rise above the general norm of fairness. Instead of demanding equal treatment of self and others, the Confucian gentleman repays iniquity with virtue, puts the welfare of others before that of self, is first to suffer, but last to enjoy life.

However, what is supposed to be a principled act, stemming from a firm interior consciousness of the self, often becomes an act that responds to external demands and other-oriented, being sensitive to others' opinions, standards, and criticisms, and trying hard to conform in order to give a good impression to others (Yang, 1995).

This attitude of attending to others first and restraining the needs of the self is reflected in many family rules. According to these rules, one does not treat others and self equally. One should be more generous and kind to others. One should repay hurt with virtue, remember for a thousand years the kindness bestowed upon one by others, but not expect any reward for the good one does to others; better be bullied by others than to bully others; better be let down by others than to let others down. And the person who can act with concern for others is not a weakling, but a person of virtue and moral strength.

Our past experience shows that we have not given much thought to the cultural context in which we practice therapy. We applied locally in the same way what was being practiced in North America. The result:

1. People steeped in traditional Chinese culture felt alienated by the model, refused to take active part in training, or did not come back to therapy.
2. The emphasis on self made them feel as if they were asked to abandon the collective. They felt being made to choose between interdependence, group solidarity and commitment to common fate on the one hand, and personal autonomy, emotional independence, and right to choose, define, and seek pleasure and personal fulfillment on the other.
3. The emphasis on individual self rather than role-self made them feel as if they were asked to abandon their ascribed roles, to give up their moral obligations and responsibilities toward family, society, country, and the world, as well as to give up their moral self and collective identity (Tam, 1999; Suen, 1983).
4. The emphasis on individualist values of self-determination and equality made them feel as if they were asked not to act filial to their parents, and to take actions disruptive of existing harmony and order.
5. The emphasis on freedom, independence, direct expression and interaction, uniqueness, and difference made them feel as if they were asked not to compromise or avoid conflicts, to be rebellious, or to break tradition and rules that have for a long time been operating in their families.

Placed in comparative cultural perspective, we came to understand more fully why some clients were not coming back to therapy. We began to look for a solution that is more culturally relevant.

In traditional Chinese society, good relationship with the other and with context is not the goal, but the pre-condition of change. Consideration for the collective and concern for the other are prerequisites for the pursuit of personal fulfillment. One does not first affirm oneself, before affirming others. It is in the act of affirming others that one affirms oneself. Pursuit of individual needs and asserting individual rights in disregard of the collective is considered selfish behavior.

The traditional Chinese gentleman knows how to keep proper balance, not by choosing one and suppressing the other, but by keeping seemingly opposing forces together in the midst of tension, loving self and loving parents, being obedient to authority and finding room for individual free space. He does not achieve self-fulfillment, individuality, independence, and freedom by abandoning the collective, but on the contrary, by upholding the collective and giving full respect to other and to context.

According to the Chinese, one may be trapped by external forces, but no difficulty in life is insuperable, as long as one's heart is free and connected (Hung, 1995). The greatest adversity in life is when one's heart is confined. One's body might be imprisoned, but when one's heart becomes free, connected (Chen & Zhao, 1999) and at peace, there is hope, and there is life. This matches Satir's congruence at Level II, with emphasis on internal peace and harmony, connectedness and wholeness.

In other words, what Satir put in her second level of congruence must become the condition of change in the very first instance in Chinese hierarchical collectivist context. So, instead of beginning congruent communication at Level I, as it is being practiced in North America, a more effective way of engaging the client and his or her significant other is to begin with Level II, where harmony with self, with other, and with context is given full consideration, and where balance, centeredness, and wholeness are given full attention.

Conclusion

What is the next step? For us, it will not be adapting and changing parts of the Satir model here and there to fit the demands of local culture. It will be the development of an approach whose basic concepts originate from local Chinese culture. We call this an emic approach. The terms *etic* and *emic* were originally used by Berry (1969) to refer to initiating research in a different culture. Now they are used to describe different approaches to cross-cultural therapy, particularly in multicultural contexts. While etic refers to concepts originating from the therapist's culture, modified when employed in therapeutic encounters with a client who is culturally different, the emic approach is based on notions and experiences indigenous to the client's culture, analyzed, processed, and then incorporated into modern therapeutic interventions (Draguns, 1996).

In our view, the etic approach can take two different forms: 1) culturally transforming itself, adapting to and working within the client's cultural framework; and 2) helping the client learn and adapt to the cultural values inherent in the approach adopted by the therapist.

When Duan and Wang (2000, p. 9) proposed that Western therapeutic practices should "be culturally transformed to serve the needs of Chinese people", that an individualism-based practice should be transformed culturally to serve people in a primarily collectivistic society, they were proposing an etic approach that adapts to and operates within the cultural framework of the Chinese people. Our description about the need to begin with Level II rather than Level I congruence when conducting clinical work with local people also falls under this category.

When the concept of culture broker is used to describe the therapist as someone who introduces the patient to new values and beliefs that will enable him or her to adjust to an ever-changing lifestyle, it is referring to an etic approach of the second type. Some of these values and beliefs introduced would include those that properly belong to a democratic society, emphasizing the right of every individual to present his or her opinion, equality between men and women in dealing with marital relationships, and need to be assertive and independent rather than passive and dependent in industrialized urban life (Tseng, Lu, & Yin, 1995). Until recently, this has been the approach we have generally adopted for the past 20 years in our training and clinical practices. Little attention was paid to clients who were non-receptive to such an approach or found such an approach not workable in their families.

The future of family therapy in Hong Kong, for us, rests with the emic approach. It is to be grounded in and to draw inspiration and resource from our traditional Chinese culture, while remaining open to the influence and stimulation of models developed in other cultures. It seeks to respond to the demands of local culture, establish linkage with traditional cultural sources, and draw from them wisdom and strength to face the challenge of the twenty-first century. It is a both/and instead of an either/or approach. It does not choose between collectivism or individualism, hierarchy or egalitarianism. It acknowledges our hierarchical collectivist traditions and at the same time seeks to protect individual quests for equality, freedom, and independence. Further elaboration, however, on this approach will be the subject of another article.

With the help of the Satir model, we have helped many people grow, and we ourselves have also grown as persons. At this point, however, we intend to return to our cultural roots. It does not mean that we will then adhere to and confine ourselves within the traditional cultural framework. It is not our intention to adapt the Satir model to the local Chinese culture. Neither do we want it to be absent from our future endeavors. The Satir model will continue to be with us, inspiring us and reminding us of certain basic, universal, human values, and stimulating us with the analysis and vehicles of change offered by the model.

In a recent initial four-day program on training and supervision in the Satir model organized by the Department for Social Work and Social Administration at the University of Hong Kong, John Banmen, trainer for the program, emphasized repeatedly the importance of attending to cultural factors and exhorted participants to be culturally reflective and sensitive when applying the Satir model in the local Chinese cultural setting. That was a much appreciated professional attitude.

For Satir, it is not the therapist who heals, but the client himself or herself, using his or her own powers. Healing comes when the person's power already present inside of him or her is unleashed. The therapist is like someone carrying a set of jumper cables. The client is there filled with energy; but the problem is, it is not working. The therapist moves in, and the energy starts flowing. It is the activation of energy that creates a movement of healing (Kramer, 1995).

Applying the same analogy at a cultural level, the greatest contribution the Satir model can offer to a culture other than egalitarian individualism lies not in its directly providing an interpretive framework, tools of analysis, and vehicles of change, but rather in its ability to stimulate the powers of a culture so that it can be re-connected to its own resources, and therein find the strength to respond to its ever changing challenges. And this is beginning to happen, in a small way, in Hong Kong.

References

Berry, J. W. (1969). On cross-cultural comparability. *International Journal of Psychology, 4*, 119–128.

Cheung, F.M. (1985). Psychopathology in Hong Kong: Somatic presentation. In Tseng, W. S. & Wu, D. Y.H. (Eds.), *Chinese culture and mental health* (pp. 287–304). Orlando, FL: Academic Press Inc.

Draguns, J. G. (1996). Humanly universal and culturally distinctive: Charting the course of cultural counseling. In P. B. Pedersen, J. G. Draguns, W. J. Lonner, & J. E. Trimble (Eds.), *Counseling across cultures* (pp. 1–20). Thousand Oaks, CA: Sage Publications.

Duan, C., & Wang, L. (2000). Counseling in the Chinese cultural context: Accommodating both individualistic and collectivistic values *Asian Journal of Counseling*, 7, 1–22.

Englander-Golden, P., & Satir, V. (1990). *Say it straight : From compulsion to choices.* Palo Alto: Science and Behavior Books.

Gadamer, H. G. (1997). *Truth and method.* 2nd ed. New York: Continuum Publishing.

Ho, D.Y.F. (1974). Face, social expectations, and conflict avoidance. In J. L. M. Dawson. & W. J. Lonner (Eds.), *Readings in cross-cultural psychology* (pp. 240–51). Hong Kong: Hong Kong University Press.

Hofstede, G. H. (1980). *Culture's consequences: International differences in work-related values.* Beverly Hills, CA: Sage Publications.

Ivey, A. E., Ivey, M. B., & Simek-Morgan, L. 1997. *Counseling and psychotherapy: A multicultural perspective.* Boston: Allyn and Bacon.

Kim, U. (1994). Individualism and collectivism: Conceptual clarification and elaboration. In U. Kim, H. C. Triandis, C. Kagitcibasi, S. C. Choi, & G.Yoon (Eds.), *Individualism and collectivism: Theory, method, and applications* (pp.19–40). Thousand Oaks, CA: Sage Publications.

Kramer, S. Z. (1995). *Transforming the inner and outer family.* New York: Haworth Press.

Lee, R. P. L. (1995). Cultural tradition and stress management in modern society: Learning from the Hong Kong experience. In T. Y.Lin, W. S.Tseng, & E. K. Yeh (Eds.), *Chinese societies and mental health* (pp. 40–55). Hong Kong: Oxford University Press.

Loeschen, S. (1991). *The secrets of Satir: Collected sayings of Virginia Satir.* Palm Springs, CA: Event Horizon Press.

Pau, G. Y. K. (2000). *Reconstructing family rules, from the Satir model to the I Tao, a trainer's interpretive account of a journey with participants of a personal growth group in Hong Kong.* Unpublished doctoral dissertation. University of Hong Kong.

Satir, V. (1983). *Conjoint family therapy*, 3rd ed. Palo Alto, CA: Science and Behavior Books.

Satir, V., Banmen, J., Gerber, J., & Gomori, M. (1991). *The Satir model: Family therapy and beyond.* Palo Alto, CA: Science and Behavior Books.

Sue, D. W. & Sue, D. (1990). *Counseling the culturally different.* New York: John

Wiley & Sons.

Sue, D. W., Ivey, A. E. & Pedersen, P. B. (1996). *A theory of multicultural counseling and therapy.* Pacific Grove, CA: Brooks/Cole.

Triandis, H. C. (1995). *Individualism and collectivism.* Boulder, CO: Westview Press.

Tseng, W. S., Lu, Q. Y. & Yin, P. Y. (1995). Psychotherapy for the Chinese: Cultural considerations. In T. Y. Lin, W. S. Tseng, & E. K. Yeh, (Eds.), *Chinese societies and mental health* (pp.281–94). Hong Kong: Oxford University Press.

Yang, K. S. (1995). Chinese social orientation: An integrative analysis." In T. Y. Lin, W. S. Tseng & E. K. Yeh, (Eds.), *Chinese societies and mental health* (pp.19–29). Hong Kong: Oxford University Press.

References (In Chinese)

Chen, Gu-ying, & Zhao, Jian-wei. (1999). *Zhou yi zhu yi yu yan jiu.* / Tai-bei : Tai-wan Shang Wu Yin Shu Guan Gu Fen You Xian Gong Si.

Fei, Xiao Tung. (1981). The social structure of Chinese society In Du Wei-ming et al., *Dang dai yan jiu yu qu xiang : Zhong-guo wen hua de wei ji yu zhan wang* (pp. 343–56). Tai-bei : Shi Bao Chu Ban Gong Si.

Hung, W.K. (1995). *Understanding I Ching.* Tai-bei: Tan Suo Wen Hua Shi Yeh Gong Si.

Suen, Long-ji. (1983). *Zhong-guo wen hua de shen ceng jie gou.* Hong Kong: I Shan Chu Ban She.

Tam, K.K. (1999). Self and consciousness of identity in Chinese civilization. In Liu Shu-xian, & Liang Yuan-sheng, *Wen hua chuan tong de yan xu yu zhuan hua* (pp. 177–88). Hong Kong: Chinese University of Hong Kong.

13

Development of a Congruence Scale Based on the Satir Model

Bonnie K. Lee

The development of measures and methods for testing existing theories and hypotheses in the field of marriage and family therapy has been identified as a research area deserving of greater attention (Liddle, 1991). Theory-based empirical research can act as feedback to refine and further develop theory and to direct theory to yet undiscovered relationships (Olson, 1976). Additionally, measures that are commensurate with the concepts, process, and goals of a theory should be useful in assessing interventions and outcomes based on such theory. This chapter reports on the development of a Congruence Scale based on the central concept of congruence in the Satir model.

Virginia Satir's contribution is recognized as a cornerstone in the humanistic-experiential school in family therapy that has made an enduring impact on the thinking and practices in the field (Gurman, Kniskern, & Pinsof, 1986; Nichols & Schwartz, 1998; Sprenkle, Keeney, & Sutton, 1982). Starting with a model of communication stances in the 1960s and 1970s (Satir, 1964), Satir further developed her therapeutic ideas and practice into an increasingly coherent system which she called the Human Validation Process Model (Satir, 1986) and the Satir Growth Model (Satir, Banmen, Gerber, & Gomori, 1991). However, empirical studies to verify the constructs and efficacy of Satir's model have been negligible. As family therapy comes of age, the use of quantitative methods along with qualitative and emerging methods will enhance theory, practice, and accountability in the field (Liddle, 1991; Nichols & Schwartz, 1998; Sprenkle & Moon, 1996). Empirical quantitative research uses a set of procedures to elicit responses from a sizable sample of participants to use as feedback on a construct or hypothesis.

To assess meaningfully a particular model of therapy and its conceptual hypothesis, the instrument used must fit the model's theoretical framework and intended goals. The goals of different approaches to marital and family therapy are by no means uniform (Alexander, Holtzworth-Munroe, & Jameson, 1994). In searching for an appropriate instrument to assess the efficacy of Satir's model and its key constructs, the author discovered that while many instruments are available for assessing clinical outcomes on problems and behaviors, no instrument yet exists that taps into the constructs and goals specific to the Satir model. The absence of such an instrument supplied the impetus for the development of the Congruence Scale described in this chapter. It is hoped that such an instrument would serve as a means to test out the validity of congruence as a pivotal Satir construct. Furthermore, the Congruence Scale could serve as a bridge to establish relationships with other therapy models and constructs, such as well-being, mental health functioning, marital satisfaction, and spirituality.

Theoretical Framework and the Concept of Congruence

Satir was more often known for her charisma and artistry in family therapy than for her theoretical contributions (Nichols & Schwartz, 1998). However, a remarkable coherence and consistency is found in Satir's model through three decades unified in her understanding of congruence (Lee, 2001). Satir's model was imparted as "theory-in-action" (Duhl, 1988) in her workshops as her concepts were explained didactically and demonstrated experientially through enactments and role-plays by workshop participants. Because of the paucity of her academic and research writings, many of her concepts and ideas are not well known to the field of family therapy, as evidenced by textbook documentation of her ideas (Becvar & Becvar, 1996; Goldenberg & Goldenberg, 1996; Nichols & Schwartz, 1998). Satir's theoretical framework and concepts, first formulated in her ground-breaking publication in the field, *Conjoint Family Therapy* (1964), were brought up-to-date and articulated with increasing systematization to an academic audience only in more recent years (Satir et al., 1991; Loeschen, 1998).

Congruence

Congruence is a core construct underlying Satir's multidimensional model of change (Davis, McLendon, Freeman, Hill, Loberg, Lester, & Huber, 1996; Satir et al., 1991). As noted by Satir's colleagues, the concept of congruence evolved with the expansion of her model and can be described at three levels: (1) in the 1950s, congruence referred to the awareness, acknowledgment, and acceptance of feelings and their expression in a nonreactive manner; (2) in the 1960s, congruence was seen as a state of wholeness and inner-centredness, corresponding to high self-esteem; and (3) in the 1980s, Satir began more explicitly to speak of a third level of congruence in relation to the realm of spirituality and universality, as an awareness and connection with a "universal life force that creates, supports, and promotes growth in human and other natural forms" (Satir et al.,1991). Congruence is a concept that characterizes the goal of therapeutic change in the Satir model.

For the purposes of this chapter, congruence is defined as a state of awareness, openness, and connection in the principal dimensions that constitute Satir's systemic understanding of the person. The three principal dimensions of the person are the interpersonal as connection between persons, the intrapsychic as connection within the person, and the universal-spiritual as connection with a universal and transcendent dimension.

Congruence and Therapeutic Change

The goal of therapeutic change in Satir's model is to transform the flow of a person's energy from a blocked, dysfunctional pattern to a more open, free, and healthy pattern, which corresponds to greater congruence in terms of awareness, openness, and connection with the key dimensions of the person (Satir et al., 1991). Therapeutic interventions in Satir's model aim at any of a number of variables in her multidimensional system leading to a shift in the entire system. To operationalize an abstract construct like congruence, one would have to go to the specific, concrete interventions and targeted shifts at each level and dimension of Satir's model. A philosophical elaboration of Satir's congruence construct based on her Iceberg metaphor has been reported in Lee (2001).

The three major dimensions of Satir's model will be reviewed briefly here.

Three Major Dimensions of Satir's Model

Interpersonal dimension. The interpersonal dimension in the Iceberg metaphor of the Satir model is characterized by the four survival communication stances of blaming, placating, super-reasonable, and irrelevant. These four stances are incomplete or incongruent stances because each leaves out an important component of congruent communication that includes acknowledgement of the self, the other, or the context. The goal of the Satir model is to foster the use of congruent communication where the self is accepted and congruently represented, at the same time that the other is allowed to be oneself, while the contingencies of the context are taken into account. Congruence is a choice at a conscious level based on awareness, acknowledgement, acceptance, and connection of self, other, and context (Satir et al. 1991).

Intrapsychic dimension

The intrapsychic dimension encompasses the various levels and dynamics that occur internally in a person. This dimension includes feelings, feelings about feelings, perceptions and beliefs, and expectations. Within perceptions and beliefs are implicit family rules we live by, such as "One must not say anything that hurts someone else's feelings," or "One must always be happy." Perceptions include the associations, interpretations, and meaning we make of a person or a communication. Expectations are what we expect of others and of ourselves, as well as what we think others expect of us. Any one of these variables can influence other variables in the intrapsychic dimension. For example, if a person interprets an action to be a punitive one, this perception could in turn affect one's feelings and expectations, as well as the interpersonal outcome. In working with these multiples levels and dimensions, Satir's interventions challenge, unblock and transform multiple internal variables that impede the flow of one's life energy (Loeschen, 1998; Satir et al., 1991).

Change is effected by bringing into a person's awareness these internal events or variables. By acknowledging them and adding on new elements, a new way of being and coping can emerge. A person can choose to update one's perceptions, beliefs, feelings,and expectations to meet the contingencies of the present, rather than remain in a limiting configuration that belonged to the past. Congruence in the intrapsychic dimension reflects awareness and acknowledgement of what one is experiencing internally, and the exercise of conscious choice for new ways of being that are conducive to manifesting one's life force.

Universal-spiritual dimension

Universal human yearnings and the Self are conceptualized as one universal-spiritual dimension because they represent experience that is common to humanity regardless of historical, cultural, and familial backgrounds. The two fundamental levels illustrated in the Iceberg are universal human yearnings and the Self or "I Am." Yearnings consist of our need to love and be loved, to be accepted and validated, and our search for purpose and meaning (Satir et al., 1991). The Self is described as our "life force, spirit, soul, core, essence" (Satir et al., 1991). In other words, yearnings and being represent a dimension of a person that transcends cultural conditioning. Yearnings are part of the human make-up, and hence cannot be denied or disregarded. Being congruent at the level of yearnings means to acknowledge one's humanity and what one longs for and strives to actualize. In the 1980s, Satir more centrally brought spirituality into her model and described congruence as harmony with our Self, our life energy, spirituality, or God (Banmen, 2003; Satir et al., 1991).

An Example of Congruence

The following example illustrates the construct of congruence involving the three key interpersonal, intrapsychic, and universal-spiritual dimensions. The wife complains that her husband is not supporting her emotionally in her stress and struggles at work and with the children. In the interpersonal dimension, she adopts a blaming stance which comes out of feelings in the intrapsychic dimension consisting of hurt, loneliness, frustration, and anger related to her perception of the lack of support. She fails to perceive the times when her husband does provide support because of her expectation of what constitutes support, which is nothing short of one hundred percent agreement with her on all issues. In her family of origin, much was expected of her and her contributions to the family, but little was given to support her in her own aspirations and striving. In the universal-spiritual dimension, it was only when she realized how her own yearnings for support and acceptance had not been met by her parents, and when she acknowledged her own disappointment and pain for what she lacked, and at the same time began to acknowledge her own worth, that she was able to update her expectation and perception of what constitutes support in the present context. With the awareness and acceptance of her own dynamics in the intrapsychic dimensions, she is then able to begin to open herself to accept the times when her husband does give her support. This example demonstrates how the three dimensions, the interpersonal, intrapsychic, and universal-spiritual, are intertwined and interactive.

Congruence and the Goal of Transformation

In summary, congruence is a core multidimensional construct that underlies Satir's model of change (Davis et al., 1996; Satir et al. 1991). As the construct evolves in Satir's formulation, congruence came to encompass openness, awareness, acknowledgement and connectedness of variables in three major dimensions: the interpersonal, intrapsychic, and universal-spiritual. The aim of Satir's model is to help persons move toward an increasingly wholistic, open, and conscious way of being that has personal, interpersonal, and spiritual implications. Thus, congruence characterizes the goal of therapeutic change in Satir's model. In this empirical study, congruence is defined as a state of integration consisting of awareness, openness, acceptance, and harmonious functioning in three major dimensions of a person's experience in a given moment.

Operationalizing Congruence

Satir's therapeutic interventions for "second-level" deep structural change beyond the behavioral level in the three dimensions are intended to increase congruence (Satir et al., 1991). For congruence to become a measurable concept to elicit responses from a statistically meaningful sample, congruence needs to be operationalized into discrete, specific items. To turn the construct of congruence into concrete descriptions of specific psychological states and behaviors, the author relied on her observations of the direction of change facilitated in Satir-based workshops, Satir videotapes, and the content of Satir meditations. Questionnaire items on congruence are based on the direction of change intended by therapeutic interventions and meditations used by Satir and Satir trainers. Items formulated as indicators of congruence are categorized into the three respective interpersonal, intrapsychic and universal-spiritual dimensions. Congruence indicators can be mental states, attitudes, perceptions and behaviors. The congruent items constructed will be tested and analyzed empirically. As congruence is an experience or process one moves toward, rather than something one possesses or attains, congruence will be conceptualized as a continuous variable.

Method

This section describes the procedures employed in the development of the Congruence Scale. An initial set of items was drafted, reviewed, modified, analyzed statistically, and grouped according to factor scores. The steps are detailed as follows:

Participants

A total of 86 participants took part in the development of the Congruence Scale. They were all participants in Satir workshops for training and/ or personal development and healing. All were from the United States and Canada. A breakdown of their demographic characteristics is listed in Table 1. The demographic profile indicates a predominance of female (73%) to male respondents (27%). The median age group is 40–59 years. Ethnicity is mainly Caucasian (87%). Religious upbringing demonstrates a predominantly Christian background (76%), including Roman Catholic, Liberal Protestant, Evangelical, and Pentecostal denominations. Current religious practice evidences a decline in Christian affiliations from 76% to 40%, with an increase from 14% to 59% in other religious affiliations, including Buddhist, Hindu, Unitarian, Native, and unspecified religious practices. Eighty percent of the respondents have masters degrees or higher. With regard to marital status, 54% of respondents are married, and 42% are single, widowed, or divorced. Thirty-five percent of respondents report family income range of $40,000 and another 35% report family income of over $70,000 and higher per annum. Among the respondents, 56% were relatively new to the Satir model, having attended only 0–4 Satir workshops, and 44% have attended 5–20 Satir workshops.

In summary, the demographic profile of the participants indicates a predominance of middle to upper-middle income, middle-aged, female participants of Caucasian background, who grew up with Christian upbringing but are shifting toward non-Christian affiliations in their current religious practices. The sample represents slightly more newcomers than those with longer term involvement in the Satir model.

Table 13.1

Demographic Characteristics of Subjects

(N=86)							
	Variable	N	%		Variable	N	%
Gender	Male	23	27	Current	Roman Catholic	11	13
	Female	63	73	Religious	Liberal Protestant	21	25
Age	20 – 39	20	23	Practice	Evangelical	1	1
	40 – 59	46	54		Pentecostal	1	1
	60+	20	23		Mormon	1	1
Place of	U.S.A.	63	73		Unitarian	7	8
Birth	Canada	20	23		Judaism	2	2
	Other	3	4		Native	5	6
Ethnicity	Caucasian	75	87		Buddhist	5	6
	Black	4	5		Hindu	1	1
	Hispanic	3	4		Other	31	36
	Asian	1	1	Education	B.A. or college	17	20
	Other	3	3		Master	58	67
Religious	Roman Catholic	23	27		Doctorate	11	13
Upbringing	Liberal Protestant	28	33	Marital	Single	14	16
	Evangelical	13	15	Status	Married	46	54
	Pentecostal	2	2		Divorced/widowed	22	26
	Mormon	2	2		Other	4	4
	Unitarian	4	5	Family	10 – 39k	26	30
	Native	2	2	Income	40 – 69k	30	35
	Other	12	14		70k+	30	35
				Satir Workshops	0 – 4	48	56
				Attended	5 – 20+	38	44

Procedure

Generation of initial pool of items. The author attended a total of 11 training and therapy workshops based on Satir's model conducted by three Satir trainers between 1995 and 1998. As a participant-observer in these didactic and experiential workshops, the author noted key and representative interventions used by the trainers in relation to difficulties expressed by participants. Based on these specific interventions and their intent, items hypothesized to operationalize congruence were constructed along the four dimensions discussed in the earlier section of this paper. A pool of 77 items was drawn up, with 37 items in the Intrapsychic dimension, 25 items in the Interpersonal dimension, and 25 in the Universal-Spiritual dimension. A seven-point scale ranging from strongly disagree to strongly agree, using a present time frame of a week to reflect currency was selected for self-reported ratings.

Refinement of item pool and establishment of conceptual validity. Three Avanta (an organization founded by Virginia Satir to continue her mission) faculty members and one local practitioner trained in the Satir model were asked to rate the 77 items on a scale of 1–5 in terms of their (1) clarity and readability; (2) goodness of fit with each conceptualized dimension; and (3) relevance of the item to the Satir model as an outcome measure. Items that were considered ambiguous, vague, or irrelevant to the Satir model were clarified, rewritten in their entirety, or eliminated. A resultant pool of 75 items representing the three conceptualized dimensions was selected (See Appendix).

First administration of the congruence scale. The preliminary Congruence Scale of 75 items and two concurrent measures, the Satisfaction with Life Scale (SWLS) (Diener, Emmons, Larson, & Griffins, 1985) and the Outcome Questionnaire (OQ) (Lambert & Burlingame, 1996) were distributed to 32 participants at the 1998 annual Avanta meeting and training in Seattle, Washington. Respondents were invited to jot down questions and comments regarding the wording or content of the items if they so chose. This feedback was intended for future development and refinements of the scale. Twenty-seven participants completed the questionnaire onsite, and two were mailed in subsequently, totalling an overall return rate of 91%.

Selection of best items by item-total correlations. Item-total correlations were performed on the 75 items from this initial administration. Thirty-eight (see items in Appendix marked with an asterisk) with item-total correlations of 0.3 and higher were retained.

Administration of the refined congruence scale. The refined Congruence Scale of 38 items and the two concurrent measures were sent to trainers at three Satir Learning Centers in the United States and Canada to be administered to Satir workshop participants. The return rates from the three centers with the mail-out questionnaires with stamped return envelopes were: 35/91 (34%), 9/13 (69%), and 13/35 (37%).

Factor analysis of the Congruence Scale. A principal components factor analysis using a quartimax rotation with eigen values set at 1.0 was conducted on the 38 items of item-total correlations of 0.3 and above, responded to by a total of 86 participants, 29 participants from the 1998 Avanta annual meeting and 57 participants from the mailed questionnaires. Results of the factor analysis were compared to the conceptualized dimensions and interpreted.

Determination of concurrent validity. Two concurrent measures were selected for validation of the Congruent Scale, using the best 38 items administered on the 86 subjects. The Satisfaction with Life Scale (SWLS) (1985) by Edward Diener was selected because of its focus on global well-being and its high positive correlation with self-esteem and negative correlation with clinical measures of distress (Pavot & Diener, 1993). This short scale (5 items) assesses an individual's subjective evaluative judgement of his or her life by using the person's own criteria. The scale is reported to display strong validity and reliability, stability and sensitivity (Pavot & Diener, 1993). The goal of the Satir model is not only symptom relief, but also growth and optimal being, with self-esteem as an important conceptual correlate of congruence. It is therefore expected that the degree of overall well-being on the SWLS should overlap with Satir's indices of congruence.

The second concurrent measure selected was the Outcome Questionnaire (OQ) (Lambert & Burlingame, 1996; Lambert, Okiishi, Finch, & Johnson, 1998), developed as a standardized measure for assessing psychotherapy outcome. Its sound psychometric properties of reliability and validity were documented in the literature (Lambert et al., 1998; Umphress, Lambert, Smart, Barlow, & Clouse, 1997). This instrument was selected because it measures intrapsychic, relational, and social role functioning, with a multidimensionality that suggests correspondence to the dimensions of intrapsychic and interpersonal congruence. Furthermore, OQ is a scale that not only assesses symptomatic complaints but also positive mental health or quality of life and well-being, which are areas expected to correlate with congruence.

Results

Factor Analysis

Table 13.2 presents the four factors extracted using a quartimax rotation on the 38 items with the 86 responses. The four factors yielded eigen values of 11.28, 3.24, 1.90 and 1.84 respectively, explaining a cumulative percentage of 48.1% of the variance. Factor loadings of items are listed in Table 13.2, representing loadings of 0.40 and higher in all of the four factors.

Table 13.2

Congruence Scale Factor Analysis Results

Congruence Scale Items			Factor 1	Factor 2	Factor 3	Factor 4
Factor 1: Intrapsychic- Interpersonal Dimension						
(24)	1	I blame myself when things go wrong.	0.768	0.088	0.017	-0.068
(67)	2	I doubt myself	0.760	0.256	0.019	-0.027
(52)	3	I feel it must be my fault if someone is not happy with me.	0.725	0.206	0.107	-0.039
(58)	4	I am conflicted within myself.	0.718	0.263	-0.191	-0.122
(10)	5	I feel guilty easily.	0.679	0.293	0.128	-0.067
(14)	6	I can say "no" when something doesn't fit for me.	0.592	0.085	0.212	0.345
(51)	7	I feel tense when I am with others.	0.587	0.269	0.080	0.200
(55)	8	I am centred in my deeper or higher self.	0.556	0.413	0.077	0.117
(69)	9	Feelings run my life.	0.553	0.013	0.229	0.020
(5)	10	I feel connected to others in our humanity.	0.535	0.149	-0.137	0.339
(17)	11	I accept my past.	0.526	0.234	0.362	0.252
(31)	12	I avoid addressing conflicts.	0.500	-0.136	0.218	0.231
Factor 2: Spiritual Dimension						
(72)	1	I trust in the goodness of God/ the universe.	0.131	0.825	-0.034	-0.050
(27)	2	I have a relationship with God.	0.244	0.816	-0.084	0.057
(35)	3	I appreciate the mystery of the "Life Force," Spirit, or God as a part of me.	0.200	0.799	0.275	0.018
(7)	4	My spirit is connected with the Spirit of the universe/God.	0.266	0.729	-0.032	0.212
(41)	5	I appreciate the mystery of the "Life Force," God or Spirit as something larger than me.	0.119	0.709	0.060	-0.046
(56)	6	I am in awe of how well put together human beings are.	0.126	0.684	-0.089	-0.028
(43)	7	I have a positive image of God.	0.173	0.672	-0.088	0.171
(74)	8	There is a life force toward wholeness inherent in me.	0.157	0.646	0.320	-0.044
(54)	9	I am a unique manifestation of Spirit/ God.	0.272	0.560	0.092	0.088
(57)	10	My life has meaning and purpose.	0.280	0.508	0.000	0.470
Factor 3: Creative Dimension						
(44)	1	I follow the prohibitions I learned in childhood.	0.250	-0.038	0.801	-0.056
(16)	2	I know I have resources to solve life's problems.	0.251	0.204	0.596	-0.010
(19)	3	I'd rather stick to the familiar than try something new.	0.359	0.269	0.558	0.002
Factor 4: Communal Dimension						
(6)	1	I express appreciation for others.	0.168	0.244	0.015	0.681
(64)	2	I relate well to people in my family.	0.060	0.173	-0.081	0.631
(62)	3	I experience myself as part of a larger human family.	0.322	0.335	-0.021	0.389
Numbers in parentheses correspond to the original scale numbers						

All except two items represented by Factor 1 correspond to conceptualized Intrapsychic and Interpersonal items. The two items were "I am centred in my deeper or higher self" and "I feel connected to others in our humanity." These were items originally conceptualized as belonging to the Universal-Spiritual dimension. Although these two items point to experience beyond the individual self, they could also represent intrapsychic experience. Therefore, these items can reasonably be accepted within the Intrapsychic-Interpersonal dimension.

Factor 2 is named the Spiritual dimension because all the items coincide with the conceptualized Universal-Spiritual dimension items. These items pertain to trust, meaning and purpose, and an immanent sense of spirit or life force within oneself, and a sense of connection with a transcendent dimension. These items form a single factor despite the use of both theistic and non-theistic language in the formulation of the items. Since the items are more reflective of spirituality than universal human yearnings, the dimension is named simply as the Spiritual dimension.

Items in Factor 3 pertain to the exercise of one's choice to update family rules and beliefs one lives by, while shedding roles, rules, and beliefs from the past that are limiting. These items, originally conceptualized as intrapsychic items, form a cluster among themselves in terms of one's capacity to exercise one's freedom and creativity to break out of old forms, family rules, and beliefs to respond to the present context and to exercise one's freedom of choice for the future. Freedom and creativity are central values in the Satir model in its existential emphasis on the present and future. Change in the Satir model is directed toward releasing and redirecting energy tied up by unresolved issues from the past toward coping with awareness in the present and in creating the future according to one's wisdom and vision (Banmen, 2003). The conditioning influence of the past can be transcended and transformed. These three Factor 3 items reflect the forward-looking, creative aspect of congruence, and this factor is named the Creative dimension.

Factor 4 brings together items from the original Interpersonal and Universal-Spiritual dimensions. "I express appreciation for others" and "I relate well to people in my family" were originally conceptualized as interpersonal items. "I experience myself as a part of a larger human family" was conceptualized as an universal-spiritual item. The commonality among these items is the participation of the self within a larger human unit and the forging of bonds between self and others. These items mark a self-transcendence that takes the self beyond one's isolated self to connect with a larger human family. This factor is therefore named the Communal dimension.

Correlations with Other Scales

Table 13.3 displays the correlations of the four factor scores and total score extracted from the Congruence Scale with subscores of the two compatible measures, the Outcome Questionnaire (OQ) and the Satisfaction with Life Scale (SWLS). Using Pearson correlations of significance, subscores, and the total score on the Congruence Scale are found to be moderately correlated with most of the subscores and the total scores on the Outcome Questionnaire and the Satisfaction with Life Scale. The correlation coefficient of the total Congruence score with the OQ total is -0.61. Correlation coefficient with the SWLS total is 0.53. In both cases the correlations are significant at the 0.01 level. These moderate levels of correlation are reasonable, as congruence is expected to relate to levels of well-being on the SWLS and to levels of functioning intrapsychically, interpersonally, and in social role adjustment on the OQ. The moderate correlations indicate that while there is overlap of the construct of congruence with life satisfaction, intrapsychic and interpersonal functioning, and social role adjustment, these variables remain different and separate constructs. Among the four factors, Factor 1 representing the Intrapsychic-Interpersonal dimension correlates highest with the OQ subscales and with the SWLS. Factor 4, the Communal dimension, correlates least with the OQ and SWLS.

Table 13.3

Correlation Coefficients of Scores on the Congruence Scale with the Outcome Questionnaire and the Satisfaction with Life Scale

	Intrapsychic-Interpersonal	Spiritual	Creative	Communal	Total Score
OQ sd	-0.66**	-0.36**	-0.40**	-0.18	-0.62**
OQ ir	-0.43**	-0.35**	-0.36**	-0.25*	-0.47**
OQ sr	-0.42**	-0.26*	-0.28**	-0.19	-0.41**
OQ Total	-0.63**	-0.38**	-0.41**	-0.23*	-0.61**
SWLS	0.53**	0.36**	0.31**	0.28**	0.53**

sd = symptom distress

ir = interpersonal relations * p<0.05 **p<0.01

sr = social role

Note: The negative correlation coefficients reflect the opposite directionalities of scoring on the OQ and Congruence Scale.

Discussion

Item Selection and Formulation

On the Congruence Scale, some items in the Spirituality dimension were reported to be difficult and confusing to one Christian respondent and two Buddhist respondents. The problem seems to be related to the use of language in referring to the spiritual dimension and whether the language is consonant with the language of their respective religious traditions. Satir used generic terms when referring to spirituality, e.g. the "Life Force," "manifestation of life." At times, she had used terms with Judeo-Christian connotations in reference to the person, e.g. "miracle," "temple." In her workshops and conversations, Satir reportedly had spoken explicitly of "a benevolent God" (John Banmen, personal interview, February 1, 1998, Ottawa, Ontario). However, naming the spiritual dimension was less important to Satir than the experience the connection with this dimension facilitated (Satir & Banmen, 1983). She saw the challenge of becoming more fully human as a capacity to "open to and to contact the power we call by many names, God being one frequently used" (Satir, 1988, p. 336).

Because the Satir model focuses on the process and experience of spirituality, respondents from a plurality of faiths seem to be able to appropriate the experience within the language of their own religious framework. In constructing the Spirituality items, a mixture of theistic and non-theistic terms was employed to test out the responses of a North American group of respondents. The results showed that theistic terminology remained meaningful to the majority of North Americans sampled in this study. As religious affiliations in demographics shift, and if the Congruence Scale were to be used with populations outside of North America, the terminology referring to Spirituality may need to be adapted.

Factors Correspondence with Conceptualized Items

The four factors extracted from the factor analysis of the Congruence Scale displayed varying degrees of correspondence with the dimensions of items as conceptualized. This leads to a reconstitution of the composite dimensions of congruence. Items conceptualized as Intrapsychic and Interpersonal were responded to by subjects as a single category. The three Interpersonal items were "I can say 'no' when something doesn't fit for me," "I feel tense when I am with others," and "I avoid addressing conflicts." On examination, the original Interpersonal items were not always sufficiently clear and unambiguous to indicate a communicative or interpersonal component that is distinctly separate from the Intrapsychic dimension. Hence it is not surprising that these items did not separate out as a distinct interpersonal factor in themselves. A more precise formulation of interpersonal items to reflect the behavior described in Satir's communication stances would be important in establishing a clear Interpersonal dimension distinct from the Intrapsychic dimension. The Interpersonal items may need to be reformulated.

Factor 2, the Spirituality factor, came out identical with the Universal-Spiritual items as conceptualized. This dimension was renamed as simply the Spiritual dimension as items referring to universal human yearnings were not represented in the factor items.

Factor 3 is interpreted as the Creative dimension. A limited number of items originally conceptualized in the Intrapsychic dimension separated out as an independent factor. The ability to take risks, to exercise the freedom to choose, to evaluate past learnings, and to be open to the present and future are salient elements to the the Satir Model and Satir's understanding of congruence, creativity and self-esteem, emphasized in her writings and meditations (Satir, 1988; Banmen & Banmen, 1991). Although this dimension is not represented in the Iceberg metaphor as depicted by Satir and her colleagues, it is nevertheless a dimension that is significant in Satir's other writings. Factor analysis makes prominent this Creative dimension.

The Communal dimension combined items originally conceived of in the Interpersonal and the Universal-Spiritual dimensions. Development of the Communal dimension, a central component of Satir's workshop experience, has not been singled out in the Satir literature as a significant expression of congruence and a feature in the Satir experience. Factor analysis has brought the Communal dimension to the fore consisting of three items: "I express appreciation for others," "I relate well to people in my family" and "I experience myself as part of a larger human family."

Through various Satir vehicles for group process, such as family reconstruction, Satir workshops provide a unique context for experiencing and witnessing one's humanity and that of others, including significant others from the past and present. Therefore, one expected outcome of Satir workshops is the recognition and experience of one's legitimate human yearnings shared by other human beings and the acceptance of one's own and others' humanity. According to Satir, our human yearnings, when legitimated, can serve to provide the impetus for positive human striving and change. Acknowledgement of our universal human yearnings breaks us out of our isolation from each other and promotes our acceptance of others in their human struggles and limitations. Taken together, these three Factor 4 items constituted by the originally conceptualized Interpersonal and Universal-Spiritual items make up the Communal dimension. Connection of the self to a larger humanity and an appreciation of our shared human yearnings is a noteworthy component of the meaning of congruence.

In summary, factor analysis of the Congruence Scale accomplished the purpose of clarifying and reconstituting items relevant to the dimensions of congruence, based on the statistical response patterns from a sample of 86 respondents. Conceptual understanding and empirical verification work reciprocally to refine the construct of congruence. Spirituality as a dimension of congruence in the Satir model is confirmed. Intrapsychic and Interpersonal items appear to be very closely intertwined. Therefore more precise clarification of the formulation of intrapsychic and interpersonal items is required. Creative and Communal dimensions appear to be more salient in the Satir model than was conceptualized.

Sample Size and Factor Resolution

Ideally, a minimum of five responses for each item is recommended for a procedure such as factor analysis. Given the sample size of 86 participants on 38 items, the ratio of two responses per item may not be sufficient for a stable factor solution. The stability of the factors therefore need to be tested further with a larger sample to see if the same factor pattern would obtain. Replication of the application of the scales with larger samples and additional populations is necessary to further confirm the factor structure of the Congruence Scale.

Uses of Scale and Future Research

The moderate significant correlations of the Congruence Scale with the Satisfaction with Life Scale and Outcome Questionnaire indicate that congruence is related to self-esteem, well-being, and levels of functioning intrapsychically, interpersonally and in social role adjustment. Since the Congruence Scale was developed using a sample of workshop participants in workshops based on Satir's model, it is particularly suited for application to evaluate the experience and outcome of Satir workshops. However, the Congruence Scale could also be applied to individuals, couples, and families in therapy, in particular for treatment that is based on the Satir model because of the alignment of the scale's dimensions with Satir constructs and dimensions. With the revival of interest in spirituality in therapy in recent years, the Congruence Scale is one scale that can be used to compare spirituality with other dimensions of functioning. The relationship of life satisfaction, well-being, and clinical symptomologies with the construct of congruence could yield useful information about the congruence construct. Since Satir training institutes exist worldwide, cross-cultural studies on the universality of the construct of congruence and the applicability of the Congruence Scale in different cultural contexts would be a reasonable and useful application of this instrument.

This chapter describes an initial step in the development of a Congruence Scale that aims to capture the important dimensions constituting the construct of congruence. The present Congruence Scale does not purport to be comprehensive or exhaustive in its representation and validation of the congruence construct. In the development of the present Congruence Scale, significant dimensions of the construct of congruence in the Satir model were highlighted for theoretical and practical consideration. With additional testing, and the use of larger samples, the construct of congruence and the Congruence Scale could be refined and further validated.

References

Alexander, J. F., Holtzworth-Munroe, A. & Jameson, P. B. (1994). The process and outcome of marital and family therapy: Research, review and evaluation. In A. E. Bergin & S. L. Garfield (Eds.), *Handbook of pychotherapy and behavior change* (pp. 595–630). New York: Wiley and Sons.

Banmen, J. (Ed.). (2003). *Meditations of Virginia Satir.* Seattle, WA, Avanta, the Virginia Satir Network.

Becvar, D. & Becvar, R. (1996). *Family therapy: A systemic integration.* Toronto: Allyn and Bacon.

Davis, B., McLendon, J., Freeman, M., Hill, N., Loberg, J., Lester, T. & Huber, C. (1996). Satir and congruence: A response. In B. J. Brothers (Ed.), *Couples and the Tao of congruence* (pp. 143–48). New York: Haworth Press.

Diener, E., Emmons, R. A., Larsen, R. J. & Griffin, S. (1985). The Satisfaction with Life Scale. *Journal of Personality Assessment,* 49, 71–75.

Duhl, B. (1989). Virginia Satir: In memoriam. *Journal of Marital and Family Therapy,* 15, 109–110.

Goldenberg, I. & Goldenberg, H. (1996). *Family therapy: An overview* (4th ed.). Belmont, CA: Brooks/ Cole.

Gurman, A. S., Kniskern, D. P. & Pinsof, W. M. (1986). Research on marital and family therapies. In S. L. Garfield and A. E. Bergin (Eds.), *Handbook of psychotherapy and behavior change* (pp. 565–624). New York: Wiley and Sons.

Lambert, M. J. & Burlingame, G. M. (1996). *Outcome questionnaire.* NJ: American Professional Credentialing Services LLC.

Lambert, M. J., Okiishi, J. C., Finch, A. E. & Johnson, L.D. (1998). Outcome assessment: From conceptualization to implementation. *Professional Psychology*, 29, 63–70.

Lee, B. (2001). Congruence in the Satir model: Its spiritual and religious significance. *Contemporary Family Therapy*, 24(1).

Liddle, H. A. (1991). Empirical values and the culture of family therapy. *Journal of Marital and Family Therapy*, 17, 227–348.

Loeschen, S. (1998). *Systematic training in the skills of Virginia Satir.* Pacific Grove, CA: Brooks/ Cole.

Nichols, M. P. & Schwartz, R. C. (1998). *Family therapy: Concepts and methods* (4th ed.). Boston: Allyn and Bacon.

Olson, D. H. (1976). Bridging research, theory, and application: The triple threat in science. In D. Olson (Ed.), *Treating relationships* (pp. 565–79). Lake Mills, IA: Graphics Press.

Pavot, W. & Diener, E. (1993). Review of the Satisfaction with Life Scale. *Psychological Assessment*, 5, 164–72.

Satir, V. (1964). *Conjoint family therapy.* Palo Alto, CA: Science and Behavior Books.

Satir, V. (1986). A partial portrait of a family therapist in process. In C. Fishman & B. Rosman (Eds.), *Evolving models for family change* (pp. 278–93). New York: Guilford Press.

Satir, V. (1988). *The new peoplemaking.* Mountain View, CA: Science and Behavior Books.

Satir, V., & Banmen, J. (1983). *Virginia Satir verbatim.* North Delta, B.C.: Delta Psychological Associates.

Satir, V., Banmen, J., Gerber, J. & Gomori, M. (1991). *The Satir model: Family therapy and beyond.* Palo Alto, CA: Science and Behavior Books.

Sprenkle, D., Keeney, B., & Sutton, P. (1982). Theorists who influence clinical members of AAMFT: A research note. *Journal of Marital and Family Therapy*, 8, 367–69.

Sprenkle, D., & Moon, S. (Eds.). (1996). *Research methods in family therapy.* New York: Guilford Press.

Umphress, V. J., Lambert, M. J., Smart, D. W., Barlow, S. H. & Clouse, G. (1997). Concurrent and construct validity of the Outcome Questionnaire. *Journal of Psychoeducational Assessment*, 15, 40–55.

14

If Depression Is the Solution, What Are the Problems?

John Banmen

Depression and anxiety are pandemic in the developed world. Depression has been called "the common cold" of mental disorders, with an estimated 10 percent of the population affected at any given time, up to 30 million in the United States alone (Segal, 2005). Unlike the common cold, depression does not run a predicable five-to-ten–day course and resolve on its own. It tends to be long-lasting, affects one's ability to love and to work, and recurs even when treated. It disrupts healthy eating and sleeping patterns and abilities to concentrate and probably even weakens the immune system. It takes an immeasurable toll on well-being, not only for sufferers, but also for their families, friends, and co-workers. Its most serious consequence, in severe cases, is death via suicide. The World Health Organization estimates that by 2010, depression will rank second only to heart disease in economic cost (Segal, 2005).

Professionals such as Klein & Wender (1993) suggest that depression is one of the most treatable illnesses. On the other hand, studies have shown the placebo effect to be powerful in the treatment of depression, so much so that psychiatrist Walter Brown of the Brown University of Medicine has proposed placebo pills as the first treatment of patients with mild or moderate depression (Lipton, 2004, p. 140). Data shows that in more than half of the clinical trials for the six leading antidepressants, the drugs did not outperform placebos (Kirsch et al., 2002). In other words, antidepressants are hardly better than sugar pills in many cases. If a substance that mimics the side effects of dry mouth in antidepressant drugs is added to the placebo, the sugar pills are even more effective, says psychiatrist Gordon Warme (Warme, 2006, pp. 12-13).

Sometimes prescription drugs are necessary to reduce the client's protectiveness and fear. Dr. Bruce Lipton (2004) says: "Using prescription drugs to silence a body's symptom (like depression) enables us to ignore personal involvement we may have with those symptoms. The overuse of prescription drugs provides a vacation form personal responsibility…Pharmaceutical drugs suppress the body's symptoms but never address the cause of the problem." We hope to do much better.

One hallmark of the Satir model of therapy is that the symptom of depression, the presenting problem, is not the area of focus. As the title of this chapter suggests, this model sees depression as a person's solution, a dysfunctional response to life stressors.

Depression has many different definitions and many competitive and conflictual treatment modalities. For this article, I use this definition:

> The buildup of suppressed feelings results in the chronic depressed and manic-depressed condition. Depression is not a disease or illness that we catch. It is not genetically acquired even though some persons are more susceptible to it. Depression is the result of misarrangement of experiences, a pattern of suppressing feelings, a depletion of energy (Ruskan, 2000).

In other words, depression is not a feeling. It is a symptom of the repression of feelings. Moreover, depression is a dysfunctional solution to numerous internal struggles, even if the struggles are often triggered by outside factors, such as one's living context or unhappy relationships. Usually dissatisfaction has been present for a long time but ignored and suppressed. We thus need to help the depressed client deal with whatever is not functioning well.

Although outcome data are not yet available on the use of the Satir Transformational Systemic Therapy (STST) model, my thirty years of clinical experience, along with that of many other therapists who use the Satir model, suggest Satir's approach can be especially effective in alleviating depression and preventing its recurrence. It appears to do so by tapping the client's own deep resources for healing, thus promoting change in not only the level of thinking, feeling, and doing, but the level of *being*.

Psychiatrists and psychologists diagnose people as being depressed if the individual indicates having five or more of the following:

1. Usual mood is dominated by dejection, gloominess, cheerlessness, joylessness, unhappiness.
2. Self-concept centers around beliefs of inadequacy, worthlessness, hopelessness, and low self-esteem.
3. Is critical, blaming, and derogatory toward self.
4. Is brooding and given to worry.
5. Is negativistic, critical, and judgmental toward others.
6. Is pessimistic.
7. Is prone to feeling guilty or remorseful.
8. Has poor appetite or is overeating.
9. Has insomnia or hypersomnia.
10. Has low energy, is fatigued.

Most of these clinical indicators of depression include feelings and perceptions. One might even say that feelings and perceptions drive the symptoms of eating and sleeping not enough or too much. Are there therapeutic ways of dealing with people's feelings such as guilt, gloominess, hopelessness, moodiness, pessimism, critical judgments, and negativity? Instead of focusing on these feelings and perspectives, maybe a better question is: Are there therapeutic ways of dealing with the processes that trigger these feelings? The Satir model says yes.

Several years ago, I had a therapeutic session with Carl, a middle-aged male who had been depressed for over twenty years. The session was recorded in front of a group of therapists studying the Satir model with me. (The session is now available on video and DVD from the Satir Institute of the Pacific. It includes a full transcript of the session. The website for purchasing the tape is www.satirpacific.org.)

Carl says, "My journey through depression began showing when I was twenty-six years old. While I was sitting in a therapist's office one day, I became acutely aware of just how much emotional pain I was in. I had always depended on my ability to distract myself by working hard, but the cost was high. At twenty-six years old, I was already tired. Depression had stolen the life of all I found important. Looking at my five-year-old daughter at that time, who was the light of my life, was no exception.

"My world became very dark, and I felt horrible inside. It felt like everybody else was making decisions for me, and I basically lost my voice and I kind of shrank inside and became very quiet and withdrawn. It is a very hard and painful place for me to be in. Things became kind of gray. I looked sad, felt tired. I am a sleeper when I'm depressed. I literally have had the experience of stopping at a stoplight and actually falling asleep. I felt so disconnected from myself. I was sad and lonely.

"I found pieces of my childhood that were very painful. I wanted my mom to hold me as a child, but that didn't happen. My dad was gone a lot. There were times when my mom would leave me as a young child—three, four, five years old—in the house by myself. I had a lot of fear at that time and a lot of anger later that I kept inside. I needed her, I desperately needed her to touch me, to hold me. I've been angry at her most of my life. I have avoided my mother most of my life. I've done the rage and full anger piece with her in therapy. I have tried many therapies over the years as well as all kinds of medication. When I'm not depressed, I'm afraid that depression will come back, as it often has."

The session shows how to make contact and how to work with the client's inner world to bring about some major changes. Impacts of the past are resolved, and the client achieves a new positive sense of self. The tape includes a lengthy follow-up interview with Carl and his wife several years later. Since his therapy session, he has returned to graduate school and completed his doctorate. He has not been depressed since the session using the Satir model. If this can happen with Carl, it might also work with many of the millions now suffering from depression.

The STST model is a humanistic, spiritual change and growth system. It states that the human being is of value beyond the materialistic mechanistic world view. Its belief is that humans are by nature good, that we have an inherent value of equality, and that at our core we manifest a common life force that is spiritual in nature. More practically, the Satir model firmly believes that change is possible, at least inside a person, even if change does not seem possible outside that inner world.

STST has a complex view of the person. It addresses a person's yearnings, expectations, perceptions (beliefs and cognition), feelings, feelings about feelings, as well as survival patterns and behavior. These components are all grounded in the Self, the "I Am," which is the core or essence of each person. As mentioned, this is often considered the spiritual base of humans. With the sense or belief that the life force has an internal drive to survive and grow, the Satir model sees human beings to strive to become more fully developed, more congruent, whole, and self-actualized.

When negative experiences interrupt such developments, our expectations, perceptions, and feelings get triggered negatively. One way to deal with such negative experiences is to suppress one's feelings and perceive oneself as hopeless and helpless. Depressing feelings also depresses life energy, the life force that helps us meet our universal yearnings of loving and being loved, belonging, and having a personal meaning of life. Depression, therefore, becomes a natural dysfunctional solution for negative feelings, negative perceptions, and unmet expectations. In other words, we avoid feeling the pain of unfulfilled yearnings.

So, how do we work with the depressed person instead of the symptom? Within this concept and approach, the first step is to learn the Satir model. The second is to develop the skills to bring about therapeutic transformations.* Two books of value in understanding, appreciating, and utilizing Satir Transformational Systemic Therapy are New Peoplemaking by Virginia Satir (1988) and The Satir Model: Family Therapy and Beyond by Virginia Satir et al. (1991). Key concepts include:

1. Human beings are all unique manifestations of the same universal life force.
2. Human processes are universal and therefore can be changed regardless of different environments, cultures and circumstances.
3. At their core, the essential level of the life energy, people are naturally positive and good.
4. The "problem," the symptom, is not the problem. Coping or not coping is the problem. The symptom is the subconscious solution to the problem.
5. Change is always possible. A solution more positive than depression is therefore possible.
6. We can learn to change negative impacts of the past and let go of hurt, anger, disappointments, and negative perceptions and projections.
7. Feelings belong to us and therefore can be changed.

Once they internalize these beliefs, orientations, and concepts, therapists are well along the road to learning skills for dealing with people diagnosed as depressed.

The Satir model also stresses two other areas in applying transformational therapy. One is the interactive process between persons, an important concept and practice of family therapy. The other is the influence of three-generational forces on the individual. The Satir model has an interactive and intrapsychic focus within a three-generational setting. Instead of focusing on the story, the narrative, or the history, the model focuses on the story's impact. The goal is to change the negative effect of family patterns from negative to positive. Changing impacts and meeting a client's yearnings are very effective in dealing with childhood abuse, trauma, and depression.

In using the Satir model with people who have been diagnosed as depressed, five essential qualities of transformational change are:

1. **Experiential**. Therapy must be experiential, which means that the client experiences the impact of a past event in the present. At the same time, the person experiences his or her own positive life energy. Triggering body memory is one way to help people experience these impacts. It is only when they experience both the negative energy of the impact and the positive energy of their life force that an energetic shift can take place.
2. **Systemic**. Therapy must work within the intrapsychic and interactive systems. In the intrapsychic system, clients experience their perceptions, expectations, yearnings, and spiritual energy, all of which also interact. The interactive systems include the person's relationships, both past and present. A change in either system<em dash> intrapsychic or interactive<em dash>affects the other. Transformational change is an energetic shift in the intrapsychic system, which then changes the interactive systems.
3. **Positively directional.** In the Satir model, the therapist actively engages with the client to help reframe perceptions, generate possibilities, identify the positive message of universal yearnings, and connect the client o his or her life energy. The focus is on health and possibilities, appreciating inner resources, and anticipating growth rather than on pathologizing or problem solving.
4. **Change focused.** As Satir therapy emphasizes transformational change, the process questions throughout the session relate to change. For instance, asking, "What would have to change for you to forgive yourself?" gives the client an opportunity to explore uncharted intrapsychic waters.
5. **Congruent**. When therapists are congruent, clients experience them as caring, accepting, hopeful, interested, genuine, authentic, and actively engaged. Thus, for clients to tap into their own spiritual life energy, congruence of the therapist is essential. Connected to the spiritual Self when in a congruent state, a therapist's creative life energy shows up in metaphors, humor, self-disclosure, sculpting, and many other creative interventions.

*This can easily be done by registering and taking a ten-day program over five months from the Satir Institute of the Pacific, whose web page is www.satirpacific.org.

A profile of a person suffering with depression includes many of the following features:

- Seems tense, irritable, restless
- Engages in self-doubt, has given up at least part of life
- Thinks negatively, feels downcast
- Lacks motivation, procrastinates, has difficulty accomplishing things
- Is self-blaming, self- critical
- Experiences fatigue, lack of energy
- Feels helpless
- Is fearful
- Is angry
- Is easily up-set, negatively sensitive
- Cannot see or implement alternatives
- Experienced rigid family rules when growing up
- Is fully self-absorbed
- Has unresolved early-childhood stressors
- Does not enjoy life, does not experience joy

As this list suggests, people with depression experience themselves within a field of great negativity. To heal, they need to deal with their own negativity as well as stimulate their life energy to emerge again. First, however, we suggest that the therapist look at such a client as a spiritual being living in a human body that strives to be wholesome. Something negative has thrown the system out of balance, resulting in negative experiences and, eventually, the diagnosis of depression. Embodying the Satir model's five essential qualities, we can connect with such a person's deeper core and stimulate the life energy to begin a process of healing. Here are some of the steps.

1. Prepare yourself for each session by centering yourself so that you can be fully present for the client. Get into a congruent state, experiencing your own positive life energy.
2. Start by making contact with the client: show interest, be accepting, and make it safe and secure for the client. Make contact with the person, not just with the client's experience of depression. This is a person-to-person connection, in which the relationship is very important throughout the therapeutic process, not just in the introduction phase. Know your client, not just everything about him or her.
3. Hear the conscious problems and experiences of the client. Hear

the problem in terms of unfulfilled yearnings.

4. Explore the person through the use of the Iceberg Metaphor, described at length throughout this book. (For additional help in exploring the iceberg, see Banmen, 2005). Be curious and accepting. You want the client and yourself to have a deeper sense of how the person experiences him- or herself in all parts of the iceberg, both negatively and positively.
5. Experientially explore the client's conscious and subconscious feelings. For this here-and-now experience, use the list presented earlier on essential qualities of transformational change. See how the person experiences him- or herself, how the feelings were triggered, what meaning the client made of the experience and of him- or herself having such feelings, and what decisions the client made about him- or herself as a result of these experiences and decisions. Have the person become more aware of his or her feelings and what led up to these feelings experientially. Have the client accept and risk his or her reactions to their feelings.<nsl>
   a. If the client is not aware of specific feelings, you might need to work to bring those hidden, suppressed feelings into awareness, ownership, and acceptance.
   b. Feelings at the subconscious level need to be brought into awareness and acceptance. Do so by focusing on unmet expectations and perceptions, especially judgments and criticisms. What feelings underlay the unmet expectations and perceptions?
   c. Feelings need to be given a voice, acknowledged, and expressed, even at the physical level.
   d. Explore the messages of the feelings. Usually this is where yearnings come to the surface.

Then work on bringing about changes. Set positive directional goals for each of the areas of the iceberg. Most importantly, work with the person to set goals for his or her yearnings. This could include letting go through reframing in each part of the iceberg, forgiving self and others, appreciating self and others, and especially savoring life itself. Helping the client connect positively with his or her life force is one of the major goals.

As part of a coping mechanism, people often resist change. Listen to any such "resistance." What is its message? Possibly fear, possibly doubt. You might have to interject some hope, trust, and acceptance before the client is willing to change. This might include empowering the client to take charge and become internally responsible. Nonjudgmental acceptance and patience are necessary attributes of the skillful therapist.

The process of changing the negative feelings and impacts, using the Satir model, often takes only a few months or less.

6. With the client, work toward a state of living in peace with the past, appreciating the present and meeting yearnings as a final outcome of therapy.
7. Some people will be able to connect with their universal, spiritual energy during the therapeutic process. The Satir model sees this important but many people do not seem to be ready for this phase of growth. Open the door but do not push the client through it.

Tapping into his or her own energy field, the therapist brings the client hope, patience, and possibly love. In summary, the Satir model, used this way, has helped many people who were using depression as a dysfunctional solution to their internal negative experiences.

References

Banmen, J. (2005). *Sample iceberg process questions of the Satir model.* Vancouver, BC: Satir Institute of the Pacific.

Kirsch, I. et al. (2002). The emperor's new drugs: An analysis of antidepressant medication data submitted to the U.S. Food and Drug Administration. Prevention & Treatment. *APA* 5, article 23.

Klein, D. R. and Wender, P. H. (1993) *Understanding depression: A complete guide to its diagnosis and treatment.* New Your: Oxford University.

Lipton, B. (2004). *The biology of belief.* Santa Rosa, CA: Mountain of Love/Elite Books.

Ruskan, J. (2000). *Emotional clearing.* New York: Broadway Books.

Satir, V., (1988). *The New Peoplemaking.* Palo Alto, CA: Science and Behavior Books, Inc

Satir, V., Banmen, J., Gerber, J., & Gomori, M. (1991) *Satir model: Family therapy and beyond.* Palo Alto: Science and Behavior Books, Inc.

Segal, Z. V. (2005). *"Mind-life dialogues on clinical application of meditation."* Presented at the Mind and Life Conference 2005, Washington, DC, Nov. 8–10.

Warme, G. (2006). *Daggers of the mind.* Toronto, Canada: House of Anansi Press.